Praise for

CITY OF LIGHT, CITY OF POISON

"*City of Light, City of Poison* is not only a serious, meticulously researched work of nonfiction, it is an irresistible story. Full of danger, mystery, and excitement, it will keep you up well into the night, marveling at this forgotten world of dark intrigue."
—Candice Millard, author of *Hero of the Empire*

"*City of Light, City of Poison* [is] a cop drama of sorts, intermingled with a historian's tenacious pursuit of the evidence. . . . Tucker's way with a lavish description will have you planning your all-star adaptation of the book. . . . Fascinating."
—Sharon Wheeler, *Times Higher Education*

"Tucker is a deft scene-setter, and there is an enjoyable whiff of *The Untouchables* about her evocation of the Parisian underworld, Louis XIV's decision to clamp down on it, and the entry of her hero, La Reynie. . . . [This] is excellent material for a romp, which is precisely what Tucker makes of it."
—Tim Smith Laing, *Sunday Telegraph*

"Holly Tucker tells [this] story . . . with great gusto and with an amazing array of facts. *City of Light, City of Poison* conjures up 17th century Paris and makes it seem close to the present day."
—Jonah Raskin, *New York Journal of Books*

"A fierce tale of conspiracy and retribution. . . . Thanks to Tucker's sympathetic necromancy and her luscious resurrection of everyday detail, even in gilded palaces the human psyche seems familiarly deceitful and self-justifying."
—Michael Sims, author of *The Story of Charlotte's Web* and *Arthur and Sherlock*

"Tucker walks the tightrope between scholarship and storytelling with practiced bravado. *City of Light, City of Poison* is as tightly structured as an Agatha Christie mystery."
—Pamela Toler, *History in the Margins*

"At once bewitching and chilling, the dark story of toxic intrigue, murder, and mayhem in the Sun King's France reads like the most gripping thriller, thanks to Holly Tucker's storytelling flair and relentless research." —Adrienne Mayor, author of *The Poison King*

"*City of Light, City of Poison* is a fascinating history of how a brilliant policeman brought light and law to Paris."
—Kate Ayers, *Book Reporter*

"A riveting tale of power, passion, and toxic lovers. . . . Tucker's account . . . read[s] like a novel." —*Bookwitty*

"A delightfully gruesome tale. . . . Tucker deftly unravels the secrecy and intrigue amid scenes that read like the best historical fiction. . . . An unforgettable read."
—Michael Ray Taylor, *Nashville Scene*

"A tour of an almost medieval world of witchcraft and poisoning. . . . Narrative history at its involving best."
—Gordon O'Sullivan, *Historical Novel Society*

"Tucker has done a phenomenal job of wading through official transcripts, court documents, confessions and more to tell this amazing story. The book is non-fiction but it reads like a historical thriller." —KV Marin, *Paris Through Expatriate Eyes*

"Tucker fuses history and mystery to create the dramatic effect of a novel while remaining true to the real-life plots and poisons of France's seventeenth century. . . . A genuinely illuminating study of a remarkably amoral moment in human history."
—Deborah Blum, author of *The Poisoner's Handbook*

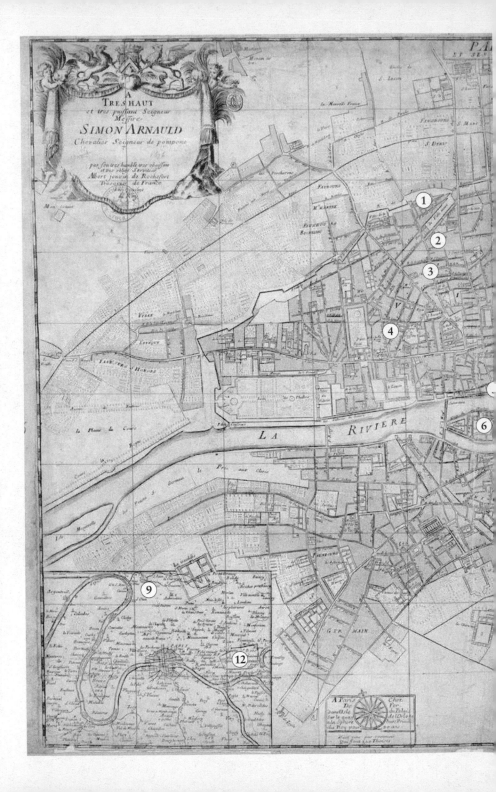

1. RUE DU BEAUREGARD: CATHERINE VOISIN'S HOME
2. COUR DES MIRACLES
3. RUE MONTORGEUIL
4. RUE DU BOULOI: NICOLAS DE LA REYNIE'S HOME AND HEADQUARTERS
5. CHÂTELET: CRIMINAL COURTS AND PRISON
6. PALAIS DE JUSTICE (*PARLEMENT*)
7. SAINT-PAUL CHURCH: LETTER DISCOVERED
8. SAINT-SÉVERIN CHURCH: FATHER MARIETTE PERFORMS CEREMONY FOR VOISIN AND LESAGE
9. SAINT-DÉNIS: FATHER GUIBOURG'S HOME AND CHURCH
10. BASTILLE
11. ARSENAL COMPOUND
12. CHÂTEAU OF VINCENNES

CITY
OF
LIGHT,
CITY
OF
POISON

MURDER, MAGIC, AND THE
FIRST POLICE CHIEF OF PARIS

HOLLY TUCKER

W. W. NORTON & COMPANY
Independent Publishers Since 1923
NEW YORK LONDON

For information about permission to reproduce selections from this book,
write to Permissions, W. W. Norton & Company, Inc.,
500 Fifth Avenue, New York, NY 10110

For information about special discounts for bulk purchases, please contact
W. W. Norton Special Sales at specialsales@wwnorton.com or 800-233-4830

Manufacturing by LSC Communications, Harrisonburg, VA
Book design by JAM Design
Production manager: Anna Oler

Library of Congress Cataloging-in-Publication Data

Names: Tucker, Holly, author.
Title: City of light, city of poison : murder, magic, and the first police chief
of Paris / Holly Tucker.
Description: First edition. | New York : W. W. Norton & Company, [2017] |
Includes bibliographical references and index.
Identifiers: LCCN 2016046270 | ISBN 9780393239782 (hardcover)
Subjects: LCSH: La Reynie, Gabriel Nicolas de, 1625–1709. | Police—
France—Paris—History—17th century. | Crime—France—Paris—History—
17th century. | Murder—France—Paris—History—19th century. | Paris
(France)—History—17th century.
Classification: LCC HV8206.P3 T83 2017 | DDC 363.2092—dc23
LC record available at https://lccn.loc.gov/2016046270

ISBN 978-0-393-35543-7 pbk.

W. W. Norton & Company, Inc.
500 Fifth Avenue, New York, N.Y. 10110
www.wwnorton.com

W. W. Norton & Company Ltd.
15 Carlisle Street, London W1D 3BS

1 2 3 4 5 6 7 8 9 0

To my parents, Louhon and Carolyn Tucker.
My journeys, across continents and through time,
would not be possible without their
love and encouragement.

⁂

And to Pat Fife, our Gam, whose adventures
are as good as any book—and whose
Moscow Mules helped the words
flow for this one.

If you judge by appearances in this place you will often be deceived, because what appears to be the case hardly ever is.

—MADAME DE LA FAYETTE,
La Princesse de Clèves, 1678

Contents

Author's Note

However dark and strange the events depicted here may seem, *City of Light, City of Poison* is a work of non-fiction. Unless otherwise noted, anything between quotation marks is taken directly from details in a court document, interrogation record, memoir, or letter as cited in the endnotes.

In the French legal tradition of the early modern period, depositions were recorded in the third person, but in such a way as to capture how a witness or suspect spoke and the words they chose. I have translated these indirect quotations into direct quotations, being careful not to change the nature of the exchange between the questioner and the witness or suspect. A few clarifications have been made, as necessary. For example, some referents are not clear in a specific sentence, but are obvious in the context of the rest of the testimony. Run-on sentences, often the result of a scribe's effort to capture fast-moving dialogue, have been shortened where needed. I have attributed no words, thoughts, motivations, or actions for which there is not documentation.

If, as I hope, the story feels rich and the characters full of life, it is because what history has left us is similarly rich and alive. Truth be told, I am comforted by the fact that I do not have sufficient imagination to conjure up a story as grim and troubling as this nonfiction account of lost souls and cruel deeds.

A Note on Currency

The main forms of seventeenth-century French currency referenced here are the *denier, sol* or *sous, livre,* and *écu.* Twelve *deniers* were the equivalent of one *sol* or *sous.* Twenty *sols* made one *livre.* Six *livres* comprised an *écu.*

In 1667, one pound of bread cost eight *deniers.* A prisoner's daily food allowance was four *sols.* A police officer patrolling on horseback made fifty *sols* a day, which included the keep of his horse. Police fines ran from six to thirty *livres.*

It cost twenty *sols* to have one's palm read or horoscope prepared by a magician in the Montorgeuil neighborhood. Midwives and poisoners there also paid fifteen to thirty *sols* for pigeons, frogs, and other ingredients to make their beauty creams and potions, which they sold for upward of twelve *livres.* The average fee to "prune a family tree" ranged from 2,000 to 10,000 *livres* (more than 1,600 *écus*).

Burn Notice

Versailles, 1709

The plumes on the guards' hats fluttered in time with the beats of the horses' hooves along the route from Paris to Versailles. Riding in formation on the hot June day, the men had been entrusted with delivering a single letter to the king. No one, not even the horsemen, knew what made the cargo so precious. But as the swords dangling at their sides and the muskets slung across their chests made clear, they would kill to protect it.

After a few hours the travelers could see the sprawling palace in the distance. Once the site of a modest royal hunting lodge, Versailles was now home to Louis XIV. Construction on the palace had begun nearly a half century earlier, just months after the king had assumed the throne at the age of twenty-three.

The palace's golden gates shimmered in the sun. Beyond them one could spy the large clock above the window of the king's bedroom. At the center of the clock sat Apollo, the sun god, his face framed by rays of light. The clock marked the king's day with precision. From the moment he awoke in the morning to the time he went to bed at night, nobles jockeyed for the privilege of attending to the king's every need, from helping him dress to removing his chamber pot.

Since 1682 nearly ten thousand souls had lived in cramped quarters in the palace in return for access, either real or longed for, to the king. This sense of connection allowed Louis XIV to retain a large measure of control over the noble class, which he had learned long ago never to trust.

As the guards entered the palace gates, a sea of carriages and sedan chairs parted to make way for them. Once inside the main gates, the horsemen traversed the place d'Armes, the expansive courtyard fronting the château. Hundreds of soldiers stood in formation to protect the king and to impress his subjects.

Dismounting, the lead horseman bounded up the massive stone staircase and headed for the quarters of the king's most trusted minister, Louis de Pontchartrain. As Louis XIV's chief of staff, Pontchartrain held unparalleled power at Versailles. All correspondence passed through him—no small task given the daily avalanche of reports and requests that flowed into the palace from across France and throughout Europe.

The guard entered the minister's quarters and, once acknowledged, placed the letter in Pontchartrain's hands. Pursing his lips, as was his habit, Pontchartrain turned the letter over. With a start, he recognized the bold handwriting of Nicolas de La Reynie.

It was a letter from a dead man.

For more than thirty years Nicolas de la Reynie had served as the police chief of Paris, the city's first. He never cared for Pontchartrain. In fact, it had been Pontchartrain's appointment as the king's counselor that brought about La Reynie's eventual retirement. After working closely with La Reynie for nearly seven years, Pontchartrain strongly encouraged the king to replace the aging police chief with a younger, more dynamic officer. Still, the ever-practical La Reynie knew that the only way to get a letter to the king—and to be sure what it contained stayed intact—was through Pontchartrain.

After decades of monitoring Paris and its inhabitants, La

Reynie knew secrets that the nobility and the monarchy alike
would have preferred to keep hidden: crimes of passion, sins of
greed. From prostitutes he'd learned of the nobility's sexual pec-
cadilloes. From matrons and nuns he'd learned the true identities
of the children orphaned at foundling homes. Nothing surprised
the police chief.

Some secrets, however, were more dangerous. La Reynie knew
of plots so dark and menacing that they posed a direct threat to
the monarchy. He promised he would protect these secrets for the
rest of his life.

Now, less than a day after the police chief's death, his letter lay
heavy in the minister's hands. Pontchartrain broke the wax seal
and unfolded the thick piece of paper that formed both letter and
envelope. A key tumbled out. Holding the key in one hand and the
letter in the other, he scanned the page and then left immediately
to find the king.

Pontchartrain did not hide his annoyance at the crowds as he
marched through the halls of Versailles toward the king's counsel
room. The interior of the château teemed with so many nobles and
their attendants that Louis XIV's late superintendent of royal
buildings, Jean-Baptiste Colbert, had fretted over whether the palace's marble floors were thick enough to withstand the constant traffic.

Congestion was always worst in the long corridor that linked
the palace's north and south wings. First-time visitors stood in
awe as their reflections ricocheted across the 578 mirrors that
lined the gallery's walls. On the barreled ceiling were thirty stunning paintings by the master Charles Le Brun that told the story of
the Sun King's economic and political successes. Pontchartrain
was now too preoccupied to look up to admire Le Brun's master-
pieces; if he had, he would have been reminded of the king's gesture of gratitude to the man whose letter he held in his hands.

Among Le Brun's works was a painting titled *The Police and
Safety Established in Paris*, an allegorical image featuring two
women in flowing Greco-Roman gowns. Holding a balance and a
sword in one hand, Justice orders soldiers to disperse the violent

gangs battling in the background. Reclining at her feet is Security, who extends an open wallet to the soldiers as a show of her support and confidence. The soldiers—armed with weapons and lanterns— point toward newly paved and lighted streets to show the fruits of their labor. La Reynie's transformation of Paris from a crime- infested city into a civilized one had been chronicled in gesso and gilt for all to see at the king's château.

An ornate mechanical clock chimed ten as Pontchartrain moved through the king's empty bedroom and into the adjacent counsel room. He walked to the large table that sat in the center of the room and stood quietly alongside a small group of other min- isters. The aging king walked slowly toward his seat. Once settled at the table, he looked toward his ministers and nodded to indicate that he was ready for his daily report.

It did not take long for the king's eyes to fasten on the letter and key Pontchartain held in his hands. Without a word, Pontchar- train slid the letter toward him.

Louis XIV read the former police chief's words and paused for a moment, weighing their meaning. He handed the letter back to Pontchartrain. There was no need to speak; the minister knew what to do.

Several days later the royal notary François Gaudion placed a large black leather box on a table in front of Pontchartrain. Thirty years of dust coated the box, confirming that its contents had not been disturbed. When La Reynie entrusted this box and others to Gaudion decades earlier, he made it clear that they were to stay in the notary's safekeeping until further notice. That moment had arrived. Pontchartrain offered Gaudion written confirmation from the king that neither he nor his family nor his progeny would be held responsible for anything that might be revealed once the box was opened.

Reassured, Gaudion bowed and left the room, shutting the door behind him. Alone, Pontchartrain inspected the black case. It was secured with not one but two sets of wax seals imprinted with La Reynie's official insignia. Pontchartrain cracked open the brit- tle seals with a small knife and inserted the key into the lock. The

mechanism gave despite years of disuse. Inside he found hundreds
of manuscript pages bundled together. Removing one large stack
of pages, he placed the papers on the table and turned each gingerly. He saw names of France's highest nobility. Alongside them
were scrawled the words "death," "poison," "murdered."

Only four other men knew the extent of the secrets that Louis XIV
had worked so hard to keep hidden for so long. The first was Jean
Sagot, La Reynie's chief notary, who was now long dead. The second, Louis's trusted minister, Jean-Baptiste Colbert, also took the
secrets to his grave in 1683. He was followed eight years later by
the marquis of Louvois, Colbert's nemesis and Louis's esteemed
minister of war. And, of course, Nicolas de La Reynie.

   With La Reynie's death, Louis XIV became the sole keeper of
the secrets surrounding the Affair of the Poisons, and he had no
intention of letting them outlive him. The king ordered his servants to start a fire in the large stone fireplace at the end of the
counsel room. For a hot July day, it was an odd request.

   Page by page, Pontchartrain handed the documents to the king,
who fed each of them into the hungry flames. The two men
watched the parchment curl and catch fire. As the smoke rose from
the chimney into the summer sky above Versailles, the king
silenced the horrors of the affair and the screams of its victims for good.

   Or so he believed.

PART I

"Day and Night They Kill Here"

1

Crime Capital of the World

ate seventeenth-century Paris assaulted the senses and rattled the nerves. Screams and yells echoed off the walls of narrow streets as Parisians lodged boisterous complaints against the insults of urban life: fistfights among angry neighbors, cutpurses racing from victims, chamber pots dumped out from upper floors onto passersby below. Carriage drivers swore and taunted one another as they jockeyed for command of the street. Packs of vendors shouted at the top of their lungs. Sounds of animals punctuated the cacophony: dogs barked, roosters crowed, cows lowed as they strolled with their bells clanking.

The filth of Paris attached itself to clothes, the sides of buildings, and the insides of nostrils. Several times a week, butchers, tanners, and tallow makers welcomed herds of cattle and sheep to the city's central slaughterhouses, located near streets with names like rue Pied-de-Boeuf (Cow-Foot Street) and rue de la Triperie (Tripe-Shop Street). On Thursdays and Fridays, Parisians had no choice but to trudge through inches of congealed blood. Even on nonslaughter days, the streets were permanently rust colored from the blood that had soaked into the earth.

There were no sidewalks in Paris. No European city had them. In a futile response to the mud, many homeowners installed a protruding iron bar at ankle height in their home's stone edifice, so visitors could scrape the foul muck from their shoes before entering. To avoid walking in the streets altogether, those who could afford to hire carriages increasingly did so. In the mid-seventeenth century, there were barely three hundred carriages navigating the streets. Within just a few decades, that number swelled to well over ten thousand, creating traffic jams in the narrow streets for hours at a time and, worse, a major safety hazard. As one Italian traveler wrote, "There is an infinite number of filthy carriages covered in mud, which serve to kill the living."

Overcrowded and dirty, Paris brought even the most levelheaded of inhabitants to the brink of violence. Conflicts were frequently adjudicated by a supply of weapons—from brass knuckles and clubs to daggers and rapiers—kept close at hand. When street "justice" was dealt, it came swiftly and often to the great shock of its victim. Only steps from the king's library on the rue Richelieu, a watchmaker encountered a former customer. Bypassing all polite greetings, the man launched into vitriolic complaints about defects in the watch he had bought a year earlier. When the watchmaker protested, his customer smashed a heavy sword into the watchmaker's head, leaving him dead.

The new accessibility of pistols across social classes turned an already dangerous city into an even more deadly one. The product of the sixteenth-century discovery of saltpeter, guns revolutionized early European warfare overnight. By the 1640s the French had perfected flintlock-firing technology, which made guns much lighter, smaller, and less expensive to produce than traditional wheel-lock guns and rifles. Armed with pocket-size pistols under their cloaks, thieves became bolder. Parisians looking to protect their homes raced to buy handguns, making the city all the more unsafe.

In response to the rising violence, the Crown issued an edict in 1660 calling for the ban of all weapons including—and especially—

handguns, by anyone other than soldiers, police officers, judges, and noblemen. The law did not have the desired effect. Another ordinance issued six years later repeated the 1660 law nearly verbatim. It also added that all handguns needed to be conspicuous, heavy, and with barrels that were at least fifteen inches long. Any person in possession of such a weapon was required to carry a lantern or a torch as he moved through the streets at night, so both law officials and citizens could see that the person was armed. Judging from the violence that filled the city after dark, few followed this mandate either.

By night Paris became frighteningly claustrophobic. At sunset, soldiers pulled shut the massive gates of the city's ramparts and lowered the barricades behind them. But the gates did little to protect those locked in with their fellow citizens. Nighttime revelers made their way across a city plunged into inky shadows, with only the faint glow of candlelight peeking through a drape or shutter illuminating a small stretch of street. Homeowners and shopkeepers battened down their homes and stores, pulling shut windows and doors for the night like sailors preparing for a storm. Here the weapons came in handy. As one Mademoiselle Surqualin said nonchalantly to the police after killing an intruder, she always kept a knife at her bedside precisely for that task.

Despite its dangers, a vibrant city still beckoned. Some heeded the siren call of the city's drinking holes. Most streets boasted at least two or three taverns of varying repute. They advertised themselves with colorful names like the Cradle, the Lion's Ditch, or the Fat Grape—and they attracted neighborhood locals eager to eat, drink, or pick a fight.

Paris did not have a centralized police force until the late seventeenth century. Instead policing responsibility for the city lay in the hands of just forty-eight commissioners—fewer than one commissioner for every fifteen thousand Parisians. In theory each commissioner maintained order in the quarter in which he lived, but the commissioners learned quickly that fighting crime did not pay. What did pay was the mountain of bureaucratic and legal tasks required after crimes were committed. A visit to a commissioner's home, which served as his office, was the first stop in the long, and often expensive, process toward finding justice. The commissioner scanned each person who walked through the door for signs of his or her ability to pay. One commissioner, Nicolas de Vendosme, certainly made such an assessment when a local laborer came to lodge a complaint on behalf of his two sons, who worked as apprentices to a woodcarver. The agitated father declared that the woodcarver had pushed his sons into the muddy street and swung a mallet at one of them. It was sheer luck, the father explained, that the woodcarver did not break his son's leg.

Vendosme explained that a simple complaint against the woodcarver would set the father back fifteen *sols,* nearly three-quarters of a day's pay. For this the woodcarver would receive formal notification that his actions were not acceptable. If the father wished to pursue the matter in court, there would be additional fees. To begin with, paper was not free. It cost well over one *sol* per page, and they would need plenty of it for letters and court filings. Witnesses also expected compensation for their testimony. Then there were the clerks who required payment when they filed the complaint with the court. All this would be in addition to the commissioner's own honorarium, which would be determined by the complexity of the case. In all, the father would be facing at least three *livres,* the equivalent of three full days of the workman's wages, to pursue litigation against the woodcarver. Still, this was reasonable in comparison to the seven *livres* in fees that the director of a royal textile factory paid, or the ten *livres* that a duchess paid for similar services. When it came to seventeenth-century justice, the more one was thought able to pay, the more one usually did.

On the Right Bank of the Seine sat the castle-like Châtelet compound, which housed courtrooms as well as a prison where convicted prisoners languished following judgment. Châtelet was divided into two bureaucratic fiefdoms. One was the dominion of d'Aubray, the civil lieutenant, who served as the overall head of Châtelet. He decided disputes among individuals and groups that had implications for the public good of the city. The other was that of the criminal lieutenant, Jacques Tardieu, who had jurisdiction over most crimes committed in Paris. Like the commissioners, the lieutenants (and their staffs) were paid by the plaintiff for their efforts. Determining the jurisdiction of a case—especially high-profile ones that involved the wealthy—brought out bitter infighting. During much of the seventeenth century the legal system at Châtelet ground to a halt as the magistrates battled, often for months on end, for the right to hear certain cases.

"Day and night they kill here, we have arrived at the dregs of all centuries," wrote Guy Patin, a doctor at the Paris Faculty of Medicine. As if things could not be any worse, the city reached its boiling point on one hot August day in 1665, when the criminal lieutenant himself was murdered in broad daylight.

René and François Touchet spent weeks spying on the home belonging to Criminal Lieutenant Jacques Tardieu, logging the comings and goings from the Left Bank household. Tardieu's home was a classic example of the type of luxurious *hôtels particuliers* (city estates) that only the most affluent Parisians could afford. A tall, imposing wall separated the Tardieu family from the filth and noise of the streets surrounding it. A pair of twenty-foot-high wooden doors opened into a large courtyard, providing yet another buffer from the violent world outside.

With each passing day the Touchet brothers became more convinced that a bounty of riches lay behind the high walls. The seventy-two year old Tardieu attended mass regularly at Notre-Dame, a short carriage ride away from his home on the quai des Orfèvres. René and François, both in their early twenties, lay in wait one Sunday morning until the large wooden doors of the compound opened to release several carriages and a stream of servants on foot. Believing the house to be empty, the brothers scaled the wall, entered the home through an open window, and began ransacking it for jewels, money, and other precious items.

They did not realize that the elderly Tardieu had chosen to stay at home that day. The thought of joining the crowds to celebrate the Feast of Saint Bartholomew was too exhausting. Instead he and his wife sent the other members of the family off, preferring to remain at home on their own.

A frightening scream pierced Tardieu's peaceful morning. It was the cry of his wife in an adjoining room. He scrambled from his bed as fast as his aging body allowed and shuffled down the long corridor in search of her. Moments later Tardieu heard a sickening series of sounds: the cocking of a pistol trigger, the earsplitting explosion of a bullet, followed by a dull thud. When he finally reached his wife's room, he saw her sprawled on the floor, blood pooling around her lifeless body.

With a strength that belied his age, Tardieu lunged at the thieves, battling the Touchet brothers for the gun. One of the brothers dropped the weapon and kicked it swiftly across the room. As Tardieu crouched to retrieve it, the second brother reached underneath his belt and removed a dagger. With four strokes to the neck, Tardieu crumpled to the floor.

Servants discovered the couple's corpses when they returned from church. Shocked, they ran into the streets screaming. The local guardsmen came and, after searching the home, they found the younger of the two brothers crouching on the roof. The elder, hiding in the cellar and covered in blood, eventually surrendered.

The brothers were charged with murder and sentenced to death. In a public spectacle not far from Tardieu's courtrooms, the criminals were executed as Parisians crowded into the square to watch.

Tardieu's murder stunned the city's nobility. If even the criminal lieutenant, the man responsible for sentencing violent criminals, was not safe in Paris, then who was? The answer arrived the following year when Tardieu's counterpart and rival, Civil Lieutenant François Dreux d'Aubray, was also murdered. This time death came not by a gun or a dagger, but by poison.

In the months following Tardieu's murder, Dreux d'Aubray's career had blossomed. The criminal lieutenant's death left no question of who was in charge of legal affairs at the Châtelet. D'Aubray was an energetic man, whose lively eyes and wry smile belied a deep seriousness in both his professional and personal affairs. From dawn each morning until well into the late evening, d'Aubray could be found in his chambers in the heart of the Châtelet. Wearing a long, black robe and triangular cap, he decided the fates of Parisians.

D'Aubray lived in an elaborately decorated estate on the rue du Bouloi, alongside many of the city's other grand legal and financial families. D'Aubray was the father of two sons, each holding high-ranking positions in the royal government. The elder, Antoine, was in line to succeed him as civil lieutenant. His daughter, however, was another matter.

Marie-Madeleine d'Aubray had been blessed with a petite frame and porcelain skin. Her intense blue eyes paired nicely with a striking air of confidence that she inherited from her father. Headstrong and passionate, she had been a precocious child with an uncanny ability to talk her way out of anything. So it came as a relief to her father when, at the age of twenty-one, Marie-Madeleine agreed to marry one of the most-sought-after bachelors in Paris, the wealthy and handsome Antoine Gobelin, the marquis of Brinvilliers.

D'Aubray was initially optimistic about the marriage, hopeful that his daughter would finally settle down. It seemed a good match with a promising future. The marquis owned an estate in the wealthy Marais quarter on the Right Bank of Paris, a gift from his family when he was just sixteen years old. With the intention that the young man would soon marry, the marquis's parents decorated the house with the best furnishings that money could buy: mahogany consoles topped with marble, silk-upholstered chairs with painstakingly carved wooden legs, and more than enough silver place settings for the long table that filled the large dining room.

The marquis's wealth also caught the eye of Jean-Baptiste

Godin, a man of "mean birth" who was biding his time in the army as a horseman until he could find a more profitable pursuit. Godin may have lacked money, but he did not lack guile and ambition. He had a lively and upbeat manner about him that was enticing, even seductive. With the flash of a smile, he could persuade just about anyone around him to yield, happily and willingly, to his wishes—especially when it came to money. Eschewing his past as an illegitimate child, Godin assumed the more noble and pious-sounding name of Sainte-Croix.

The marquis of Brinvilliers found a kindred spirit in Sainte-Croix and invited him to live in his sprawling Marais home. Sainte-Croix did not question his luck in attracting such a profitable friendship. Instead he immediately looked for a way to exploit it, which did not take long.

Despite his family's wealth, Brinvilliers seemed incapable of managing his own finances. With the encouragement of Sainte-Croix, the marquis denied himself and his friends nothing at the gambling tables or for their mistresses. Soon the only assets that remained were the house in which the couple lived and the marquise de Brinvilliers's generous dowry from her father. Dreux d'Aubray worried that this too would disappear.

Protective of both his reputation and what was left of his fortune, d'Aubray used his connections to make a legal arrangement that disentangled his daughter's wealth, and that of the d'Aubray family more generally, from the couple's marital property. Now nearly penniless and made a social outcast by the more powerful d'Aubray, the marquis de Brinvilliers had little choice, if he wanted to maintain a semblance of wealth, but to allow the marquise de Brinvilliers to live her life exactly as she wished. To her father's dismay, she became swept up in a passionate affair with her husband's best friend, Sainte-Croix.

It did not matter to Sainte-Croix whether the marquise's interest in him was born of spite for her husband's reckless infidelity or whether it came from a font of untapped desire. In the marquise of Brinvilliers, Sainte-Croix saw a bounty of riches he could exploit.

Playful flirting soon turned into regular romantic interludes, often in her own home. "I am," the marquise confessed to Sainte-Croix, "yours with all my heart."

No amount of shaming or threats from her father could separate the marquise de Brinvilliers from the man she claimed to love. Her two brothers, Antoine and François, also made similar entreaties to their sister, all to little effect. Seeing no other choice, the elder d'Aubray turned to the king for help.

Members of the nobility could, and frequently did, petition the king for a *lettre de cachet* (letter of the signet). For well-connected members of court, it took just a strategic whisper and an offending person would quickly be ushered away, never to be heard from again. The letters were a convenient means for dysfunctional noble families to settle scores. As one aristocrat wrote in support of *lettres de cachet*, "The honor of a family requires that anyone who, by vile and abject morals, brings shame be made to disappear." These letters were executed on the simple signature of the king or his scribe, perfunctorily countersigned by a royal minister, and then folded and sealed with wax and embossed with the royal insignia. Letters of the signet were used so often that the king's secretary designed preprinted arrest requests in which a name and a date need only be inserted.

In March 1663 d'Aubray received notice that the king approved his request to separate Sainte-Croix from his daughter. A group of royal guards on horseback surrounded the marquise's carriage as it made its way across the Pont Neuf. The bridge had a reputation for drawing some of the city's most unruly crowds, and it did not take long before gawkers, drunks, and cutpurses swarmed around the carriage to watch the show. Ignoring the marquise's loud protests, the guards pulled Sainte-Croix from the coach and carted him off to the Bastille.

The marquise de Brinvilliers never forgave her father for his actions. Still, she had little choice but to rebuild her relationship with him, as she relied on his largesse to finance a noble lifestyle that her husband could now ill afford. Also, her father was getting on in years. There would be more money to come in the future if she made peace with him.

Three years after Sainte-Croix's arrest, d'Aubray felt relief that his daughter seemed to have come to her senses. Not only were they on speaking terms again, but also by the end of June 1666, they embarked on a trip to the family's country estate together.

D'Aubray had been unwell for several days. He fought bouts of nausea and fatigue that came in unpredictable waves, but he resolved to undertake the journey. There were important matters that he needed to discuss with the farmers at his estate. The château in Offémont sat in a densely wooded region about fifty miles northeast of Paris. It took a full day of traveling to get there, and d'Aubray was eager to leave as early as possible. The journey did not start well, however. The marquise arrived late at their meeting point and refused to allow a large leather vanity case to be strapped to the top of the carriage with the other valises. She insisted it must remain at all times in her sight, even if it meant less room in the carriage for the two of them.

By midday d'Aubray and his daughter reached the small village of Senlis, where they planned a short rest at the Pewter Kettle. Their arrival at the *auberge* caused a stir, as it was not often that such an elaborate carriage was seen in these parts. Several locals leaned out of the inn's upper windows to catch a glimpse of d'Aubray and his daughter as they regained the road to Offémont.

When they arrived at the estate late that night, the exhausted d'Aubray collapsed into a chair. Despite his lack of appetite, he took comfort in the kindness of his once-estranged daughter, who ordered the servants to prepare her father a warm and soothing broth. She even spooned the liquid into his mouth. He did not eat much, just enough to restore him before announcing that he was ready to retreat to his room in the hope of getting a good night's sleep. The marquise joined her father as he made his way upstairs. She took her vanity case with her.

Hours later d'Aubray screamed in pain, which woke the servants. Running to their master's room, they found him clutching his stomach and moaning about "strange heat in his entrails." He began to vomit violently.

In better days the isolation of the family estate within the wooded forests of the Oise region provided respite from the busy world of Paris. Now its remoteness brought only panic. The civil lieutenant seemed to be near death, and there was no doctor nearby. The marquise stayed by her father's side as the servants carried him down the stone stairs of the château and into the main courtyard, where a carriage waited. Once they were settled inside, the driver raced back to Paris.

For two months after his return, d'Aubray languished in bed, his days marked by pain. Friends, family, and doctors rotated in and out of his home to offer care and support. No amount of bloodletting seemed to improve his condition. Nor did efforts to strengthen him through wine, broth, or herbal tinctures. The civil lieutenant refused to eat, and when he did he was often not able to hold the food down. With every day that passed, hope dimmed.

Barely able to speak but practical to the end, d'Aubray dictated his last will and testament on September 7, 1666. He divided his assets among his daughter and her two brothers. D'Aubray's son François traveled from Orléans, where he worked as a lawyer, to be at his father's bedside. "You cannot know," he wrote at six o'clock in the morning on the day before his father died, "just how difficult and upsetting it is to see a person who is so dear to me in such extreme peril." At eleven o'clock the next morning final rites were administered; by that evening d'Aubray was dead.

Friends and family speculated whether poison had been to blame. D'Aubray's symptoms suggested it. But as quickly as they brought forward the possibility, they also dismissed it. D'Aubray had been ill before the trip to Offémont. Moreover, the only person close enough to poison d'Aubray at Offémont was the marquise. The very idea was preposterous. Surely a woman "raised in an honest family, who had such a pleasant face and complexion, and appeared so good natured" could not be capable of poisoning her own father. Equally reluctant to pursue the question, the civil lieutenant's doctors declared that the sixty-six-year-old man had died of a sudden return of gout, an illness he had battled several years earlier.

It would take another ten years for the full truth of d'Aubray's death to be uncovered. Once it was, no one could have imagined the many more murders still yet to emerge from the shadows.

2

City of Light

aris was an embarrassment to Louis XIV. The criminal lieutenant had been murdered, and the civil lieutenant lay dead under suspicious circumstances as well. The king knew that a ruler who was unable to control his capital could be perceived as inefficient or, worse, weak.

He charged Jean-Baptiste Colbert, his trusted minister and controller-general of finance, with the gargantuan task of reforming the police. Nicknamed "le Nord" (the North) for his icy demeanor, Colbert had proved his unwavering dedication to the king when he uncovered a large stash of hidden assets that his predecessor, Cardinal Jules Mazarin, had left behind following his death. Not long after, the king appointed the financially cautious Colbert superintendent of buildings, giving him responsibility for all construction efforts in Paris and at Versailles. A year later, in 1665, his portfolio expanded to include the Ministry of Finance. Colbert had dominion over every area of royal administration except the military—a restriction that would eventually cause much infighting between Colbert and the marquis de Louvois, the minister of war.

Working from his house on the rue Vivienne, just a block from the Royal Library, Colbert built a massive archive that could be drawn on to help both the king and himself make key policy decisions. As "information master" he created a system of state intendants, or bureaucratic informants, who collected and curated reports of activities of interest to the Crown in every aspect of French political, economic, and social life.

Despite his thirst for information, Colbert recognized that there was no way that he could read every report and missive sent by his intendants. He instructed each intendant to distill intelligence into concise and meticulous summaries that he could scan quickly and, on occasion, share directly with the king. Colbert did not disguise his frustration when presented with disorganized or indecipherable reports. "You must make sure to write in large letters," he told one intendant, "or have your dispatches transcribed, because I am having too much trouble reading them." In addition to the external intendants, Colbert supported learned academies, such as the newly established Academy of Sciences, with the understanding that he would be the first to hear of their discoveries. He also enlisted an army of scribes, accountants, mapmakers, and couriers to ensure the efficient functioning of his information machine.

For several years Colbert had been impressed by the work of Nicolas de La Reynie, a lawyer from Limoges who had risen methodically through the ranks of the *parlement*, the highest royal court. The son of a long line of lawyers and magistrates, La Reynie was already well positioned for success in his chosen career. His marriage in 1645 to Antoinette de Barats, the daughter of another well-placed legal family in the region, had strengthened his standing. Still, given that Antoinette's dowry was relatively small, the twenty-year-old La Reynie likely married her for love rather than social, political, or economic advantage. Whatever the case, the marriage brought good fortune. The following year La Reynie was appointed head of the Bordeaux courts, where he had the final say in the region's most complex court cases.

While La Reynie set to work establishing his career, the couple wasted no time in starting a family. Within three years Antoinette bore four children. Of the four, only one survived past infancy. Their mother followed them in death in 1648, very possibly from complications in childbirth.

Whether heartbroken, driven, or both, La Reynie plunged himself into his work. It earned him many supporters, and many enemies, in the years following the country's bitter civil war, the Fronde. The monarchy barely escaped intact from violent uprisings initiated by the nobility between 1648 and 1653 in its effort to take control of the country. To clamp down on dissent, the prime minister arrested three lawyers at the *parlement* who were leading the movement. The capital exploded with protests. Over the course of two days in late August 1648, Parisians put up more than twelve hundred barricades throughout the city. Soon after, the royal family fled from the Louvre to the safety of the royal residence in Saint-Germain-en-Laye, northwest of Paris.

Ten-year-old Louis was well aware that his life was in danger and could be ended by the *frondeurs* at any moment. During the five years of conflict that followed, watching his mother, the queen regent, Anne of Austria, and her prime minister, Cardinal Mazarin, fight to save the monarchy, left an indelible mark on the boy.

During the uprisings, La Reynie made his alliance to the Crown clear and refused to allow political troubles to cloud the work of his courts. The powerful duke of Épernon, also a royalist, offered support and protection. When riots broke out in Bordeaux, the two men had little choice but to flee or risk execution. They survived the mob and the Fronde, garnering rewards for their support of the monarchy. The duke of Épernon brought La Reynie's loyalty to the attention of Cardinal Mazarin. Impressed, Mazarin soon offered La Reynie the position of master of requests (*maître de requêtes*), responsible for high-level judicial proceedings, in the Paris *parlement*.

Following the prime minister's death in 1661, La Reynie's merits also caught the eye of Mazarin's successor, Colbert. In 1665, the same year as Tardieu's murder, La Reynie wrote a meticulously detailed summary of what the country's disgruntled farmers were saying about the king. "I have learned," he wrote, "that to save time, you allow your staff to provide you with written reports about matters that you should know about...I would like to take the liberty to share other observations with you, if this is agreeable to you." The report impressed Colbert. Shortly thereafter he charged La Reynie with the task of reviewing maritime trade and security protocols at the country's most strategic ports: Marseille, La Rochelle, Nantes, and Rouen.

As La Reynie dug into the work with his characteristic dedication and quiet seriousness, Colbert tackled the problem of how to ensure the safety and security of the country's most important city. Following the shocking deaths of Tardieu and d'Aubray, the king himself took action. Paris was out of control; it was time to "purge the city of what was causing its disorders"—starting with the archaic and labyrinthine system of policing.

On March 15, 1667, at Colbert's urging, Louis created the position of lieutenant general of police. Its far-reaching powers included overseeing "city safety, gun control as prescribed by royal ordinances, street cleaning, flood and fire control." He would police the city's major markets as well as control any unsanctioned gatherings in Paris. The lieutenant general would also have full supervision of the prisons at the Châtelet complex.

The challenge lay in finding someone who was not so ingrained in the system as to be incapable of the creativity and determination required to assert control over an unruly city. Such a man, Colbert explained to the king, would have to be exceptional if not almost superhuman. The new lieutenant general of police must be "a man of the robe and a man of the sword and, if the doctor's learned ermine must float upon his shoulder, on his foot must ring the strong spur of the knight." Colbert continued, "he must be unflinching as a magistrate and intrepid as a soldier; he must not pale before the river in flood or plague in the hospitals, any more than before popular uproar or the threats of your courtiers."

As Colbert scanned the list of possibilities for a lieutenant general of police, Nicolas de la Reynie's name rose to the top. No person showed as much dedication to duty and loyalty to those he served as did La Reynie. Although the Fronde was long over, Louis stored in his memory the names of those anti-frondeur nobles who had dared to support the monarchy and stand firm against the uprising. He knew La Reynie had been one of them. The king swiftly approved Colbert's recommendation, declaring that he could think of no "better man or a more hardworking magistrate" for the job.

Soon after meeting with Colbert on March 20, 1667, La Reynie was appointed lieutenant general of police. In June, La Reynie sat at his desk, quill in hand, and began a letter to Pierre Séguier, the king's chief of staff. "We are making progress every day on police matters. Much good will come of it, even more so because it will be done without resistance. This will give all inhabitants of this city reason to be grateful that the king wanted to establish law and order in Paris."

Eager to transform unruly Paris into an idyllic "new Rome" that would serve the glory of his image as the all-powerful Sun King, Louis XIV granted La Reynie unprecedented authority. Operating as police chief and as the equivalent of mayor, La Reynie reached into nearly every corner of late seventeenth-century Parisian life. In this once-dark world, whose inhabitants had been scared to leave their homes after nightfall, lanterns now dotted every throughway and intersection. Newly built fountains relieved residents from their daily trips to the Seine to siphon off its foul waters. A series of well-publicized and forceful police measures were put into place to stave off organized crime—including recently codified procedures for arrest and interrogation sufficiently painful to give even the most hardened criminals pause.

Much of La Reynie's success came from a tireless work ethic, coupled with an insatiable thirst for information. At all hours of the day and night, couriers on foot and horseback arrived at his compound-like home near the Louvre, on the rue du Bouloi. The couriers delivered updates from the wardens in charge of supervising the city's overflowing prisons, whose names—the Bastille, the Grand Châtelet, the dungeon of Vincennes—filled Parisians' hearts with dread. They also brought handwritten accounts from each of the city's forty-eight commissioners responsible for reporting the daily activities in their local quarter and for enacting La Reynie's far-reaching orders.

La Reynie received daily updates from a web of civil servants, lawyers, judges, doctors, and merchants from whom he collected endless bits of information. But by far the most interesting missives came from the army of spies and informants that the police chief employed in his efforts to keep crime at bay. Their reports arrived written in invisible ink, stuffed into wigs, or sewn into jackets.

La Reynie reviewed all the reports personally, initialing each page in his unmistakable looping handwriting. He studied every report, deciding which crimes required further investigation and plotting a detailed plan of action for his officers. He also penned daily summaries of his efforts for the king—who studied the police chief's briefs just as attentively.

Law and order: From his first days as lieutenant general of police in the spring of 1667 to his retirement thirty years later, this was and would remain La Reynie's prime objective. He started his campaign with a series of ordinances designed to establish unequivocally who was now in charge of cleaning up the streets of Paris. To the grumbling of citizens, La Reynie imposed a "mud tax" on every Parisian who had a lodging or a business within the city—from shops to churches to counts and countesses to the king himself. The tax was intended to offset the substantial costs related to street maintenance. Officials calculated the mud tax based on the length of the facade of the building in which principal owners and renters lived or worked. The tax was paid, in advance, twice a year. There were swift and steep penalties for late payment or refusal to pay, including the immediate confiscation of the inhabitant's furniture.

La Reynie reached out to well-placed nobles across the city and encouraged them to demonstrate their support. In return the police chief appointed them directors of their quarters. The strategy played into what La Reynie knew to be two common characteristics among the upper classes: a need for recognition and a need for power. The job was more than honorary. Once a year each director submitted a detailed list of all homeowners and their property. It was on the basis of these lists that their fellow inhabitants were taxed and daily expenses for an area's street cleaning paid.

But what fully set La Reynie's efforts apart from prior attempts to keep the streets clean was the requirement that every inhabitant of Paris participate. At precisely seven o'clock every morning, hundreds of men ringing large bells moved through the city announcing that it was time for collective cleaning efforts. Parisians young and old, some still rubbing the sleep from their eyes, stumbled out of their houses, brooms in hand, to sweep the filth in front of their homes into the middle of the street. Thirty minutes later thousands of trash collectors were deployed to collect the refuse and haul it outside the city walls.

To aid street-cleaning efforts, new ordinances forbade residents from tying animals outside their homes or leaving the carcasses of dead beasts in public pathways. The long practice of emptying chamber pots from windows was also prohibited. A first offense earned a fine; a second resulted in a beating.

However, La Reynie soon learned with frustration that what residents could no longer throw into the streets they kept in their houses. A commissioner surveying the neighborhoods to the north of the Louvre described the "infection and stink" permeating the insides of homes. They were full of "fecal material and dead animals, a putrefaction that was as large in their homes as it was in the countryside." Inhabitants continued to relieve themselves on walls, in the streets, and even in the well-populated halls of the Louvre. The call of nature knew no social hierarchies, as some theatergoers learned in 1670 when two noblewomen chucked the contents of a chamber pot from their balcony loge onto the public below "in order to rid their box of the unpleasant smell."

Still, La Reynie claimed victory over filth a mere three months into his appointment. He crowed that the mud tax had been extraordinarily successful: "Horses are slipping around on the pavement because the streets are so clean now." It was perhaps a bit of an exaggeration, but no one could argue that the streets weren't much cleaner.

La Reynie's first months as lieutenant general coincided with the summer, when the long days kept the nights at bay. But with fall approaching and the dark days of winter to come, the police chief faced another problem: Where there was dark, there was crime. La Reynie decided the time had come to end the saga of nighttime thefts and murders occurring throughout the fall and winter. His first course of action was to issue an ordinance imposing public lighting in the city.

In the new ordinance, written in capital letters, La Reynie declared: "We order that, starting the last day of this coming October, candles will be lit in all streets and public places of the city and its surroundings. To this effect, commissioners of each quarter will determine...where lanterns shall be installed and determine the amount that each person in the quarter shall contribute."

Wanting to leave nothing to chance or misunderstanding, La Reynie provided detailed instructions. The lanterns, which were to be made of sturdy glass in metal housing and stocked with enormous multiwicked candles, should be mounted on the facades of buildings on a flagpole mechanism, allowing for lighting and extinguishing. Once the location and the cost of the lanterns had been decided, each quarter would hold elections to select those responsible for installing and maintaining them. Failure to perform elected duties would result in a stiff fine, which would increase after each instance of neglect. Moreover, property owners would be required to place a lamp in each of their windows and ensure that it remained lit—even on nights when a full moon shone brightly.

"We order," La Reynie further declared, "that the present ordinance be read and posted everywhere, so that no one can ignore it." The police chief knew that in a short time his declaration would be typeset and hundreds of copies printed. Within hours, the sounds of drumbeats would fill every quarter as the populace gathered in the streets to listen to public criers read aloud the declaration, which would be on public kiosks, pasted over ever-thickening layers of other official decrees. Members of La Reynie's police force also fanned out to deliver the ordinance to each of the city's churches and ordered priests to recite it in their Sunday sermons.

In just a few months, more than one thousand lanterns were installed on the city's busiest streets. An ornate rooster was painted on each lantern, the symbol of timely vigilance. When La Reynie was done, 2,736 lanterns illuminated the majority of Paris's streets.

The new lanterns quickly became a target for vandals. In many cases theft or damage was the result of the negligence by a member of the lighting brigade, who had not raised the lantern high enough up and out of reach after lighting the candle. Still, even when they could be raised as high as possible, the lanterns functioned as convenient marks for lackeys, pages, and carriage drivers who saw a tempting target for their whips, canes, and swords. Deeply frustrated by the vandalism, La Reynie issued another ordinance in January 1669 giving anyone who witnessed the destruction of a lantern the right to make a citizen's arrest. The offense would be considered a felony and punished to the fullest extent of the law.

La Reynie cleaned the streets; he conquered the night. His legacy continues today in Paris's reputation as the City of Light. The first major European city to be illuminated at night, Paris inspired awe. "Until two or three in the morning," marveled the journalist François Colletet, "it's almost as light as daytime."

Despite the transformation of the Paris night, La Reynie still needed to rein in the thieves, thugs, and other undesirables who made movement around the city a dangerous proposition. The challenge lay in changing the city's culture of violence. Deadly fights still broke out between carriage drivers jockeying for space in the congested streets, or as packs of men—drunk, armed, and looking for trouble—roamed the city after the taverns closed.

La Reynie issued still more new ordinances to reduce the number of weapons on the streets. He forbade coachmen and other servants from carrying swords, and watched eagerly for opportunities to make an example of offenders. He didn't have to wait long. When the duke of Roquelaure's coachman and one of the duchess of Chevreuse's pages stabbed a student to death on the Pont Neuf, the police chief swiftly had the two men apprehended. They were tried and condemned to a public death by hanging. La Reynie's intervention met with outrage on the part of the nobles, who complained that the police chief had ignored their long-held rights to control and punish their own servants. The executions took place anyway. As a result La Reynie demonstrated that he held the sole power, with the support of the monarchy, to make all decisions when it came to the collective good of the city.

Like the king, La Reynie was a devout Catholic. He supported, fully and with fervor, the king's growing interest in policing the morality of his subjects. He imposed a system of fines on the "morally corrupt," offering up to one-third of the fines as finders' fees to anyone who reported questionable activities of their fellow city dwellers. One simply had to go to the home of the neighborhood commissioner and make a formal complaint. The commissioner then interviewed witnesses, questioned the accused, and determined guilt. The offenses ranged from swearing to public intoxication and prostitution. In many cases La Reynie got directly involved.

In one of his daily reports to the king, La Reynie shared the case of a man named Orléans who had shouted "execrable blasphemies" after being hit, in his tender parts, during a handball match. Witnesses reported his actions to a local commissioner, who forwarded the case to La Reynie. Knowing that their friend was in trouble, several men raced to La Reynie's headquarters at Châtelet to offer excuses on the man's behalf. La Reynie said he would take the matter to the king. However, the man's fate was by then all but sealed. In his letter La Reynie recommended "a long stay in prison, ordered by His Majesty, [to] allow the man to recognize his error and give him an opportunity to repent." No record of the ultimate outcome survived, but the odds are very good that the king approved the recommendation.

As part of his effort to address Parisian morality, La Reynie similarly showed no sympathy for the homeless. The earliest forms of hospitals—the *hôtels-Dieu* (houses of God), as they were called—had originally been established to heal tired and sick

Christians traveling on religious pilgrimages. Now, the *hôtels-Dieu* provided a convenient place to incarcerate the poor, the mentally ill, and prostitutes in order to "reform" them. Living in cramped and unhygienic spaces, they received only minimal sustenance and were threatened with beatings if they did not obey the rules. To ensure full police involvement, La Reynie appointed himself to the board of directors overseeing hospitals, public charities, and orphanages.

Despite some grumbling about La Reynie's heavy-handedness, the early years of his work as police chief earned him much praise and goodwill throughout the city. "Thanks to your talents," an appreciative Parisian wrote La Reynie, "everyone feels more secure in Paris...we don't hear 'Catch that thief' anymore. Valets, who are sometimes so insolent, don't carry swords, don't insult anymore, and don't hit people. The number of assassins, poisoners, prostitutes, and blasphemers has decreased, and the streets are much less muddy." The *Mercure Galant,* France's most influential society paper, also praised La Reynie: "Monsieur de la Reynie attempts nothing that does not pass; he has done things since he has been Lieutenant of the Police that were thought impossible, and which many ages attempted in vain. No judge could be more equitable, uncorrupt, or zealous in the service of his King. The populace is so obliged to him, they ought to contrive a way to eternalize his memory."

Louis XIV agreed, making his own contributions to the praiseworthy propaganda of La Reynie's work. Two years after the police chief's appointment, he commissioned a commemorative medal. It featured a woman, the allegorical representation of Paris, holding one of La Reynie's lanterns in her hand, with the inscription: "Security and Clarity of the City 1669."

3

The Street at
the End of the World

As much as La Reynie's efforts transformed daily life in Paris, many things remained frustratingly out of his control. The Montorgueil quarter was one of them. The most impoverished and godforsaken place in Paris served as home to a violent network of criminals who catered to every dark desire imaginable.

Meaning literally "mount pride," Montorgueil sat at the northern outskirts of the city. Ramshackle homes leaned precariously against one another in the tangled network of alleyways and narrow streets. Inside, families took turns sleeping on a single, shared mattress in their crowded quarters.

For the even less fortunate, the streets were home. Men, women, and children made gaunt from hunger roamed the neighborhood dressed in dirty and tattered clothing that barely covered their skeletal frames. Some had found ways to fashion makeshift shoes from odd pieces of leather gathered from a nearby tannery, wrapping the leather around their feet with twine. Others trudged barefoot through the rank-smelling, ankle-deep mud as they pleaded with passersby for a coin or a scrap of bread. The desperation of the situation was captured in the very name of one of the quarter's streets: *la rue au Bout du Monde* (the Street at the End of the World).

In a darkened cul-de-sac steps from the Street at the End of the World lay the Court of Miracles. A place of legend, it inspired both fear and curiosity in onlookers. An old and rotting house half buried in the ground served as the only entry point to the most notorious den of organized crime in Paris. To get there, visitors descended a steep and winding bridge that led to the front door. Inside, the shack opened into a large subterranean network of tunnels extending all the way to the city's ramparts. Rumor had it that more than five hundred men, women, and children lived together "without faith and laws" in these squalid underground caverns.

Every day a motley army emerged from the Court of Miracles and fanned out across the city in search of loot. It ranged from elderly men and women who stood hunchbacked and quivering on crutches to children whose deformed limbs required them to be carted around in wheelbarrows: The more dramatic the show of suffering, the easier it was to profit from the guilty charity of the bourgeoisie and nobility. Indeed, the Court of Miracles got its name from the beggars, for whom the show of their infirmities was mostly an act. At the end of the day, wrote one observer, "they clean themselves up and become healthy and jolly in an instant—without any miracles."

Senior members of the Court of Miracles devised a system for training neophyte criminals in the fine art of petty theft. An apprentice thief began by practicing cutting a purse suspended from rafters—while standing precariously on an unstable platform. If the apprentice stole the purse but fell off, he was beaten—and made to repeat the drill until successful. Once the apprentice passed the first test, his mentors took him to a public place—a market, a church exit, a busy passageway—and told him to steal something. To teach him how to "maintain his sangfroid" his elders would yell into the crowd without warning: "Stop thief!"

While the apprentice was being beaten by the victim and other witnesses, the older thieves used the distraction to steal cloaks, jewelry, money, and whatever else they could get their hands on.

Nothing that took place at the Court of Miracles, however, could compare with the strange and troubling things that occurred a few streets away. At the heart of Montorgeuil stood the house of Catherine Voisin, palm reader, fortune-teller, and poison maker. Every day, women dressed in elegant clothing arrived at Madame Voisin's door. They teetered precariously in their silk-covered high-heeled shoes as they exited their carriages. With one hand the women held a fan in front of their faces to protect their identity; with the other they hoisted their skirts to protect their dresses from the mud and the filth.

Voisin dressed the part of the mysterious and powerful witch she claimed to be. She wore a long embroidered tunic over a green velvet robe, which she topped off with a flowing crimson cloak. Like most people of her day, Voisin believed in the power of herbs, charms, and spells. The intervention of otherworldly forces, whether God or the devil, determined all things in early European culture: success and failure, love and loss, health and sickness, life and death. Despite centuries-long efforts by the Church to tamp down superstitious practices, the distinctions between religion and magic were far from clear. Illiterate peasants and well-educated nobles alike consulted astrologers and believed in their prognostications. An astrologer had even been present at Louis XIV's birth to draw up the new king's chart. Silver and gold charms inscribed with protective symbols, called sigils, dangled from the necks of those who could afford them; and *grimoires*, or spell books, containing incantations to ensure achieving desires from clear skin to winning at cards, were often nestled among household remedy manuals.

The women seeking Madame Voisin's mystical help chased after the same dreams: love, passion—and when it all fell apart, coldhearted revenge. In whispers they confessed their deepest secrets to Voisin. But it was when words failed that Voisin demonstrated her uncanny ability to guess what troubled the distressed woman who sat across from her: unrequited love, an unfaithful lover, an illegitimate pregnancy, a miserable marriage, an abusive husband.

Many of Voisin's best clients were women of the nobility. Marriage, especially among the upper classes, was rarely based on love. Instead it served to merge political and economic interests between families. A seventeenth-century priest reportedly told one of his penitents that loving one's husband was something better left to the lower classes: "It is only six months since the sacrament joined you, and you still love your husband? I dare say your dressmaker has the same weakness for her own [spouse], but you, Madame, are a marquise."

During her initial meeting with a client, Voisin often shrugged as the woman shared her woes, telling her to take her troubles up with God. In fact there was a church right next door where she could pray and make confession. It was usually after Voisin's perfunctory first dismissal that the desperate woman quickly got down to business and pressed Voisin for her assistance, the payment offered increasing with each rebuff.

The many beauty products that Voisin sold from the ground floor of her home represented the most benign aspect of her profitable business. She offered fake eyebrows made of mouse hair and moleskin. She distilled herbs, such as argentine, known for removing red marks and sunspots. Voisin also mastered recipes for skin-whitening waters and washes, using traditional ingredients such as eggshells, milk, oil of poppy, or the juice of white melons.

If beauty alone was insufficient to capture the heart of a potential lover, Voisin offered a wide range of love potions. She sold lip balms infused with special herbs that would make any man fall in love with the woman who kissed him while wearing them. She also crafted creams and perfumes made of the powder of dried moles, roosters' combs, and menstrual blood—all of which were believed to have aphrodisiac properties. Another of Voisin's arcane techniques involved taking pigeon hearts, drying them, and then crushing them into a love powder that the wishful client could then sprinkle onto the man's dinner plate.

It was, however, the shimmering powder of cantharis that was most prized as an aphrodisiac. Also called Spanish fly, cantharis came from an iridescent green beetle found on olive trees and honeysuckles. The beetle secretes a substance called cantharidin, which when ingested could cause a person's blood vessels to swell—including and especially those in the genital area.

Cantharis was usually administered as a powder or in a tincture mixed with other substances known for their aphrodisiac properties. An early treatise on sex and venereal disease offers the following recipe: "Take of civet, eight grains; amber-grise, six; the best musk, five; Indian oil of cinnamon, eight drops; distilled oil of nutmegs and mace, each four drops; tincture of cantharis, ten drops...with which anoint the nut of the yard and perineum before engaging with your wife, which will be of extraordinary efficacy for procreation for it stimulates and mightily prompts venery, causes titillation and delight." Mixtures such as these apparently worked so well that the sixteenth-century surgeon Ambroise Paré reported the case of a man who suffered from a perpetual erection (the "most frightful satyriasis") after swallowing a mixture of ground cantharis and nettles.

Despite its presumed libidinous attributes, Spanish fly could also be poisonous if administered in too high a quantity, which it often was. An overdose of cantharis produced stomach ulcers followed by a "burning fever, vertigo, madness, restlessness, the brain being disturbed by...vapors lifted from the corroded and burnt parts of humors."

While Voisin was smart enough not to sample her own elixirs, she liked to drink. In those moments when alcohol numbed her discretion, she sometimes bragged about what happened in the shack in the courtyard of her home. It was here that Voisin frequently escorted women of all ages who worried about protecting their honor, their marriage, or both. "Voisin could make a lady's bosom more bountiful or her mouth more diminutive," wrote one contemporary familiar with what happened at the woman's house. "She also knew just what to do for a nice girl who had gotten herself into trouble."

In the small dirty shack Voisin gruffly instructed her nervous clients to hike up their heavy skirts and lie on a bloodstained wooden table. Next came an order to take a deep breath and remain still. Some moaned, others stifled screams. But in every case, entrance to the shack was invariably followed by pain and loss.

A lodger in Voisin's home claimed to have discovered the remnants of her procedures. Finding himself alone in the courtyard, he lifted the stained fabric curtain that served as a door to the small wooden hut. Inside he saw something he would never forget. Countless fragments of tiny bones sat charred in piles of ash: a miniature skull here, a tiny jawbone there. Perhaps Voisin had not been exaggerating, the lodger later recalled, when she estimated with pride that she had burned the corpses of more than 2,500 aborted children.

In theory, abortion was a crime punishable by death. In 1660 the noble classes of Paris were abuzz about the death of Mademoiselle de Guerchi, one of the queen's ladies-in-waiting. Finding herself pregnant with the child of her married lover, Monsieur de Vitry, she turned to a midwife for help. While it is not exactly clear what type of procedure the midwife performed, Guerchi died in her care several hours later. A court case followed. Under intense interrogation the midwife admitted that she had helped Guerchi abort her unwanted child. For the crime of killing an unborn fetus, the midwife was sentenced to death by hanging. Denied a Catholic burial, her body was burned publicly on a funeral pyre as a cautionary tale for other women.

Yet if Voisin's constant stream of clients was any indication, she was willing to take the risk. Voisin worked in partnership with a midwife named Catherine Lepère. When a woman worried about late periods, Voisin sent her first to Lepère's home. The elderly widow, who wore all black and looked the image of a witch, usually sold her a small bottle filled with ruby-red liquid in exchange for money, splitting the profits with Voisin. "Take this," the old woman would say, "You'll see soon enough if you're with child." In those cases where the client was visibly pregnant, Lepère would nod to her adult daughter, Madame Leclerc, to retrieve a large clay pot from a high shelf filled with bottles, jars, and other containers. Setting the pot onto the table, Leclerc scooped a bit of powder into a small sachet and handed it to the woman, instructing her to add it to her next meal or glass of wine.

The partnership between Lepère and Voisin had been lucrative, but Lepère groused on slow days that she was not making enough money. With a smile, her daughter bantered back, "So what you really want is that all women and girls be whores?" The mother never answered, but her silence was as good as a resounding yes.

When Lepère's powders did not work, the woman's next stop was Voisin's courtyard shack. "The secret [to a successful abortion]," Voisin later revealed, lay in "a little hollow syringe with a button that has a lot of holes in it." The syringe was filled with warm water mixed with "a white substance" and injected into the woman's uterus. The historical record does not indicate what Voisin and Lepère's various powders and potions contained and how they worked. However, there was no dearth of "recipes" to end a pregnancy circulating in herbal manuals and in oral tradition. Plants such as celery, fern, juniper, and parsley were long believed to stimulate menstruation; and marjoram, peony, marigold, and pennyroyal were also lauded for being "wonderful for the womb." Knowledgeable practitioners knew exactly what that meant, especially given that pennyroyal was most frequently used in a tincture or through intrauterine injections for abortions.

In early modern Europe, both lay and learned people alike were convinced that the bodies of newborns—whether stillborn, aborted, or murdered immediately after birth—had mystical properties. Placentas were used as aphrodisiacs when dried into a powder or a cure for infertility when eaten raw, practices the Church condemned. Tradition also had it that the fat of children was what made witches' brooms airborne, and dried umbilical cords served as wicks in the candles that illuminated their black Sabbaths.

So as not to be accused of witchcraft, Voisin made a show of baptizing the aborted fetuses, sending her servant, Margo, to the church next door to fill a small pewter pot with holy water from the font. She also burned the evidence of her business in a small oven in the garden.

While some women came to Voisin for help with love and its consequences, others came looking for revenge. The priestess who could make a love potion could also, if she were so inclined, make a poison. And Voisin was always so inclined, for a good price.

To help a client determined to get rid of her husband, Voisin asked for the man's shirt. She would then bid adieu to her guest and pass the shirt to a trusted laundress, who washed it thoroughly with an arsenic-based soap. (In a pinch, the man's shoes were also an option.) Buttoning his freshly pressed *chemise*, the husband unwittingly sealed his own fate. The rash appeared a few hours later, followed by blisters, nausea, vomiting, and finally death. For the husband whose skin resisted the poison, a second shirt would be ordered up nine or ten days later. In the meantime the family physician would diagnose the man with a pernicious case of syphilis, whose telltale sores earned the wife, his murderer, the sympathy of friends and family.

In early Europe arsenic had long been the poison of choice. Also called *mort-aux-rats* (death to rats), it was easy enough to acquire in local apothecary shops for domestic purposes. Colorless, odorless, and tasteless, it could be used on clothing, in food, or via an enema (a staple in early household medicine) without detection. When administered in small doses over a long period of time, arsenic—as well as other common poisons such as opium, sulfur, antimony, and quicksilver—proved difficult to pinpoint with certainty in criminal investigations. Its symptoms were frustratingly similar to those of common illnesses, such as food poisoning, gastric ulcers, and dysentery. It would not be until the mid-nineteenth century that a British chemist, James Marsh, discovered a way to test for the presence of arsenic in liquid by creating a yellow precipitate (arsenic sulfide).

Voisin prepared her own brand of exotic poisons in the same courtyard shack where she performed abortions. Toads were her ingredients of choice. All species of toads produce toxins in varying levels of potency, which are released as a defense mechanism against predators. When the venom is mixed with arsenic, as was often done in early modern Europe, it produces intense convulsions, vomiting, and death. Like arsenic, there was no definitive way to test for toad poisons.

Another one of Voisin's colleagues, named François Belot, claimed he had a foolproof way of poisoning his victims. First he force-fed arsenic to a frog and placed it in a silver goblet. Pinching the frog's head, he made it urinate and then smashed it to death. Belot claimed that by coating the cup with the liquids produced, it was possible to ensure multiple deaths, even if the goblet were washed and rinsed between uses.

Voisin preferred a different method. Her neighbor Madame Vautier delivered large pots full of toads to Voisin's home on the rue Beauregard. Together the two women retreated to the secluded garden behind the house and lit a large fire, stoking it until the logs burned bright red. Once the fire was ready, Voisin reached her hand into the pot to grab one of the toads, which puffed up its neck in resistance. Holding it firmly in one hand, she milked the toad of its venom. Using her thumb and forefinger, she also squeezed the porous glands on the toad's legs as well as at the base of its neck. A viscous white liquid oozed from each of the glands and dripped onto a glass dish. Within minutes the venom dried to form a thick, rubbery substance that could be easily scraped off and added to other ingredients to create a deadly mix.

Once the toad had been milked, Voisin wrapped the animal tightly in muslin and tossed it, alive, onto the coals. Wearing a scarf around her nose and mouth to block the putrid smell, Vautier cooked the toads, turning them over and over until their bodies were crisp enough to be ground into a toxic powder, ready for their next customer.

4

To Market

Catherine Voisin often sent her nine-year-old daughter, Marie-Marguerite, into the dangerous Montorgeuil neighborhood to run errands. Stepping out of the family's house, the child joined the swirl of activity in the streets outside, a coin clutched tightly in her fist. Errands for her mother required her to hurry, otherwise she would suffer her mother's wrath. She did not know kindness from her mother, who maimed just as easily with a sharp word as she did with a kick or a punch. Catherine did both, and often.

Marie-Marguerite frequently made her way to the largest market in the city, Les Halles, a ten-minute walk south from her home. The same chaos that reigned in the city streets lived here, but with much greater intensity. Fruit and vegetable merchants competed with one another as they hawked their wares to the crush of shoppers who funneled into the market's narrow rows from all parts of the city. Pickpockets and beggars roamed about, nipping a piece of fruit here, a cloak there, while prostitutes rubbed up against male customers to let them know that vegetables were not the only thing for sale.

Marie-Marguerite ducked and elbowed her way through the stalls until she found the right vendor. Cages of birds—hens, quail, ducks, and pigeons—were stacked several layers high and lined the perimeter of the small space. Some of the animals were sold alive. The days of others were numbered, if the plucked birds hanging from the wooden beams were any indication.

The child trotted toward the pigeon cages and scanned the clusters of bobbing heads until she found precisely what her mother wanted: a single white bird. Marie-Marguerite relinquished her coin and rushed home as quickly as she had come, holding the bird protectively under her arm. She did not know what her mother planned to do with it, but whatever it was, it would not be pleasant. Not much of what happened in her family's run-down home ever was.

Arriving home, she walked through the darkened entry hall and into the courtyard. Her mother waited there impatiently. Next to her stood an ugly, older man wearing a bright red wig and a gray cape. Without a word the man yanked the pigeon from her arms. In one deft move, he sliced the bird's neck and collected its blood in a glass goblet. When there was nothing left, he tossed the pigeon onto the ground. With a gruff scowl, her mother told her to go, to get out. Marie-Marguerite ran from the courtyard.

The name of the man who wore the red wig at Voisin's house was Adam Coeuret. A longtime charlatan, Coeuret changed his name not once but twice: first to Dubuisson and then to Lesage (the wise one).

Lesage claimed to be able to communicate with the devil. For a fee, clients wrote their most secret wishes and desires on a small slip of paper. After noting that he had not read what was written on the paper, Lesage crumpled it up into a tiny ball, rolled the ball in wax, and tossed it into the fireplace. Together Lesage and his client watched it smoke, catch fire, and turn to ashes. A few days later, when the client returned for an update on the status of their request, Lesage produced the original, unburned piece of paper. It was a sure and favorable response from Satan, he claimed: Their request would be granted. Unknown to the fee-paying dupe, Lesage had switched the original request for a fake, and by sleight of hand, burned that one in the fire.

Always on the prowl for new avenues of income, Lesage decided it was time to create a small partnership among similar-minded entrepreneurs who traded in making dark desires come true. He heard rumors that Voisin's clientele had become decidedly more illustrious in recent months. Some speculated that many of her customers even moved in the same orbit as the Sun King himself. As Lesage knew firsthand from his ruses, there were plenty of people for whom Voisin's earthly interventions would not be enough. Some wishes could be fulfilled only with the help of otherworldly forces. What Voisin's network needed, Lesage calculated, was someone who could take her clients' desires to a higher power— not to God but rather his hellish counterpart.

Lesage believed there was no better person for the job than a priest. Like many people in the early modern period, he believed if religious ceremonies allowed one to commune with God, their perversion could conjure up the devil instead. With this in mind, he partnered with a Father Mariette, a priest at the Church of Saint-Séverin, to expand his range of services.

Hopeful that they might merge their client lists, Lesage called on Voisin at her home with Mariette at his side. Voisin was not a trusting person by nature or profession, but she found Lesage strangely seductive, and it did not take long for the two to become lovers. Deciding she had found a kindred spirit, she revealed to Lesage that several high-ranking women of Louis XIV's court were regular customers, and they wanted to do everything within their means to ensure that they took a place in Louis's heart and bed.

Voisin showed Lesage and Mariette an envelope containing some herbs that she prepared for one of her royal customers. Unable to hide his enthusiasm, Lesage explained to Voisin that he knew a way to make the herbs even more powerful and to increase her profit margins—for a cut. He took the package from her and handed it to Mariette. The priest nodded. A silent pact had been made. To seal the arrangement, Voisin brought out a bottle of strong alcohol, eau-de-vie [aquavit], and handed it to Mariette.

The priest lifted a pouch from under his cassock and removed a small chalice. Murmuring prayers, he solemnly poured the liquor in the chalice, and they took turns drinking from the holy cup.

A few days later Voisin ventured across the Seine to the narrow and twisting streets of the Latin Quarter. Her destination was the hulking Church of Saint-Séverin, which stood across the river from its more elegant sister, Notre-Dame. Scores of gargoyles stared down as Voisin and Lesage lumbered up the five stone steps and entered the fourteenth-century church. Once inside, the pair knelt in the direction of the altar and made the sign of the cross. It did not take long for Voisin to spot Father Mariette. He was now dressed in religious vestments and preparing for Holy Communion at the altar.

Despite its colorful and delicate stained-glass windows and Gothic flourishes, there was something ominous about the church, making it the perfect home for a man like Father Mariette. Its twisting pillars, meant to evoke palm trees and the Christian symbolism of peace and eternal life, looked instead like gnarled arms crawling their way through the stone floor. The dim light of the nave and the murky shadows cast by the small chapels heightened its strange ambience. The priests who presided over this church lived not in the light, but twilight.

With somber focus, Mariette prepared the sacrament in front of the faithful. Voisin watched as he carefully lifted the chalice and intoned prayers in Latin. She joined the other worshippers in the long line that snaked toward the altar to receive the sacrament. She knelt in devotion when it was her turn, and made the sign of the cross. She then looked up knowingly at Father Mariette, who blessed the host and laid it into Voisin's open hands. Placing it in her mouth, she then reached both hands toward the chalice to sip the wine that Mariette offered her. As she did, she felt the priest's hands slip a small package into her palm. It was the packet of herbs. Nodding toward the altar, he signaled that they received the same blessing as the host and the wine.

As they left the church Lesage reassured Voisin that, because Mariette had now performed his "conjurations" on the packet, the herbs would have the full and intended effect. "Indubitably," he added.

Ostensibly pleased with the results of the spell, a few months later Voisin's customer contacted Lesage and Mariette directly to request additional services from the priest. The men traveled by coach to the King's château in Saint-Germain-en-Laye, his main place of residence from 1666 to 1682.

Perched on the banks of the Seine to the west of Paris and surrounded by a thick forest, Saint-Germain had long been one of the favorite residences of French kings when they wanted to escape from daily life in the more centrally located Louvre. Saint-Germain held an especially important place in Louis XIV's life. He had been born at the palace and, during the Fronde, found safety there when residence in the Louvre proved too dangerous for the young king.

The men were escorted discreetly to the woman's quarters. Once there, Mariette pulled a small bottle filled with holy water from a pouch and sprinkled it on the woman's head. A few steps away, Lesage lit incense in a small thurible and began swinging it with smooth motions through the richly decorated room. Handing the woman a small scrap of paper, Mariette instructed her to read the incantation aloud. When the short ceremony ended, the woman provided the men with a small package containing two pigeon hearts, recently excised.

The next time the two men saw their client, it was in the private sacristy of Saint-Séverin. Taking a chalice in one hand and holding the pigeon hearts in the other, the priest recited prayers in Latin as he passed the offering under the sacred vessel. Lesage held open a gold box. Mariette placed the pigeon hearts inside. He then added the paper with the incantation, a drawing of a pentagram, and a consecrated host. Closing the box and handing it to the woman, the two men sent her back on her way to the Château of Saint-Germain.

Over the weeks that followed, Lesage and Mariette bragged too loudly about the demand for their services, and word of their deeds traveled quickly. "There is much talk about a priest at Saint-

Severin," The doctor, Guy Patin, wrote. "They say he is a magician, but I don't believe it."

Lesage and Mariette were soon arrested. Accused of impiety, they were put on trial in the criminal courts of Châtelet, which lay in La Reynie's jurisdiction. Both Mariette and Lesage admitted to participating in mystical ceremonies, with the priest going so far as to give the name of their noble client. No one paid much attention to the two men, or to their ridiculous-sounding claims that a member of the king's entourage had employed them to cast magic spells. When the two men found themselves on the stand three months later, they wisely chose to make no further mention of their client. Preferring to put the matter quietly to rest, the court exiled Mariette from Paris for nine years and sent Lesage to the galleys.

PART II

King of Hearts

5

Agitation without Disorder

I n June 1667, two months after La Reynie's appointment as
lieutenant general of police, Louis XIV traveled through the
Low Countries in a gold-encrusted coach drawn by six Anda-
lusian horses. A regiment of 3,200 soldiers, three hundred carriages, and a swarm of noblemen on horseback accompanied the
king. By one count the procession included more than thirty thousand horses.

The sound of horse hooves could be heard from miles away as
Louis XIV's cortege snaked its way through the countryside. Peasants working in the fields raced to the main road to witness a
spectacle unlike anything they had seen in their lives—and likely
never would again. "Everything you have ever read about the mag-
nificence of King Solomon or the grandeur of the King of Persia,"
wrote one observer, "is nothing compared to all of the pomp that
accompanies the king on this trip."

The army of carriages rocked back and forth along the pock-
marked dirt road. The noblewomen in the entourage wore sumptuous, décolleté dresses with sleeves that dipped low off the
shoulder and opened widely just below the elbow. Even on an

extended rural expedition, their hair was piled high on their heads, meticulously coiffed, and adorned with lace bows. Alongside the carriages, their sons and husbands rode stiff-backed on fine horses, handsome in their knee-length jackets, brocade pants, and wide silk victory belts tied around their waists.

Yet the most interesting show was the one the thousands of onlookers could not see. It took place in the sumptuous interior of the king's coach, where Louis sat next to his wife, Marie-Thérèse. Louis's brother Philippe and his wife, Henrietta Anne, joined the royal couple, as did two of Louis's mistresses: Louise de La Vallière and Athénaïs de Montespan.

The king and his court were on their way to declare victory over the Spanish in the first major military campaign of his reign. It was not so much a war as an incursion, a bold attempt by the king to assert claims over Spanish-controlled territories in what are now Belgium and the Netherlands. The previous fall, some fifty thousand French troops had massed along the border, near the river Somme. They had little trouble overtaking the towns of Douai, Tournai, Charleroi, and eventually Lille.

Louis declared ownership of the territories in the name of his Spanish-born wife. Curious observers could catch a glimpse of the twenty-nine-year-old as she sat next to her husband in the royal coach. If they were looking for a woman of style and sophistication, they were sorely disappointed. Marie-Thérèse was a plump woman, whose bottom lip jutted out from her round face. She lacked the sense of elegance that had long defined life in the French court. Following instead the Spanish style, she wore her hair in tight curls and had not yet abandoned her enormous and outmoded hooped skirts, so large that they made climbing into a carriage or passing through doors a challenge.

The death of Marie-Thérèse's father, King Philip IV, eighteen months earlier had put the ownership of the Low Countries in question. Louis did not dispute that Spain now belonged to Marie-Thérèse's eldest brother, Carlos. However, he argued that according to the local laws of the contested territories, Marie-Thérèse's rights as Philip's firstborn child from his first marriage took precedence over those of Carlos, Philip's son from his second marriage. In other words, the Spanish Low Countries actually belonged to Marie-Thérèse—and thus to her husband, the Sun King.

Marie-Thérèse was hardly the type of wife one might have imagined for a handsome and gallant young king. The marriage, arranged some seven years earlier, made great political sense, offering "peace as a dowry" at a time when Spain and France seemed forever at odds. Anne of Austria, Louis's mother, who was also Marie-Thérèse's Spanish-born aunt, orchestrated the match.

It was not the first time that Anne had inserted herself into her son's love life. She coordinated the young king's initiation into the world of physical pleasures when he was sixteen. A practical woman, the queen regent knew that sex and love were often easily confused, especially in the young. She did not want Louis to become so enchanted with his first sexual experience that he would fall in love with a girl who would not be suitable, socially and politically, for the monarchy.

To thwart this Anne hand-selected one of her servants to educate her son. The young king lost his virginity to forty-year-old Catherine Bellier. One-Eyed Kate (*Cateau-la-Borgnesse*), as she was called, was "old, short, ugly,...fat, and round all over." Rumor had it that the woman had taken the handsome youngster's virginity one day as he was getting out of his bath, and that there had been many more encounters between Cateau and her pupil. The experience must not have been entirely unpleasant, as the king was said to owe his impressive repertoire of sexual skills to Cateau. For her services Anne's servant received the title baronne of Beauvais, a house, and a pension.

No doubt heartened by her success with Louis and Cateau, Anne worked on finding an appropriate bride for her son. Twelve years earlier, in 1655, she had set her sights on Henrietta Anne of England, the youngest daughter of the English king Charles I and his French-born queen, Henrietta Maria. Louis would have none of it. Instead Louis tested his mother's patience with his affections for not one but two of Cardinal Mazarin's five nieces. Olympe Mancini, the second eldest, caught his attention first. They were both the same age and shared a deep love of the theater and ballet. The possibility of a marriage between Anne's son and the niece of her prime minister did not go overlooked. "It would be a shame to not marry two young people who get along so well," Queen Christina of Sweden declared during a visit to the French court. As much as Anne appreciated Mazarin, she rejected the idea of uniting their families and refused to hear another word about an unworthy pairing for a king. A realist, however, when it came to her son's increasingly obvious sexual needs, Anne did not stand in the way of letting Louis make Olympe his mistress.

In an early sign of the king's fickle nature when it came to women, he quickly tired of Olympe, whom he found delightful but not especially pretty, and focused his efforts on her younger sister Marie. Olympe did not take the rejection well and threw frequent tear-filled temper tantrums in the hope that he might change his mind. It did not work. Her uncle soon set to work finding her a suitable spouse. Mazarin turned first to the prince of Conti, who rejected Olympe in favor of her cousin Anne-Marie Martinozzi. He then tried to unite Olympe with the duke de la Meilleraye, the grand master of the French artillery. Meilleraye also refused, preferring to marry her other sister Hortense instead. When a prince from Savoy offered to marry Olympe, Mazarin readily agreed because the alliance would strengthen the French in the contested region. To soften the blow to his niece, he gave her and her husband the new titles of count and countess of Soissons.

While Olympe grieved the end of her affair with the king, Louis fell in love with Marie. To the king's heartbreak, Anne of Austria again refused to entertain any talk of a royal marriage to a girl from a modest family of Italian nobles. It would do nothing to strengthen France politically. Marie returned to Italy and was promised in marriage to Lorenzo Onofrio Colonna, an Italian prince.

After several false starts the young king soon showed himself more receptive to his mother's suggestions. The Treaty of the Pyrenees, signed by France and Spain in 1659, divided up a number of contested territories along France's southern and northern borders. As part of the treaty, it was understood that Louis XIV would marry the Spanish infanta Maria Teresa. The princess was immediately smitten with her first cousin after seeing his portrait. Seeing her from a distance during the first formal meeting of the future couple's parents, the young French king declared simply that she would be "easy to love."

Even though the marriage between the gallant Louis and the frumpy Maria Teresa in 1660 was one of political convenience, the king wasted no time in bedding his new wife following the wedding ceremony. He urged the court to speed through the normal pomp and circumstance that usually preceded the consummation of a royal marriage: undressings, bathings, and blessings. Not long after, he was in bed making love to a shy but willing Maria Theresa, now known by her French name, Marie-Thérèse.

Yet it would not take long for Louis's romantic interests in his new queen to dwindle. He found wordplay and suggestive repartee thrilling, especially when followed by physical conquest. The quiet and devout Marie-Thérèse, who spoke little French, offered none of that. All the same, Louis demonstrated a deep respect for his queen throughout their marriage. Despite his dalliances and affairs, he could be brutal to anyone who did not show his queen the proper deference. He also made it a point of pride to sleep each night next to his wife—even if it meant slipping into bed at a very late hour after having enjoyed the company of one of his lovers.

As for Marie-Thérèse, she preferred to live with willful blindness toward her husband's infidelities. In return Louis made it a priority to spend intimate time with his wife on a regular, even scheduled, basis. Lovemaking was usually followed by a very public demonstration by the queen the next morning. Blushing with pride, she took Communion in view of the entire court and prayed that a royal child would soon be on its way. By the time of the trip through the Low Countries after seven years of marriage, she had given birth to four children.

Philippe and his wife Henrietta Anne sat across from the royal couple in the coach as it rumbled through the countryside. The two brothers were a study in contrasts. The king radiated handsome confidence and control. Philippe, on the other hand, wore his frustration and insecurities for the world to see.

As the second child, Philippe had little choice but to live in the shadow of his elder brother. After Louis made a public refusal of Henrietta Anne, she was paired with Philippe as a way to solidify strategic alliances between England and France. The marriage had gone badly from the start. The king taunted his brother about wedding "the bones of the Holy Innocent," as he had called Henrietta Anne when she was still a thin and awkward young girl. The couple had also been unable to consummate their marriage immediately because "*Monsieur le Cardinal*" (a contemporary term for menstruation) made an appearance on their wedding night. When the couple finally did have a chance for intimacy, Philippe failed to "entertain" his new wife. Although Henrietta Anne gave birth to their first child almost exactly one year after their marriage, rumors swirled that Monsieur, as Philippe was known, preferred men.

All the same, Philippe had been unable to hide his frustration and anger when, only months after his marriage, Louis developed a sudden interest in Philippe's wife. "All of France," wrote one commentator at the time, "find themselves with her [*chez elle*]." Having successfully morphed from an awkward eleven-year-old to a beautiful young woman, Henrietta Anne charmed everyone around her. Her eyes brightened when she laughed, which she did often. Sharing the king's devotion to dance and the arts, Madame— as she was known—turned the Château of Fontainebleau into a haven to which the nobility eagerly flocked. Upbeat and lively, she had "something about her that made one love her." Henrietta Anne further earned the adoration of one of the period's greatest playwrights. "The court regards you," wrote Jean Racine, "as the arbiter of all that is delightful."

Philippe witnessed with irritation a close friendship, one that seemed to teeter toward love, slowly developing between his brother and his wife. Still, there was little he could do; his royal brother's wishes had always come first. He watched resentfully as brother- and sister-in-law, both talented equestrians, galloped through the countryside together in the forests of Fontainebleau. He sat quietly seething among the other spectators when the two danced together, as principal performers, in open-air ballets. And it was hard to miss his disapproving glare when they chatted gaily together over luxuriously prepared meals followed by quiet strolls around the château's reflecting pools, as music by court composer Jean-Baptiste Lully filled the air.

While the affection shared between the two appeared chaste, it did not take long for the king's wife, pregnant with their first child, and his deeply religious mother to join Monsieur in his concerns about the impropriety of the situation. Recognizing the need to avoid scandal but unwilling to stop spending time with Louis, Henrietta Anne proposed that the king make a show of courting one of her ladies-in-waiting. This would allow him to spend as much time as he liked at Fontainebleau with her.

6

The Dew and the Torrent

The woman whom Henrietta Anne had chosen as Louis's next mistress sat uncomfortably in the coach on a narrow bench between the king and his wife on one side and Philippe and Henrietta Anne on the other. Louise de La Vallière had first been introduced to the king when she was a naive and religious-minded seventeen-year-old. With long blond hair that cascaded in loose curls over her shoulders, Mademoiselle de La Vallière possessed a graceful beauty that was reminiscent of a "Greek statue." Other young women at court were all too aware of the usefulness of their good looks. In contrast Louise appeared pure and fresh—which earned her the nickname "the Dew" among court insiders.

Although she did not know it at the time, her arrival at Henrietta Anne's court as a maid of honor had been part of the carefully orchestrated plan to detract attention from the rumors swirling around Louis and his sister-in-law. Skilled in the art of seduction, the young king played the role of gallant admirer well. He smiled nervously when Louise entered the room; he listened with rapt attention as she spoke to the other ladies-in-waiting; he found opportunities to stroll, alone, with the young woman in the lush gardens of Fontainebleau and at his sister-in-law's home at Saint-Cloud—making sure the ostensibly private, stolen moments played out in full view of the court.

A graceful tomboy, Louise only had one fault, according to late-seventeenth-century standards—she was flat-chested. Fooling no one, the young woman often wore long, floppy cravats that she tied loosely into two bows to hide this fact. But what she lacked in physical endowment she overcame in sharing the king's passion for dance and horseback riding. Soon Louise took the place of Henrietta Anne on the king's long rides in the countryside.

The ruse worked all too well. The king fell in love with Louise and set about attempting to bed her, but the young woman did not yield easily. Chaste and inexperienced, she rebuffed his advances; she wanted to save herself for marriage. Undeterred, Louis was said to have enlisted the help of the court poet, Isaac de Benserade, who, in his telling, wrote three letters to La Vallière on behalf of the king. She refused the first letter. She hid the second in her dress—where there was, as one snide court observer remarked, "more than enough space." After she received the third letter, she begged the poet to reply in her place: "You have the art of saying no, as if you were saying yes," she explained.

Despite her best efforts Louise soon lost her virginity to the king. The king claimed to be genuinely in love with her. Soon La Vallière fell in love with him. Yet this did little to assuage her guilt for her sins.

For her part Mademoiselle de La Vallière tried to remain discreet and careful when it came to her intimacy with the king, but in 1663, two years after Louis had first set eyes on her, she discovered that she was pregnant. With the help of his minister Colbert, both the king and Louise did everything they could to keep the birth of the child a secret. The greater the attempts to hide the impending birth of the king's first illegitimate child—there were soon to be many others—the more speculative the court grew. On Christmas Eve the court buzzed with stories that a blindfolded doctor had been taken to the bedside of a masked woman. No doubt it was Mademoiselle de La Vallière, the gossips speculated. In a heroic yet futile effort to defuse rumors, a "pale and very changed" Louise rose from bed just a few hours later and attended midnight mass in full view of the court. Colbert had already tendered the child to a family to raise as their own, a service he repeated for Louise in 1665 and again in 1666.

As the coach rumbled across the fields of northern France, Marie-Thérèse and Henrietta Anne looked upon Louise with loathing. Pale faced and exhausted, Louise was four months pregnant with her third child. While she was still in love with the king, he had made it clear that he was done with her. Louis had recently named her a duchess and also legitimized their youngest child. But his generosity had been little more than a public parting gift, Louise was sure. If there were any doubt, that the king had not initially invited her on the journey was proof enough. He instructed her to remain at Versailles instead.

In fact the only reason she was in the carriage at all was that she had ignored the king's orders and followed the royal cortege to Flanders anyway to beg for his attentions. On news of the mistress's imminent arrival, the queen sobbed so violently that she became ill.

Although both the king and his wife refused La Vallière an audience, she insisted—going as far as to ride on horseback at a full gallop alongside the royal carriage. Whether out of sympathy for his former lover or in an attempt to take control of the situation, Louis ordered her into the carriage. But his cold demeanor told Louise everything she needed to know. As if she had not been sufficiently humiliated, she now found herself sitting uncomfortably next to Athénaïs de Montespan, a woman who wanted nothing more than to become the king's next mistress, if she was not sleeping with him already.

In sharp contrast to the slender and reserved Mademoiselle de La Vallière, Montespan was outgoing, curvaceous, unapologetically sensual, and above all ambitious. Married and the mother of two children, Montespan had been serving as lady-in-waiting to the

queen for three years, since early 1664. Louis made such household appointments, not Marie-Thérèse, and he surrounded the
queen with some of the most beautiful women at court.

Blonde with azure blue eyes and unblemished skin, the twenty-
seven-year-old Athénaïs was stunningly gorgeous by most contemporary accounts. Yet Louis nearly passed her over for the position.
Montespan tried very hard to sway the king. "She does what she
can," Louis complained to his brother Philippe, "but I myself am
not interested." Unable to leverage her beauty, she found a way to
use to her advantage the good name of her sister, the marquise of
Thianges, who had a close friendship with Philippe. Philippe facilitated the appointment, looking for affirmation of his influence on
his brother while also taking perverse pleasure in the drama to
come of it.

The position came with lodging and a salary—a most welcome
benefit, as the marquise was in desperate need of money. The year
before her appointment, Athénaïs had married the marquis of
Montespan. From the start things had been difficult. Athénaïs
came to the marriage with a respectable dowry agreement, but her
father, the duke of Mortemart, promised much more than he could
pay up front in order to assure a good marriage for his daughter.
He agreed to pay a portion at the time of the marriage, the remainder to be distributed from her father's estate after his death.

Still, her husband was hardly ideal. The marquis of Montespan
had the same trouble managing his money as Athénaïs's father did.
A large portion of the dowry was put to use to pay the marquis's
debts, leaving little in the way of assistance as the couple set up their
home on the Left Bank of Paris. Further, there was little hope that
the outstanding dowry amount would find its way to them. The
dowry agreement stipulated that payment would be paid directly
from the bride's father to the groom's parents, and they had made it
clear to the couple not to count on ever seeing one *denier*.

Debts accrued. Eighteen hundred *livres* for carriage-seat
repairs, another eighteen hundred for silk sheets, plus 2,150 *livres*
for dress lace: The couple lived a life they could not afford. Creditors knocked on their door. In an act of desperation the marquis

de Montespan borrowed money to pay off the most urgent debts. Slowly household items disappeared—including the marquise's most precious and expensive pair of earrings. Athénaïs was hurt and humiliated, doubly so when her husband decided to join the army and leave her holding their debts.

Madame de Montespan had been among the first to ridicule Louise for her shameless show of desperation. The other ladies-in-waiting followed in their derision: "Heavens keep me from ever being one of the king's mistresses!" Montespan exclaimed with no small amount of feigned righteousness. "Because if I were, I would be embarrassed to present myself in front of the queen."

Truth be told, however, there was nothing that Athénaïs wanted more. In her cleverness and ambition, the marquise had already turned her sights on the one man who could change her situation in an instant: the king. As lady-in-waiting to Marie-Thérèse, she found herself in an ideal position to seduce him. It was just a matter of waiting for the right time.

Few believed the king's claim to be focused solely on matters of war rather than those of the heart. With the court watching his every move, the fact that La Vallière had not been initially included in the travel party left many to wager that the king intended to take a new lover. All bets were clearly on Montespan, and for good reason. A full six months earlier the Duke of Enghien announced to the queen of Poland that "the king is dreaming a bit about Madame de Montespan, and to tell you the truth, she deserves it. No one has as much wit or beauty as she does."

As the coach pushed its way through the fields of the Low Countries, Athénaïs was inclined to believe the rumors she knew were now swirling around her. Just days earlier Louis had invited her to take a carriage ride alone. It would not be long before they arrived at their encampment; and if things went as she hoped, the king would soon be hers. The Torrent, as the court later named her, had every intention of trumping the Dew. She would do whatever it took to make sure of it.

7

The Door Marked 1

It is not known when the king and Madame de Montespan consummated their affair, but it most likely happened during the trip to the Low Countries. Each evening a legion of soldiers and servants set up camp, creating in just a few hours a bustling village larger than most towns in France. At the center of the encampment sat the king's enormous quarters, composed of a network of interconnected tents, each subdivided into separate rooms. A gold-leafed chandelier hung from the center of every room, illuminating armoires detailed with brilliant gold leaf, as well as silk-upholstered beds and chairs.

The fact that the king now traveled not only with his wife but also two of her ladies-in-waiting, both Louis's mistresses, brought headaches for Louis's minister of war, Louvois, who had to find ways to accommodate the "three Queens" in the royal tents. The arrangements proved as complex as the most detailed battlefield mission. "You should accommodate the room marked V for Madame de Montespan," Louvois explained to his head officer in Dunkirk, "and make a door in the place marked with a number 1. There should be a hallway from her room into the room marked 2.

This will serve as her garderobe." Lest La Vallière be forgotten—
or more likely, get in the way—Louvois went on to say that
"Madame la Duchesse de La Vallière will be housed in the room
marked Y, from which you need to make a door, marked here as
3...and another marked 4, which will serve as her closet."

As passionate dramas played out both privately and publicly, the
women had little choice but to pretend to enjoy one another's company as they spent their days moving from village to village together
in the coach and their evenings indulging at banquets. After dinner
the king went for a ride on horseback in the fields of Northern
Europe. Depending on the weather, the women rode alongside him,
mounted or in a coach. "If all wars were done like this," wrote one
observer, "there would not be as much to complain about."

Louis XIV continued his military conquests in the Low Countries, which he undertook in the name of his Spanish queen. He
also spent as much time as possible with Athénaïs. The princess of
Montpensier, Louis XIV's cousin, recalled suggestively that she
and others in the court noticed that "the King was often alone in
his quarters, and that [during those moments] Madame de Montespan was not with the Queen." On days when the troops
remained at camp, the king instructed Marie-Thérèse to visit the
newly conquered towns, villages, churches, and convents. Her
lady-in-waiting, Athénaïs, often pleaded fatigue and preferred to
stay in her quarters. In the evenings Montespan claimed disin-
genuously that she had "slept all day long."

Montpensier also remembered that, while dining with the royal
couple one evening, the queen turned to her and said, "The King
did not go to bed until four o'clock. It was already light out. I do
not know what he could have been doing."

"I was reading dispatches," Louis explained, turning his head
toward his cousin with a sly smile. Montpensier found the exchange
entertaining but, out of respect for the queen, lowered her eyes and
stared silently at the plate in front of her. Montpensier remarked
that the king appeared to be in an "admirably good mood" after
the meal as he set out on his evening walk in the company of his
wife—and his lover, Madame de Montespan. If Marie-Thérèse

was aware of the affair, she chose not to confront the king. "I see many things," the queen later explained to a confidante. "I am not the dupe that everyone thinks I am, but I am prudent."

On September 3, after three months of military action and travel in the company of his court, the king declared victory over Spain in the Dutch provinces. Four days later he returned to his château in Saint-Germain-en-Laye. Now back at home, Louis quickly returned to his regular activities: dancing, horseback riding, hunting, parties, and other sensual pleasures.

Louis found ways to see Montespan alone at Saint-Germain, sometimes more than once a day. He visited her quarters, and especially her bed, every afternoon. They danced together publicly at the court's many evening balls lasting well into early morning. Montespan also joined the king, along with the queen and La Vallière, at the royal table for dinner every night.

Although Louis's timid mistress Louise de La Vallière had fallen out of favor with the king, Louis needed to make a show of still being in love with her in order to distract attention from his relationship with the lively but married Montespan. However, the king's feigned love extended only so far. While La Vallière gave birth to their fourth child one night in early October, Louis attended a ballet in the company of Athénaïs. The infant was immediately whisked away as maids tidied the room and La Vallière rushed to make herself presentable for the *medianoche*, the midnight meal, which the king had decided to take in her quarters. The ruse fooled no one.

As much as Louis enjoyed life at Saint-Germain, the king set his sights on constructing a larger residence more fitting for a valiant and virile king. Three years earlier, in 1664, Louis undertook a massive expansion of the gardens at Versailles, his father's former hunting lodge. He did so in anticipation of the seven-day celebration, which he called the "Island of Pleasure," of his love for Louise. Another wave of construction came in the fall of 1667, in anticipation of another, even more elaborate celebration—this time for Athénaïs.

Louis instructed his architects to expand the view from the palace's windows. To this effect, they widened and lengthened the Allée Royale (Royal Path) behind the château, adding more fountains, statues, and perfectly sculpted trees and bushes. Still not satisfied with the view, the king consulted members of the Academy of Sciences to study whether it would be possible to create a canal at the end of the Allée Royale. The canal would serve two purposes. First, tapering ever so slightly and appearing much longer than it actually was, the canal would trick the eye into believing the king's gardens were infinite. Second, through an ingenious system of aqueducts, the canal would collect water from a distance in order to feed Louis's growing collection of fountains. A massive army of laborers moved earth and lifted stones as big as buildings to make the king's wishes come to fruition. Each day Louis inspected their work. During visits, he often stopped for a quick ride on the rustic wooden roller coaster—one of the first of its kind.

Viewing Versailles as little more than a place for the king's pleasure, Colbert lamented—as he often did—that the massive expenditures involved were a missed opportunity to move the court back to Paris and the Louvre. Colbert's preference for the Louvre over Versailles was not at all surprising given his ongoing desire to turn Paris from a crime capital into the jewel of the Crown. "Your Majesty has spent such huge sums on this house [Versailles]," Colbert told the king, "that the Louvre, which is assuredly the most superb palace in the world and most dignified for the grandeur of Your Majesty, has been neglected." Fueling the conflict between domestic and military affairs, Colbert complained, "Your Majesty knows that, in addition to stunning successes on the battlefield, nothing marks more the grandeur and the spirit of princes than buildings.... Oh what a pity, that the greatest and most virtuous king would be measured by Versailles!"

Ignoring Colbert, the king forged ahead on construction at Versailles. By mid-July 1668, the palace hosted a "great royal entertainment" like none ever seen before to celebrate the Peace of Aix-la-Chapelle, which heralded still more success in the Low Countries and netted France both Wallonia and Flanders (more or less the equivalent of modern-day Belgium). However, all who attended knew that the elaborately choreographed fete served mostly as a joyful acknowledgment of the one-year anniversary of the king's relationship with Madame de Montespan.

At precisely six o'clock Louis invited his guests—fifteen hundred in all—to experience the "pleasures of the walk" with him. On cue hundreds of engineers lying in wait in bushes and behind statues had inserted heavy metal T-bars in the deep holes where the valves for the palace's many fountains lay. When opened, the valves sent jets of water soaring toward the late-evening sun.

Accompanied at every step by the music of the court composer Lully, the king strolled down the long path behind the château toward another fountain, surrounded by a grove of shady trees. Around the fountain stood an immense and edible "mountain" made of cured cold meats. A palace-shaped sculpture made entirely of marzipan and sugar cakes sat next to it. Vases contained live trees from whose branches hung brightly colored candied and real fruit. The court stood entranced as they watched the king and the queen delight in the whimsical yet impeccably presented buffet. The king then invited his subjects to "pillage" the beautiful arrangements that had been prepared for them. Mountains toppled, and the châteaux fell. Noblemen and -women laughed with delight as they nibbled sweets and threw candied fruit at one another.

Supper took place inside a tent that soared fifty feet in the air and had been embellished to look like an ancient temple. Sitting proudly at the table of honor, the king surrounded himself with forty-eight of the most notable ladies in his kingdom, with Montespan proudly holding court next to him.

Sitting among the ladies was La Reynie's new bride, Gabrielle de Garibal. In the twenty years since the death of his beloved Antoinette, the police chief had not considered remarriage. However, he knew that having a widower at the helm of the police force would only be a distraction to the court, inclined to gossip as it was. Less than a year after his appointment, he married the wealthy daughter of the late Jean de Garibal, a former president of the *Parlement*, in a perfunctory ceremony and got back to work clearing the way for law and order in his city of light.

Louis, on the other hand, relished the pleasures of his new love. After an evening of dance lasting into the wee hours of the morning, guests marveled at a fireworks display that "filled the air with a thousand twinkles brighter than the stars." For the grand finale, two intertwined L's—Louis's insignia—lit up the night. Montespan by his side, the king was in love.

8

"He Will . . . Strangle Me"

When Monsieur de Montespan heard rumors of his wife's infidelities, he exploded with outrage. Leaving his military post in the South of France, Montespan returned to Paris, where he launched into a vitriolic and public campaign against his wife and the king. He began by showing the king's cousin and court gossip, Mademoiselle de Montpensier, a written diatribe that he intended to read aloud to the king. In it he demanded that Louis return his wife to him or "suffer the punishment of God." Montpensier counseled him to desist in his protestations, but to no avail.

The next day Montespan showed up unannounced at the Château of Saint-Germain. Resting in her quarters, Athénaïs could hear her estranged husband yelling and cursing as he approached the room. Witnessing the exchange, Montpensier reported that Athénaïs was "nearly speechless." Monsieur de Montespan entered his wife's chambers "in a fury" and spewed "every insolence imaginable." He boasted that he frequented brothels just so he could catch a disease and have his wife "spoil" the king with it. The king's guards scuffled with Montespan, stopping him before he forced himself on Athénaïs.

Furious, Louis signed a *lettre de cachet* instructing the Paris police to throw the belligerent husband in jail, where he remained for a week. In a show of public "kindness," Louis allowed the cuckolded husband to depart to his home in the provinces with the agreement that he would never be seen or heard from again. Montespan announced to family, friends, and the couple's five-year-old daughter and three-year-old son that the marquise was dead and, following a symbolic funeral at the local church, ordered the household to wear black in a gesture of mourning.

While the matter with her husband had been resolved quickly, Athénaïs had lingering concerns about her position at court and, more specifically, in the king's heart. At best her husband's behavior caused annoyance for Louis and at worst, embarrassment. To complicate matters, she had just learned that she was pregnant with the king's child. In a desperate attempt to delay the inevitable scandal her pregnancy would cause, she inaugurated a new dress style at court, *la robe battante,* for the purpose. The royal mistress's loose, flowing dresses fooled no one, and the style was soon christened, tongue-in-cheek, "L'Innocente."

Athénaïs worried Louis might go looking for other ways to fulfill his passions during her pregnancy. Seventeenth-century doctors and midwives considered sex during pregnancy dangerous for the developing child and therefore to be avoided by couples. Her rival, Louise de La Vallière, was still the official *maîtresse-en-titre* at Saint-Germain. As always, Athénaïs feared that if she made one false step, La Vallière could find a way back into the king's bed and heart.

Athénaïs was not the only one with marital problems. The marriage between the king's former love, Henrietta Anne, and his younger brother had been fraught for years. Their troubles began with Philippe's festering outrage at his wife's antics with his brother early in their marriage. Tensions intensified as rumors spread of his predilection for men.

The marriage became an arena where each partner fought bitterly for power and control over the other. The duke of Orléans's latest strategy involved treating his wife's most loyal friends and supporters inhospitably at the couple's home at the Château of Saint-Cloud, in an obvious effort to humiliate his spouse and isolate her from the rest of the court.

At a ball at the couple's home, Philippe appeared in a dress and joined a cluster of women who stood nervously waiting for an invitation to dance. A smartly dressed man approached and bowed to the group. Henrietta Anne's husband lifted the sides of his dress demurely and curtsied to the chevalier of Lorraine. Penniless but handsome and of high birth, the chevalier of Lorraine had become a fixture in Philippe's household. Philippe provided him with luxurious apartments in the Palais-Royal and the Château of Saint-Cloud, along with expensive gifts of jewels and art. Now, in the presence of Henrietta Anne and others, Philippe accepted the offer to dance. The two men glided into the center of the ballroom and performed a perfectly choreographed minuet.

Fortunately for Henrietta Anne, Philippe's blind affection for the chevalier had not been lost on the king, who refused to allow the chevalier to receive income from the lands given to him by his lover. In turn the chevalier directed loud complaints and insults in Louis's direction. It was a fatal misstep.

In early January 1670, the duke of Orléans and the chevalier of Lorraine were asleep in bed together in the prince's quarters. Between three and four in the morning, a team of musketeers burst into the room. Rustling the two men out of bed, the guards grabbed Philippe's lover. Howling loudly, Philippe protested as they forced Lorraine down the stairs, out of the palace, and into a waiting carriage. Soon the chevalier was en route to a prison outside Lyon, two hundred miles away.

Sobbing and distraught with grief, Philippe threw himself at his brother's feet begging him to return the chevalier. Louis refused. In a flurry of rage, Philippe stormed out of the king's chambers, spewing threats of leaving the court for good. Hours later and somewhat calmer, he tried to persuade Colbert to intercede on his behalf. "What [would] the world think of me if it saw me merrily enjoying the pleasures of Carnival while an innocent prince and the best friend that I have on earth for the love of me languishes in a wretched prison far away?" he wrote. Philippe pleaded that he was being forced to choose between his brother and the man he loved. "I ask you to inform the king that, in an extremity of grief, I am required to either leave his presence or to remain in his court in shame." When no response came, Louis's younger brother gathered up his household and left Paris, without the approval of the king, for his home in Villers-Cotterêts, northeast of Paris—taking Henrietta Anne with him.

Brotherly connections or not, angry outbursts and threats rarely worked, if ever, with the Sun King. Louis demanded that Philippe return to the court, or else he would move the chevalier from the Pierre-Encise Prison in Lyon to the isolated Château d'If, an abysmal fortress on a desolate island off the coast of Marseille. Philippe refused.

More than three weeks into the standoff, Colbert traveled to Villers-Cotterêts to meet with Philippe. They struck a deal: Shortly after the visit the monarchy announced Monsieur decided of his own accord to return to court. In return, Louis released Lorraine from prison. In a cruel twist, however, Louis also banned him and forbade him ever to return. The chevalier settled in Rome after his release.

Angry and brokenhearted, Philippe was convinced that his wife used her influence on the king to separate him from the man he loved. Mademoiselle de Montpensier confirmed his suspicions. After a friendly chat with Henrietta Anne, she reported that Philippe's wife seemed to show sympathy for his plight. "I have no reason to love the Chevalier de Lorraine," Henrietta Anne told her, "yet I pity him, and I am heartily sorry for Monsieur's vexation." Montpensier, however, saw right through her. "In her secret heart," the court chronicler claimed, "she was very glad of it; she was in complete union with the king, and no one doubts that she had a share in his disgrace."

Philippe's anger reached new heights when Louis enlisted Henrietta Anne in his war efforts. For years following France's annexation of Spanish-occupied portions of the Low Countries, Louis had been waiting for an opportunity to wage war against the Dutch and seize the rest of the territories. It had been a long wait; the alliance between Holland, England, and Sweden was too strong. But now England suffered a financial crisis that put Charles II at odds with Parliament. Money could tempt the English king to break the alliance, but Louis needed someone Charles II trusted to help broker the deal. There was no better person for the job than Henrietta Anne, the king's own sister.

Henrietta Anne was happy to lend a hand. Her role as a high-stakes intermediary between two kings would enhance her reputation at court. The negotiations were initially kept from Philippe, but when he learned of the secret, he boiled over with rage. Philippe had long been upset about his exclusion from significant state matters. The king's decision to include his wife, and not him, in the treaty negotiations proved more than he could take. For two weeks Henrietta Anne helped craft a treaty on which the "fate of Europe had depended," while her husband seethed. Frustrated and now clearly fearful, Henrietta Anne confided in a friend: "If I make one misstep, he will likely strangle me, all the while saying that he missed me."

PART
III

"She Will Turn Us All into Poisoners"

9

The Golden Viper

For more than a decade Moyse Charas and his wife had been owners of the Golden Viper, a well-known apothecary shop in the Latin Quarter. The fifty-eight-year-old Charas had made a name for himself in Paris by embarking on a well-publicized study on snakes—their anatomy, physiology, behavior, and toxicology—as well as their pharmacological uses. He ordered upwards of five or six dozen snakes delivered to his home, located just above his apothecary shop. For weeks a multitude of visitors streamed through his apartment to witness the sight of so many vipers in one small space.

Delighting his curious guests, Charas pulled large snakes from wide barrels in which he kept his new pets. When a foreign tourist asked Charas if he might hold one, Charas watched appreciatively as the reptile wrapped itself around the young man's limbs for nearly a quarter hour without showing any sign of wanting to bite him. The next day the newly emboldened man reached for a snake as it slithered on Charas's dining-room table. The apothecary shouted at him to stop, but it was too late. The snake, irritated from having been picked up with metal tongs moments earlier, raised its head, bared its fangs and with lightning speed, bit the tourist on his thumb.

Charas quickly pulled out a small knife and grabbed the man's thumb to gash the area of the injury and release the venom. The man resisted, saying that it was nothing, just a little bite. Charas persisted, and the man agreed instead to have the bite cauterized with a red-hot metal spoon. As doctors believed at the time, hot metal applied to the skin burned poison from the skin. Moments later the man collapsed. Pale and weak pulsed, he began convulsing.

The apothecary raced downstairs to his shop. A large vase marked "Theriac" sat on the shelf among scores of decorated porcelain jars. A cure-all, theriac served as treatment for everything from menstrual cramps and fever to epilepsy and plague. Each apothecary created his own proprietary blend that contained upwards of eighty different ingredients, many exotic and imported from the farthest corners of the known world: cinnamon, saffron, rhubarb, sage, aniseed, ginger, myrrh, opium, and above all, snake flesh.

Charas lifted the heavy vessel to his mixing table, scooped out a generous amount of the powder, and emptied it into a mortar. Given that the tourist was in a particularly bad state, Charas sprinkled a hearty amount of "salt of viper," venom extracted from a snake's fangs and evaporated into a crystalline substance, to add punch to the mixture.

Charas mixed his impromptu antidote with wine, honey, and castor oil. Running back upstairs, the apothecary administered the thick mixture to his patient in small portions. With each dose the man became violently ill. Undeterred, Charas continued to force the man to take the theriac spoonful by spoonful until on the eighth try he was finally able to keep the medicine down. Over the next five hours the man slowly improved—"happy in his unhappiness," Charas bragged, "to have been saved so quickly and efficiently." Whether his recovery actually resulted from Charas's mixture or from the purging it caused remains unclear, but the apothecary, and his special blend of theriac, was now famous.

In May 1670, La Reynie accepted an invitation from Charas to witness the preparation of theriac. In the interests of keeping Paris safe from poisoners, the police chief agreed to certify the authenticity of the apothecary's mixture. For this the police chief invited the dean of the Paris Faculty of Medicine, as well as two senior professors at the medical school. Joining them were three representatives of the king's Corps of Royal Apothecaries.

In preparation for the visit Charas ordered substantial quantities of the ingredients needed to make the theriac. Large boxes sat on the floor around an enormous marble mortar. Once opened, the boxes filled the shop with heady scents and contained a hodgepodge of materials of all colors and textures. Some of the ingredients were recognizable by their smell (cinnamon, ginger, pepper, fennel, licorice, myrrh, and musk) or their appearance (dried irises and rosebuds, poppyseeds, thorns); others were more mysterious—or at least sounded as much: dried root of spikenard; terebinth resin (extracted from a flowering cashew plant native to Africa), earth of Lemnos (which looked to be little more than dirt, despite its alleged medicinal properties), along with other plants reputedly hailing from Macedonia, Libya, Egypt, the Americas, and places between.

Vipers' teeth, skin, and flesh held, of course, a prized place among the ingredients. Charas preferred collecting the snakes in the late spring and early summer, rather than the winter when the creatures were too thin and too lethargic. The best ones, he claimed, came from the areas around Lyon or Poitiers. He disagreed vigorously with traditional practices of whipping the snakes before cutting off their heads and tails in order to stir up as much venom as possible. He also resisted the idea that the snakes should be boiled, as this produced only a "stinking, phlegm-like" stew having no medicinal effect whatsoever. Instead Charas proposed that the snakes be treated kindly beforehand in order to extract the maximum amount of venom. Once killed, they should be skinned, gutted, and then carefully dried and reduced to a fine powder.

Charas's precision was not limited to his snakes. Every ingredient, all sixty-five of them, came with complex prescriptions. Moving from box to box, Charas scooped a small amount of each into a bowl, offering a description to La Reynie and the other observers: the name of the ingredient, its weight, its origins, where it was harvested, how it was prepared, and its "proven" medical uses.

La Reynie listened carefully, but with some impatience. The police chief had many other things to do, most pressing of which were the stacks of reports from his commissioners and detectives piling up in his absence. When the apothecary finished his presentation, La Reynie nodded to the inspectors who then weighed each ingredient and poured it into a small mortar, pulverizing it to assess its quality. They agreed unanimously that Charas's "drugs were as beautiful in the middle and back of the box as they were on top," suggesting the freshest and highest quality possible.

Inspection after inspection, Charas transferred the full contents of each ingredient into a mortar—large enough to hold the entire contents of the sixty-five boxes, weighing in all over several hundred pounds. La Reynie could not stay for the entire process; it would take hours to mix the theriac properly. Reaching for an enormous pestle, Charas began pounding, crushing, and stirring the ingredients in the equally enormous mortar. Pausing only to take a breath and to wipe his brow, he talked the observers into helping him sift the mixture over and over through a large screen made of delicate silk. Only when the entirety of the mix could pass through the screen without leaving any small chunks behind did the apothecary declare his hard work over.

At the end of the long day, and on behalf of La Reynie, the inspectors issued Charas a formal certificate of authenticity, which the apothecary posted proudly in the window of his shop: "We certify that Monsieur Moyse Charas has crafted in our presence three hundred pounds of theriac...with an exact and very curious selection and preparation of ingredients. We have been very satisfied and approve with praise...this preparation which has been made according to the best pharmaceutical rules."

Once the deaths started, all of Paris soon lined up in front of the Golden Viper in search of Charas's certified theriac.

10

"Madame Is Dying,
Madame Is Dead!"

enrietta Anne was not feeling well. For several weeks she had suffered from frequent and excruciating pains in her stomach and been unable to eat. The court gossip Montpensier observed that she resembled "a dressed-up dead person, on whom someone had put some rouge." Henrietta Anne tried to maintain appearances, going so far as to ask the queen during a visit to Versailles if they might dine a little earlier than normal together because she had not eaten all day and was famished. When the two women sat down to eat, Henrietta ate her food as if there were nothing wrong. But the "tears in her eyes" gave her away.

A few days later, as she rested at the Château of Saint-Cloud in the company of several other noblewomen, a servant poured Henrietta a glass of chicory tea. No sooner had she taken a sip than she placed one hand on her side and exclaimed, "Ah! What pain. I cannot bear it." Her face turned crimson and then drained of color. Friends and servants helped Henrietta Anne to her room, where she collapsed on the bed. They unlaced her corset, reassuring her with every loosening of the ribbon that all would be well. The fear and doubt in their own eyes told another story.

Now dressed in a loose fitting gown, Henrietta Anne writhed in pain as she waited for the royal doctor to arrive. As Philippe stood beside Henrietta Anne's bed, the doctor declared she likely suffered from a simple case of indigestion or colic and prescribed a standard course of bloodletting and herbal enemas to soothe the cramping. Delirious with pain, she moaned that it was not indigestion: She believed the glass of chicory water she drank contained poison.

Between cries of pain Henrietta Anne murmured to her estranged husband, "Hélas, Monsieur, it has been a long time since you've loved me, and this is unjust." Philippe appeared "neither moved nor embarrassed by Madame's opinion." As the pain continued she whispered, "I shall not be alive tomorrow."

At the news of her illness, Louis rushed from Versailles to her bedside. As she gasped to breathe, Henrietta Anne said again, "I have been poisoned." The royal doctors conveyed their condolences to the king, explaining that there was little more they could do. A priest administered the last rites, making the sign of the cross over a once-vibrant woman, gasping now for breath.

Visibly distressed, Louis said his final farewells to the woman who had brought so much light and happiness to his life and to the court. Whispering in her ear, Louis gave Henrietta Anne permission to slip away. Her breathing slowed; her fingers turned cold. The king lifted his eyes to the heavens and offered up a prayer before he left the room. Henrietta Anne died not long after.

The rumors began immediately. Philippe's hatred of Henrietta Anne was legendary, but was he—or his exiled lover, the chevalier of Lorraine—capable of such a horrific deed?

Henrietta Anne's brother King Charles II, newly restored to the English throne, was distraught upon hearing the news of his sister's death. The peace between France and England, recently brokered with her help, remained tenuous. The English had long viewed the French as untrustworthy and corrupt, and the death of one of their own, possibly at French hands, brought Londoners onto the streets to protest and demand vengeance.

As for Louis XIV, he could not bring himself to believe that his own brother could be involved. To help minimize the potential diplomatic disaster and to learn the truth, Louis demanded an immediate autopsy. Two esteemed French physicians, Pierre Bourdelot and Antoine Vallot, joined two English counterparts whom the English ambassador selected: the royal doctor, Hugh Chamberlain, and the royal surgeon, Alexander Boscher. Henrietta Anne's unclothed body was laid on a table. As the ambassador watched, one of the French surgeons reached for a large lancet. A "fetid vapor and bad odor" stung the air as he sliced through the middle of her body, between the breasts and down through to the stomach. The English physicians cringed not because of the stench, but because of what they perceived as the clear ineptitude of the practitioner. They muttered that he would damage the organs they were there to examine if he did not pay closer attention.

Boscher leaned in for a better look. The intestines were gangrenous. The liver was of a grayish-yellow color and crumbled between the fingers like "breadcrumbs." Holding his breath, he moved his head still closer toward the inside of the body and observed a hole in the upper part of the stomach. The careless surgeon had indeed nicked it. The stomach was full of "an extraordinary quantity of bile." Boscher remarked nonetheless that there was no "excoriation or corrosion...or lesions of any part." From this he concluded that the cause of death could only be an overproduction of bile.

After arguing a bit about the sloppy work of the French surgeon, all those in attendance—French and English alike—signed a joint report asserting that it had been "very boiling bile, very corrupt and malign, and very impetuous, which caused all the disorders in the above said parts." They concluded that ill health, rather than poison, caused Henrietta Anne's death. If it had been poison, her stomach would have been "pierced and rotten."

Few at court, including the king, ever forgot the heartbreaking oration given by Bishop Jean-Benigne Bossuet at Henrietta Anne's funeral. His words captured the overwhelming grief that consumed the court in the wake of her violent and unexpected death. "O cruel night, tragic night, night of terror!" exclaimed Bossuet, raising his arms in distress. "When there rang out, sudden as a clap of thunder, that shocking report: Madame is dying, Madame is dead!"

The king wept for his loss. The death of Henrietta Anne devastated him. He had rebuffed her as a girl, but grew to care deeply for the woman she became. While the doctors dismissed accusations that she had been poisoned at the hands of her own husband, the very possibility had been unsettling.

The next time he would shed no tears and spare no sympathy.

11

Poison in the Pie

enrietta Anne's death was not the only story of poisoning swirling among the nobility. The memory of the sudden illness and death of Civil Lieutenant Dreux d'Aubray
in 1666 was resurrected after the equally dramatic deaths of his
sons, Antoine and François.

The d'Aubray brothers were both highly respected lawyers. In
spring 1670 they had traveled to their country estate in Villequoy
for the Easter holidays with their sister, the marquise of Brinvilliers. They also invited along friends from Paris, all eager to escape
the noisy city.

One night the family and their guests gathered for dinner. A
fire blazed in the great stone hearth at one end of the long table
where François d'Aubray and his brother traded stories and gossip
with their friends. The convivial yet formal conversations among
the nobility around the table contrasted with the frenzied activity
in the kitchens. Cooks wearing smeared aprons scurried to and fro
as they prepared the dishes well-dressed servers brought out to
the table.

Among the servants was a man named La Chaussée, who was

responsible for decanting the wine served at the d'Aubray family meals. He descended into the cellar, examined the many bottles of wine lining the walls, selecting one. Upon returning to the kitchen, he opened the bottle and poured one glass. Looking over his shoulder, La Chaussée slipped a small vial from his vest and quickly sprinkled a bit of white odorless powder into the glass. As La Chaussée walked toward the family dining room, he swirled the wine in the glass, holding it up briefly in front of a candle lantern. Some grit had settled in the bottom of the glass, but not much more than would have been expected from any bottle at the time.

La Chaussée bowed with respect as he placed the glass in front of his master. François d'Aubray paused in his conversation long enough to bring the glass to his nose to appreciate the wine's bouquet. François handed the glass to his brother, who brought it to his lips and took a small sip. Antoine's eyes widened in panic. "Brother, your men would poison me!" he exclaimed. La Chaussée, thinking on his feet, apologized profusely to his master, explaining that the glass had been used earlier to give a servant a dose of medicine, which may have left a residue of bitterness. Unhappy that the glass had been used by a servant and also not washed properly, the brothers nevertheless seemed satisfied with his explanation.

One afternoon not long after François d'Aubray's close call, La Chaussée lingered in the noisy, bustling kitchen as the other servants prepared the elaborate dishes to be served that evening. From the corner of his eye he spied a cook preparing a hearty meat pie. He chatted with her as she cooked the filling for the tart—prized *ris de veau* (sweetbreads, or calves' pancreas) and *rognons de coq* (rooster kidneys)—and poured it into the piecrust. When the cook turned her head, he reached into his pants pocket, pulled out a tiny vial, and emptied its contents into the pie.

That night seven people who ate the pie became violently ill—but no one was sicker than François and his brother Antoine. Those who accompanied them back to Paris in the cortege of coaches could not be sure whether they were bringing the men back to their homes to recover, or whether the trip would soon turn into a funeral procession. When the elder d'Aubray was finally carried by stretcher from his carriage, his family and employ of servants barely recognized him, so much had the poison ravished his body. In a show of feigned devotion, La Chaussée did not leave the man's side once. François succumbed to death two painful months later.

Two surgeons and an apothecary arrived at his home shortly afterward. As the lancet pierced François's bloated belly, the men recoiled from the putrid smell that arose from the incision. Plunging his hands wrist deep inside the abdominal cavity, one of the surgeons extracted the stomach. It was black and riddled with ulcers. François's liver was also verdigris from the gangrene. Still, the doctors were reluctant to conclude that he had been poisoned.

While the doctors pondered the causes of François's death, brother Antoine also took his last breath. An autopsy revealed that both men had died of very similar conditions. Their deaths were identical in symptoms and circumstances to those of their father several years earlier. Physicians speculated that the deaths resulted from an extraordinary disease "so rare and unknown, and yet common to a whole illustrious family," while also remaining open to the possibility of poisoning.

The medical investigators did not explore at the time whether La Chaussée had had a hand in the deaths. He had conducted the poisonings so slowly and artfully that for two years investigators overlooked him as a potential suspect. They were soon to discover how shortsighted they had been.

1 2

An Alchemist's Last Words

The death of Godin de Sainte-Croix in 1672 would have gone unnoticed had he not been broke. In the days that followed, his cramped living quarters felt even tighter as they filled with witnesses to the process: the man's widow, her lawyer, a lawyer who represented various creditors, and local commissioner Sébastien Picard. Two notaries also sat in small chairs, balancing a portable table laden with a stack of parchment paper and an inkwell on their knees.

Wearing a long black robe and square tam, Picard scanned Sainte-Croix's small home. Despite the size of the space, the commissioner noted that the task would require several days. Further complicating matters, there was no doubt that Sainte-Croix had dabbled in alchemy. In fact there seemed to be little space in the home for much else. Every nook and cranny was stuffed with bottles and vials, cups and spoons, alembics and drying racks. The space could easily have been mistaken for an apothecary shop or an alchemist's laboratory.

After the inventory got under way, the commissioner heard someone knocking insistently on the main entrance door below.

Picard walked to the window and peered down to see a man dressed in a long gown. While he could not see his face, the tonsure indicated that he was a member of the clergy. Picard went to the door and greeted the man, who introduced himself as the family's priest.

In his hand the priest clutched a key, which he claimed Sainte-Croix had entrusted to him before his death. Recognizing the key, Sainte-Croix's wife led the priest and the commissioner to a small closet, where her husband kept his most precious possessions. She was just as curious as the others to learn what it held. For years her husband had banned her from this precious space, making it clear that she should never attempt to enter it. With Picard's approval, the priest inserted the metal key and turned the lock.

A set of papers rested on top of several closed boxes. The priest recognized it as Sainte-Croix's final confession. In an era when death could and often did strike without warning, it was not unusual for men and women to write detailed confessions of their sins in life, in the hopes of being forgiven for them in death. Both Picard and the priest agreed that the confession should be burned without reading it. Sainte-Croix's sins were between him and his God.

The confession now in ashes in the fireplace, the commissioner explored the contents of the closet as the creditors and notaries looked over his shoulder. A leather box about fifteen inches long and twelve inches wide, covered in calfskin, caught his eye. Lifting the lid slowly, Picard discovered a collection of powders and liquids of assorted colors. A half sheet of cloth paper lay on top of the contents. The commissioner scanned the letter: "I humbly pray those into whose hands this Cabinet may fall, do me the favor to restore it with their own hands to Madame the Marquise of Brinvilliers...seeing that what is in it concerns her, and belongs to her only." It had been written and signed two years earlier, in May 1670.

Picard replaced the letter inside the box, closed the lid, and looked around the room once again. The many mortars, pestles, alembics, and glassware now took on new meaning. This was no longer a matter for creditors. It was instead a crime scene. And he had just burned the confession.

Not far from the box Picard spotted another small package wrapped tightly with thick string and closed by eight wax seals. Another cryptic notice accompanied it: "Papers to be burnt in case of death, not being of any consequence to any person. I humbly pray those, into whose hands they may fall, to burn them...without opening the packet."

Resisting the temptation to crack open the seals, Picard followed established procedures. He collected the incriminating materials and placed them in a box. He reached for a small ball of jute cord and wrapped it around the box several times. He lit a candle and dripped a large pool of wax where he had tied the string. After imprinting his silver commissioner's seal in the wax, Picard placed the box in the safekeeping of Creuillebois, one of his trusted sergeants, and set to work drafting a detailed letter to the lieutenant of police.

Madame de Brinvilliers's grief at the news of Sainte-Croix's death was quickly replaced by her drive for self-preservation. For as much as Brinvilliers claimed to love Sainte-Croix, she had no illusions when it came to his trustworthiness. In the four years since her father's poisoning, she and Sainte-Croix had remained lovers. Brinvilliers had even given birth to three children, passing them off as her husband's. Still, Sainte-Croix's financial problems were nothing new. During one of their many passionate meetings, Sainte-Croix had assured Brinvilliers that no one would ever know about their secret desires and dark actions—as long as she helped pay his expenses. He promised Brinvilliers that he would keep every shred of evidence that could be damning to her in a small box at his home, under lock and key.

On learning of Sainte Croix's death, she remembered these not-so-subtle references to the hidden box. The marquise may not have known what secrets the box held, but she did know that she had no time to waste. She raced to her dead lover's home.

Sainte-Croix's widow opened the door. She confirmed that the police had found a very intriguing box at the house and it had Brinvilliers's name on it. She did not know what was in the box, but she clearly delighted in the prospect that the woman with whom her husband had been conducting an affair would soon pay for her sins.

The marquise tried to remain calm, but her voice betrayed her panic as she asked Sainte-Croix's widow if she might come in. The widow refused but made sure to give her the address of Officer Creuillebois's home so that Brinvilliers might ask that the box be returned to its rightful owner.

Brinvilliers may have been methodical in her poisoning techniques, but she stumbled in her initial dealings with the police. She went immediately to Creuillebois's home, only to discover he was not there. She returned two hours later, pounding on the door. When Creuillebois greeted her, she begged for the items she claimed Sainte-Croix had intended for her only to see. When he declined she shoved fifty *livres* into his hand in return for the box. When he rebuffed her again, Brinvilliers realized that she was in great danger. An hour later she packed her belongings and fled the country.

13

The Faithful Servant

When news of Sainte-Croix's death reached La Chaussée, he went not to Officer Creuillebois's home but instead directly to Commissioner Picard. The valet claimed that he had given Sainte-Croix a large sum of money to hold for safekeeping, and he wanted his name added to the rolls of creditors claiming restitution from the dead man's estate.

Sensing something strange about the man's demeanor, Picard told the servant that many odd things had been found among Sainte-Croix's belongings. La Chaussée spun around toward the door and sprinted out of the commissioner's house. He quickly made his way back to the home of Monsieur Gaussin, where he had been employed since the deaths of the d'Aubray brothers, collected his belongings, and disappeared into Paris.

La Chaussée roamed the streets by night and hid out by day. La Reynie wanted him arrested for interrogation and assigned a number of *mouches* (spies or, literally, "flies") to flush the man into the open. Two months later, at six o'clock in the morning on September 4, 1672, La Reynie's men captured him as he walked through the streets, with "his nose in his coat" attempting to avoid detection. When they searched him the officers found a number of papers as well as a small bottle filled with suspicious liquid in his cloak.

Now that La Chaussée had been captured, La Reynie needed to determine exactly what was in the calfskin box found in Sainte-Croix's home and whether there was a link between the box's contents and the bottle found on the servant. La Reynie brought in an apothecary, Monsieur Lebel, to examine the box's contents.

Settling into an inspection room in La Reyie's compound on the rue du Bouloi, Lebel placed the case on the table and began a methodical examination. Pausing frequently to take notes, he noted that the small box was divided into twelve different compartments, or "cells," each lined with muslin. In the first compartment he found a medium-size flask containing about six ounces of clear liquid. It was corked and coated with a thick layer of red wax. An odd yellowish sediment floated at the bottom of the flask. Lebel cracked open the seal and smelled the mixture gingerly before dipping his finger into the liquid to taste it. It was both odorless and tasteless. Placing it back in the case, Lebel turned his attention to the other compartments. Two of them contained what seemed to be identical paper envelopes filled with a flourlike white powder. Another held a small box that, once opened, revealed two tiny packets also made of paper. Whatever was inside had singed the paper and turned it black. Still more packets contained powders that the apothecary quickly recognized as two common poisons: opium and antimony.

In another compartment Lebel found a small porcelain pot containing something black, which he assumed from its smell and taste was laudanum, a sleep-inducing herb. He identified one packet as mercury chloride and dismissed another holding a thick gray powder as "nothing that one could have used as poison." How he knew this he did not say. He also did not explain how he knew that three of the envelopes in the case contained arsenic—preferring instead to note that "because its nature and effects are too well known," no further tests were necessary.

Initially Lebel assumed that the contents of a glass vial were benign. Both in smell and appearance, the liquid seemed to be little more than rosewater. Just to be sure, he gave a rooster one and a half spoonfuls of the fragrant water. The rooster died within a few hours. An autopsy revealed that the liquid burned five separate holes in the animal's stomach.

In the days that followed, Lebel's assistants brought a menagerie of animals upon which the apothecary could test the preparations they could not immediately identify. In one experiment they dripped a small bit of yellow-colored liquid onto a morsel of bread and fed it to a turkey. The turkey died the next day. When they opened the bird up, nothing appeared unusual. In case the timing of the turkey's death was a coincidence, they repeated the experiment on a pigeon. It died, too, again without any visible sign of damage to its organs.

In another trial they mixed a few grains of a brownish-black powder into some bread crumbs and fed them to a turkey. Clearly corrosive, the powder had burned holes in the paper envelopes in which it was stored. To Lebel's surprise it did not kill the animal right away. The turkey languished in pain for two more days. During the autopsy they discovered the animal's intestines were filled with a watery, bile-like substance and its heart filled with "curdled blood." A large cat was next in line for the experiment. It ate the doctored bread greedily. While the cat seemed "a little sad" the next day, it continued to eat. By the fourth day the cat refused the bread, so Lebel slipped some tripe in with the powder, which the cat ate "slowly and sadly." On day five the cat could barely move. Strangely, Lebel did not explain what happened next, but it is safe to assume that the animal died.

In one of the compartments Lebel found a white powder with a blue tint. He suspected that it was vitriol, most likely a copper sulfate, which is deadly if ingested. To test his suspicion the apothecary fed the powder to a red hen. Within two hours the hen died. Lebel performed an autopsy and found that the hen's stomach was "substantially altered in color and completely wrinkled as if it had been burned."

Having completed his review of the materials found in Sainte-

Croix's box, Lebel turned to the items the police officers found on La Chaussée at the time of his arrest. From inside the man's leather side-sack, they retrieved a small envelope containing a bluish-white powder. Lebel noticed it was similar to the powder he had tested. To be sure, he repeated his original experiment on a new chicken. Again the animal died and its stomach changed color, as if burned from the inside out.

Lebel returned to the notes he took during his experiments on the powder in Sainte-Croix's case. Dipping his quill in the inkpot sitting on the table, he underlined "bluish-white powder." He then reread his notes on La Chaussée, again underlined the words "bluish-white powder," and wrote, "we found this material to be similar to the one contained in the case described above." This could not be explained by coincidence alone, Lebel deduced: La Chaussée clearly trafficked in the same poisons as Sainte-Croix did. After a short trial La Chaussée received a death sentence, which would be preceded by interrogation under torture.

French law allowed for the use of torture before trial (*Question préparatoire*) in order to persuade the accused to reveal the names of accomplices. However, in France, torture most often took place following sentencing. There were two levels of postsentencing torture, the *Question ordinaire* and the *Question extraordinaire*, depending on the level of intensity and amount of pain to be inflicted.

Torture methods took four main forms. The first, the *strappado*, consisted of hoisting the criminal into the air by his shoulders using a rope and pulley. His hands would be tied behind his back and held in place by ropes held by two men, one on each side. On cue the torturers let the ropes go slack, dropping their victim violently toward the floor. As one observer explained, "The velocity of his descent…generally dislocates his shoulders, with incredible pain. This dreadful execution is sometimes repeated in a few minutes on the same delinquent; so that the very ligaments are torn from his joints, and his arms are rendered useless for life."

The *question d'eau* (water torture) forced water down the throats of criminals with a tube while they were tied down by their wrists and ankles. The English diplomat John Evelyn witnessed the torture of a condemned thief at the Châtelet in 1651. The quantity of water "so prodigiously swell'd him, face, eyes, breast, & all his limbs," he explained, "one would be almost affrighted to see it. They let him down, & carried him before a warm fire to bring him to himself, being now to all appearances dead with pain."

The third and preferred form—*brodequins*, or torture boots—consisted of enclosing each leg in a wood or metal casing wrapped tightly with rope. The torturer then hammered wood shims into each corner of the casing (four for the ordinary question, eight for the extraordinary question). The muscles often burst and bones shattered. Interrogators frequently chose *brodequins* over water torture because the pain was more localized and carried less risk of unintentional death, particularly for more corpulent criminals, whose fleshy bodies increased the water's pressure on the stomach. They wanted to be sure convicts experienced the full horrors of their execution just a few hours later.

La Chaussée was sentenced to the rack, the last form of torture, which was also frequently used as a form of execution. In preparation, guards stripped La Chaussée to the waist. They shaved his head and searched his body cavities for hidden charms that could be used to cast spells to help withstand the agony. He had also been closely watched over the preceding days to ensure that no one slipped him any herbal drugs, such as mandrake, henbane, wild lettuce, or opium, to dull the pain.

As La Chaussée begged for mercy, the interrogators instructed men on each side of the rack to tighten the mechanism, stretching the servant's body to its limits. La Chaussée's cries were quickly followed by a mournful sobbing that echoed off the chamber's stone walls. Overwhelmed by pain, La Chaussée was, wrote one witness, "touched...with remorse," the kind that "ordinarily closes the last minutes of a wretched life." He promised to tell them everything they needed to know, if only they would take him down from the rack and bring the scribe back to record his confession.

Thirty minutes later, crumpled in the corner of the prison cell,

La Chaussée admitted his guilt. Madame de Brinvilliers had provided him with poison, claiming she got it from Sainte-Croix. She ordered the servant to administer it to her father and, later, her brothers. For his efforts he received a high-level position in Brinvilliers's household, along with a handsome salary. Despite his initial reluctance, La Chaussée accepted the arrangement and agreed to do whatever she asked of him. He added powders and liquids to water and broths. He poured a reddish water into Madame de Brinvilliers father's glass. He slipped a clear poisonous liquid into the brothers' pies at their country home. And as he watched Brinvilliers delight in the slow deaths of her family, he came to loathe her; he said he had a "great mind to poison" her as well.

14

"Brinvilliers Is in the Air"

In the four years since Sainte-Croix's death, rumors surfaced from time to time that Madame de Brinvilliers had been spotted in England, Germany, and many places in between. Stories abounded of multiple identities, false names, and disguises. The truth was much less romantic. For the previous three and a half years, Brinvilliers had hidden herself in a quiet convent in Liège, a city in what is now Belgium. Thanks to the minister of the military Louvois's network of spies, however, her pious life was about to end.

Extracting Brinvilliers from Liège proved no easy task. At the time the city was an independent principality, which made any effort to seize her a difficult proposition. Fighting between the French and the Spanish for the contested territories at the borders of France and Holland had intensified. Sitting strategically on the banks of the Meuse, its guns facing in all directions, the citadel of Liège had successfully fought off assaults by both sides. The last thing Louvois wanted was to have Liège rethink its neutrality or have the Spaniards read the extradition efforts as an act of aggression. The stakes were too high.

Louvois and La Reynie agreed to send one of La Reynie's officers, François Desgrez, north to track down Brinvilliers and bring her to justice in Paris. On March 16, 1676, he carried a letter from Louvois to the head of the Liège citadel requesting help. "The King wishes very much," wrote the war minister, "to be able to arrest a person who is presently in the city of Liège. The name of this person will be indicated to you in person by the man who presents this letter to you, and that person should be arrested."

The soldiers of the citadel obliged. That evening Desgrez accompanied troops to the convent where Brinvilliers was hiding. They found the marquise sitting quietly at a long table with several nuns, eating dinner. Brinvilliers had just reached for the water pitcher, refilled her glass, and brought it to her lips when Desgrez and the soldiers broke into the dining room to arrest her. An instant later she smashed the glass on the table and frantically shoved the glass shards into her mouth in a suicide attempt. After a short struggle, the officers stopped her before she had a chance to swallow the fragments.

As much as Desgrez tried to return Brinvilliers to Paris, the journey home proved complicated. To support the French extradition efforts, Louvois wrote to Spanish officials, requesting that "one hundred soldiers on horses, an officer, and ten archers" accompany the prisoner from Liège to the Spanish-controlled town of Dinan. From there they would go to Maastricht, then to French-controlled Rocroy, and finally on to Paris.

While Louvois and the troops waited anxiously for a response, Desgrez and his colleagues guarded Brinvilliers's cell around the clock. They watched Brinvilliers as she paced in her cell. She often fell into fits of rage, banging at the door and shouting obscenities and accusations. The guards confiscated all of her belongings, save for a small hairbrush and dish of hairpins. In one of several more suicide attempts, the desperate Brinvilliers lunged toward the dish, grabbed a handful of pins, and shoved them into her mouth. Desgrez leaped into action, holding her down, prying her mouth open, and pulling the pins out one by one. With the help of a guard the two men searched the room again for other items she could use to kill herself. They found five more hairpins at the bottom of her chamber pot.

Her next suicide attempt was as crude as it proved to be scandalous. Monsieur de Coulanges described the incident to Madame de Sévigné, a highly respected member of the French literary elite. "She stuck a stick"—he gossiped salaciously—"guess where? It wasn't in her eye. It wasn't in her mouth. Not in her eye, not in her nose. Guess where? She would have died, if someone had not called for help." One of the guards present reported that the stick was "very smelly," a foot and a half long, and wrapped with cords and hairpins.

En route to Paris for her trial, she begged guards to put her out of her misery. According to a guard named Barbier, she offered to "make him a fortune" if he would tie her up with a rope to a pair of horses and have them drag her to death as they ran. If he was feeling generous, she said hopefully, he could also slit her neck beforehand. The guard refused.

For as long as Brinvilliers remained in the Low Countries, Louvois oversaw her fate. With his characteristic assertiveness, he had gladly taken the matter into his own hands. As usual this did not sit well with Colbert, who had oversight of the *parlement* courts where Brinvilliers's case would be heard.

Colbert and Louvois had long been bitter rivals. Louis's war efforts rankled Colbert, who had argued emphatically against invasion of the Spanish Low Countries in 1667 and still bristled at the king's hawkish tendencies. War was costly and dangerous, its outcome anything but certain. Colbert argued that the king should exhibit greater restraint, both at home and abroad.

Despite his dedication to the king, Colbert also had difficulty quelling his frustration with Louis's outrageous and often impulsive expenditures to display the glory of his reign. Many expensive, high-profile construction projects were now under way in Paris. The addition of massive northern and southern facades to the Louvre gave the palace new and imposing neoclassical lines. Directly across the river from the Louvre, the heavy Corinthian columns and the soaring dome of the Collège des Quatre-Nations (now the Institut de France) signaled the permanence and power of the king who built it. The construction of a state-of-the-art astronomical observatory south of the Luxembourg Gardens similarly announced the king's presence on earth, as well as his ability to reach far into the heavens.

Though these projects carried eye-popping price tags, they were nothing compared with the expenses related to the king's personal project to build a palace in the marshes of Versailles, which was nowhere near complete after six years of construction. Even a single, small fountain outside the king's bedroom at the new palace required an underground system of lead pipes "like nothing else in the world," and a team of more than 150 horses to power the pumps needed to push water through them. With growing concern, Colbert tried to keep the country from impending financial ruin at the hands of a visionary but spendthrift king.

To Colbert's consternation, Louis chose to follow the counsel of the untested yet bold Louvois—a man decades younger than Colbert. The king would demonstrate his strength to the whole of Europe and go to war. "I could not believe," Colbert exclaimed, "that such an important affair would be confided in a young man of just twenty-one years old [Louvois], without experience in this area, and who believes that he has the authority to ruin the country, and who wants to ruin it because I am the one who wants to save it."

In the years that followed, Louvois flaunted the king's clear preference for war over peace, and for him over Colbert. With every new battle won, and every new financial contribution to Louvois's war chest, Colbert had little choice but to seethe in silence as Louvois moved deeper into the king's inner circle. "My court," Louis XIV later wrote, "was divided between peace and war according to their various interests. If I inclined slightly for war, it was because of natural inclination, not because of favoritism." Still, Colbert had his doubts.

Colbert informed the attorney general of the *parlement*, Achille de Harlay, that the Brinvilliers matter would be handled solely by the *parlement*. Harlay sent a colleague to Dinan to take depositions from the marquise. Further establishing his jurisdictional authority, Colbert explained to Harlay that the attorney general could "confer with Monsieur de la Reynie on all things regarding the Madame de Brinvilliers affair." However, "Let it be known that the affair has been committed to your care in order to satisfy the king and the public."

Brinvilliers's circumstances preoccupied Parisian society for months. "The only thing one talks about here [in Paris]," wrote Madame de Sévigné, "are the words, the actions, of La Brinvilliers." When Sévigné left Paris to visit her family in the provinces, she lamented to a correspondent, "Alas, what good will I be . . . ? I pity you for not having me in Paris any longer so I can send you the latest on La Brinvilliers." She rejoiced to her daughter when she returned to the capital a month and a half later. "This affair occupies all of Paris, at the expense of matters relating to the war. . . . My dearest, rest assured that I will leave you in the dark about nothing relating to such an extraordinary matter."

On June 28, 1676, Louis made it clear that he expected the courts to show no mercy. The king still carried vivid memories of the last moments of Henrietta Anne. While surgeons had confirmed that Henrietta Anne's death was the result of an illness, rumors of poison still persisted. "It is important," the king stressed to Colbert, "[that] you tell the First President [of the *parlement*] and the *Procureur Général* [attorney general] on my behalf that I expect they will do all that they should to diminish those who . . . are involved in such a villainous commerce. Send me everything that you have been able to find out."

Brinvilliers remained in prison in the Conciergerie complex on the Île de la Cité while the Tournelle, the highest tribunal of France, tried her case. The court met twenty-two times between April 28 and July 16. As witness after witness testified, the stories of Brinvilliers's wretchedness mounted. Françoise Roussel, one of Brinvilliers's servants, testified that years earlier her mistress entered the kitchen with a jar of preserves in hand. She offered the servant a taste from the point of a knife, and Roussel fell ill shortly afterward. It had been three years since that unfortunate tasting, and still she continued to suffer from intense stomach pains and a sensation that her "heart was pricked."

During the court proceedings an apprentice to the apothecary Christopher Glaser testified that he saw Sainte-Croix talking to his master on many occasions, often accompanied by a woman who fitted the description of Brinvilliers. Moreover, Brinvilliers herself mentioned using *la recette de Glaser* (Glaser's recipe) as a poison in one of the many letters found in Sainte-Croix's belongings after his death.

The references to Glaser raised the scandal to new heights. The German-born Christopher Glaser was personal apothecary to Philippe, the king's brother and Henrietta Anne's widower, as well as owner of The Red Rose, a shop and laboratory in Paris. He wrote the first textbook for laboratory preparations in chemistry, which was published in multiple editions and languages across Europe from its first publication in 1663 until well into the eighteenth century.

Despite the incriminating evidence against Brinvilliers, few believed that a woman of high birth could commit such heinous crimes. "The advantages of quality, birth, and fortune of Madame de Brinvilliers must strongly argue that she would not be capable of the cowardly and horrible crimes of which she is accused," the marquise's lawyer asserted.

Madame de Brinvilliers finally took the stand on July 15. In the marathon session that lasted eighteen hours, she bitterly denied everything, using rank and privilege as her principal alibi. One witness, she claimed, was nothing more than a valet—and a perpetually drunk one at that. Another had been kicked out of his house because he was a morally corrupt libertine. As for the most damning evidence, the poisonous box: It "did not belong to me," she insisted, "a man like Sainte-Croix is not one to be trusted."

When the questioning ended, the judge summarized the court's response to Brinvilliers's arguments: "She disgusts us." The following day the court sentenced Brinvilliers to death by beheading.

The court requested that Father Edmé Pirot, a professor of theology at the Sorbonne, console Brinvilliers during her final days and "exhort her to think about the salvation of her soul." The morning after her sentencing, Harlay, the attorney general, met Pirot at the Conciergerie. There was little need to explain the details of the marquise of Brinvilliers's case to the priest; his parishioners talked of little else after his masses.

"We are putting her now in your hands," Harlay said. "We hope that God will touch her soul, of course. But with the public interest in mind, we also want her crimes to die along with her. We need her to declare all that she knows about other crimes that could happen. Without this, we won't be able to stop them, and her poisons will outlive her."

The priest entered Brinvilliers's prison cell and nodded to the guards who stood watch there at all times. The cell was larger than he expected, taking up a full floor of the Conciergerie's Montmorency tower. The furnishings were sparse. A curtained bed sat at one end of the room, and two chairs at the other. The priest gestured Brinvilliers toward the chairs, away from the guards. "I have come to prepare you spiritually as best I can," he said. "I wish that it were for another occasion than this one."

Pirot spent the next few days developing a rapport with Brinvilliers. They took meals together and spoke at length about matters of faith and religion. Pirot purposely steered clear of discussing the specifics of the case, other than confirming that he knew she had been sentenced to death for poisoning. From time to time the priest peppered in reassurances that God forgives all sins. "But you cannot hope for God's pardon if you do not declare to the judges what your poison was, who made it...and who your accomplices are."

Slowly Brinvilliers's cold heart showed signs of melting. Her eyes welled up regularly as she thought about her impending death and, to the priest's surprise, she sobbed uncontrollably while reading the Ten Commandments. He reported his progress to Harlay, who declared the woman ready for the Question.

At seven thirty the following morning, the guards arrived to escort Brinvilliers to the torture chamber. She held a small prayer book, a gift from Pirot, in her hands. As she left the cell she turned toward him and asked, "you are not coming with me?" Pirot shook his head, but he would be waiting nearby should she need him.

Once in the torture room two magistrates in crimson red gowns read aloud the order for her execution. Behind them bloodstained handcuffs, chains, levers, pulleys, as well as several buckets of water stood at the ready. Staring at the buckets of water, Brinvilliers turned to the magistrates. "Messieurs, there is no need for this. I will tell you everything without the need for the Question. Father Pirot persuaded me to tell you everything as it is, even when you haven't asked, and to declare everything I know. This is what I will do, Messieurs."

As proof of her contrition, she blurted out a litany of her crimes: "I poisoned my father twenty or thirty times with my own hands, and with the help of La Chaussée, with the poisons that Sainte-Croix gave me.... I also had La Chaussée poison my brothers...and I tried to poison my husband five times." The words tumbled from her mouth as she described her method. She used arsenic, in a dose no bigger than a button each time, so that the effects would not be immediately noticed.

When she was done talking, the torturer stepped forward, a length of rope in his fist. She presented her hands to him, which he tied together tightly.

History leaves us neither any formal record of Brinvilliers's being administered the Question, nor precise documentation of the tortures to which Brinvilliers was subjected. What we do know is that, seven and a half hours later, Father Pirot was called to the chamber to attend to her. On his way to see the marquise, he passed Monsieur Paluau, one of the magistrates who attended the interrogation. She said little, Paluau explained, besides what they already knew. When the priest entered the chamber, he found her weak but not physically broken, lying on a dirty mattress in front of the fire. Attendants were changing her clothes and preparing to serve her several raw eggs, intended to bolster her strength. She would need it for her execution.

At six o'clock on the morning of July 17, prison guards fetched Madame de Brinvilliers from her cell. Outside the prison the crowd buzzed with excitement. People came from all over the country to catch a glimpse of the infamous poisoner. Street vendors hawked crudely produced newspapers and broadsides claiming to tell the true story of Brinvilliers's deeds in all their gore. The windows of buildings along the route Brinvilliers would walk to her death spilled over with onlookers who paid homeowners a tidy sum for the privilege to watch above the crowds.

When the main doors of the Conciergerie swung open, a front flank of guards pushed the crowd out of the way, preparing the way for the open cart containing Brinvilliers. Wearing only a linen sack dress, she held a lit torch in her hands in a show of penitence. Her confessor Pirot, who walked alongside the cart, noted the "continuous murmur in the streets along our route, lasting all the time until the scaffold."

The cart stopped first at Notre-Dame. As guards pushed back the crowds, Pirot helped the woman to her knees in front of the cathedral's large, closed doors. Fulfilling the duties of the *amende honorable* (literally, "honorable amends") and a symbolic donation to the Church, she confessed her sins. "I recognize that wickedly and for vengeance, I poisoned my father and my brothers...in order to obtain their goods. I beg pardon from God, from the King, and from Justice." Following her prayers, the guards shoved Brinvilliers back into the cart, which rumbled slowly across the narrow Notre-Dame Bridge toward the Hôtel de Ville and the place de Grève.

For more than four hundred years, criminals had been punished or executed for crimes both quotidian and spectacular in this public space in front of city hall. In the following century the installation of the guillotine solidified the place de Grève's macabre reputation.

Arriving at the place de Grève, the driver of the cart struggled to cut a path through the unruly mass of people waiting to see Brinvilliers meet her bloody end. "Never were there so many people nor Paris so moved or so attentive," wrote one witness. Despite the excitement of it all, however, "in truth, it made me shiver."

The marquise ascended the stagelike platform where the execution would take place. Showing no resistance, Brinvilliers fell to her knees, allowing the executioner to turn her head from side to side like a rag doll's as he cut her hair. The crowd's excitement intensified as the executioner ripped Brinvilliers's sack dress off her shoulders, exposing her breasts. He grabbed her wrists and tied them behind her. The marquise showed no expression, acting as if this were as natural as wearing "gold bracelets or a pearl necklace."

Holding a large cross high in the air, Father Pirot heard the woman's second and final confession as she knelt. With a nod, he signaled that it was time. The executioner blindfolded Brinvilliers and placed her head against the chopping block. He placed his fingers against her neck, gauging its span. In a moment and with a dull thud, it was over; the executioner "swallowed her head with a single strike of the ax."

Taking a swig from a large jug of wine, the executioner turned to the priest. "Father, wasn't that a nice job?" he asked. The priest nodded absently. For as dramatic and as charged as the morning's events had been, he felt nonetheless "consoled." Brinvilliers met her death with as much "sentiment of piety and contrition" as he could have hoped for her.

Brinvilliers's head and body were burned; the ashes thrown to the wind. "And so it is," wrote Sévigné in one last commentary, "Brinvilliers is in the air...we will now breathe her, and, with this, she will turn us all into poisoners."

Father Pirot may have been reassured by Brinvilliers's pious death. La Reynie, however, could not have been more unsettled. As she raged in her prison cell, Brinvilliers made ominous statements suggesting that she was far from having been alone in her poisonous acts. During her questioning, she muttered in passing that "half of the nobility have done the same things, if I felt like talking, I'd ruin them all!"

La Reynie shuddered at the thought that Brinvilliers would never have been caught had it not been for a few lucky breaks. "Who would have thought that a woman raised in an honest family, with such an apparently gentle demeanor, could have been capable of such a long meditation [of] such a list of crimes?" he wrote. What would have happened, he asked himself, "if God had not permitted that Saint-Croix die of an extraordinary death and leave his papers" so that they were found by the authorities?

By the grace of God, Brinvilliers had also been found. She had been convicted, tortured, and executed. La Reynie worried what would happen if they were not so lucky next time.

PART
IV

"Cease Your
Scandals"

15

House of Porcelain

In March 1669 Athénaïs delivered her and Louis's first child in secrecy at a small house near the Tuileries Gardens. Within minutes of the delivery, the doctor took the baby girl to a nearby carriage, where a woman named Françoise d'Aubigné waited.

For Athénaïs the thirty-four-year-old woman seemed the perfect choice as governess for her illegitimate children with the king. Abandoned by her parents at a young age, Françoise was raised by nuns in a convent. Without any dowry to speak of, she had little choice at the age of sixteen but to marry Paul Scarron, a well-known yet physically deformed author twenty-six years her senior. Scarron died six years later, leaving her destitute but with many connections at court. Athénaïs's cousin César d'Albret had long been a supporter of Scarron and took Françoise in after his death. In return the young woman handled domestic matters at d'Albret's home with efficiency and discretion, which impressed Athénais.

Though Françoise was "beautiful…sweet, grateful, secretive, faithful, modest [and] intelligent," her religious upbringing kept her from being easily swayed by potential suitors. Athénaïs took special note of this rare quality—a necessity for the mistress to a king who strayed easily—and offered her the position of governess. In a turn that would later come to characterize the relationship between the two women, Françoise refused. She insisted that she would accept only if the king, not Montespan, made the request personally, which he did. Only much later would Athénaïs understand that she had put, once again, a formidable rival in the path of her beloved king.

Cradling the newborn in her arms, d'Aubigné signaled to the driver to set off for the remote home where she would raise the child as her own. The scene repeated itself a year later, in 1670, when Athénaïs gave birth to a second child, the future duke of Maine, and again in 1672 and 1673. As one court observer noted, "The lady is extremely fertile and her powder lights very quickly."

Six years after Louis and Athénaïs first consummated their relationship, the king legitimized their three children. In what should have been a dry legal statement, Louis used the announcement to document publicly his love for Montespan, explaining that at the heart of his actions lay a "tenderness that nature has given His Majesty for his children and for other reasons that augment considerably his sentiments."

While Françoise kept herself off limits to the king, Louis hardly remained celibate during his mistress's frequent "indispositions." He continued performing his husbandly duties for the queen on a weekly basis. He also surveyed the court for other potential partners. The dark-haired Claude de Vin des Oeillets caught his eye. Claude Oeillets possessed a dramatic flair, having grown up in the theater. Her parents had lived a nomadic life as actors, roaming from theater to theater, city to city, with their children in tow. By the early 1660s her parents had settled into the Théâtre de Bourgogne in Paris, where Molière's troupe also performed. Within a few years Oeillets's mother, Alix Faviot, had established herself as one of the most praised actresses in the capital, earning accolades for her roles in plays by Pierre Corneille and Jean Racine. Members of the Théâtre de Bourgogne frequently entertained the king at Saint-Germain and Versailles, giving Oeillets's mother the opportunity to make the connections necessary to ensure a place for her daughter in Montespan's household.

Although successful actors often circulated among members of the court, their home lives could not have been more different from those of the nobility. Considered to have questionable moral values and denied Christian burial, actors lived at the fringes of society, in poverty or at least very close to it. Despite her renown, Faviot lived on the rue Saint-Denis in the destitute Montorgeuil neighborhood. Her daughter Claude lived nearby on the rue du Regard, also in the same neighborhood, but once employed by Montespan, she was rarely seen by her neighbors. Busy attending to the king's mistress, she was a rare success story of a local woman having found her fortune at court.

The details of Louis's intimate encounters with the thirty-three year-old Oeillets are not well documented. But it is likely that the two became lovers as early as 1670 and most certainly no later than 1672. In the months before the birth of Montespan's second child in 1670, the king transferred a substantial sum of money from the royal coffers to Oeillets. Two years later, around the time of Athénaïs's third child, he deeded property to Oeillets near Clagny, north-east of Versailles, with the intent that she would eventually build a home there. A royal maid later confided to a court insider that she and the king spent time together when Madame de Montespan was either "busy" or sick. She also suggested that Oeillets also gave birth to one of the king's illegitimate children, though documents do not confirm this.

To Athénaïs's relief, the king always came back to her when she was no longer indisposed. In 1671 the king instructed the architect Louis Le Vau to design an elaborate villa for the couple on the outskirts of the Versailles estate. The Trianon of Porcelain, as it was called, was true to its name. Thousands of blue-and-white Delft porcelain tiles protected the facade and roof of the building. Inside, porcelain covered every inch of the floor, and delicate vases and figurines imported at great expense from China decorated the interior. From the windows or while strolling outdoors, the king and his lover could admire gardens bursting with rare plants and flowers—Spanish jasmines, tuberoses, hyacinths, and narcissuses imported from Constantinople. And in each room, bouquets arranged in enormous porcelain vases filled the villa with their heady fragrance. But the most exquisite place in the Trianon of Porcelain was the Chambre des Amours (lovers' room), which housed the sumptuous bed to which the king and his mistress retreated, spending endless hours in intimate escape.

As Louis and Athénaïs frolicked, Françoise d'Aubigné raised their children. Having ordered them away from court from the moment of the birth, the king himself had never met his children. On Christmas Eve 1672, Louis sent for the three children to be brought to the Palace of Saint-Germain. Smiling at the first glimpse of the trio with their governess, he asked her who their father was. Françoise responded playfully, "I have no idea. I imagine it's some duke or big lawyer at *parlement*." Both Athénaïs and Louis doubled over in laughter at Françoise's feigned ignorance. In a demonstration of the king's newfound interest in his children, Louis legitimized them in 1673, and Françoise moved with them to court, where she became a regular and privileged fixture in the royal family.

As Athénaïs's star continued to rise, Louise de La Vallière continued to suffer. In an ultimate act of cruelty, Louis made La Vallière godmother to his third child with Athénaïs. The couple named the baby girl Louise-Françoise in a sly reference to her mother, Françoise-Athénaïs de Montespan, and Louise de La Vallière, the woman whom Montespan had replaced. By the end of June 1674, Louise could not take any more humiliation at court. After attending a mass with the king in the company of Marie-Thérèse and the ever-present Athénaïs, she dropped to her knees and begged him to let her leave the court forever. Louis waited a full year to approve her request. In the spring of 1675 Louise ate her last dinner at the palace in the company of the king and Madame de Montespan. The next day she entered the Carmelite convent on the rue Saint-Jacques, where she remained until her death thirty-five years later.

The departure of her main competitor solidified Athénaïs's hold over the king. Committed to pleasing his demanding mistress, the king instructed Colbert to arrange for "a pearl necklace, which I want to be beautiful, two pairs of earrings, one in diamonds, which I [also] want to be beautiful, and all of the other [earrings] in [precious] stones." To this list, the king added four dozen buttons, each with a jewel in the middle surrounded by diamonds, and a third pair of earrings made of pearls. He also wanted the jewelry to be presented in a box covered in diamonds and precious stones of all colors.

In 1674 the king had a country home built for his mistress in nearby Clagny. When Athénaïs complained it was "fit for a chorus girl," Louis had the house razed and instructed the Versailles architect, Jules Mansard, and chief gardener, André Le Nôtre, to design something much bigger and more elaborate. From the battlefields of the Low Countries, Louis kept careful watch over the construction of his mistress's new palace, making sure that her every wish was fulfilled. "Madame de Montespan mandated me to order you to buy orange trees [for Clagny]," he wrote on June 5 to Colbert. In response to Colbert's grousings, the king conceded three days later that the cost was "excessive," but insisted "to please me, nothing is impossible." One year later, in August 1675, Madame de Sévigné exclaimed to her daughter, "The eye sees [the palace] rising in the distance. [The gardens] are assuredly the most beautiful, the most surprising, and the most enchanted novelty one can ever imagine."

As triumphant as Montespan—whom the court now called "Quanto" (How much?) and "Quantova" (How far will she go?)—felt, the victory proved fleeting. Montespan soon faced another, more formidable competitor.

To acknowledge her dutiful service, Louis had gifted Françoise d'Aubigné a large fortune, a château, and a new title, Madame de Maintenon, after the village where the château was located. Montespan did not make a secret of her disliking for her new rival. Athénaïs bristled with jealousy at Maintenon's close relationship with her children, fearing as well the governess's deepening relationship with Louis.

As for Maintenon, she remained committed to raising Montespan's young family, but refused to support the woman's loathsome behavior. She complained loudly, avoiding her nemesis's name, that "*one* only consults me after a decision has been made, wanting me to approve and not wanting me to give my opinion. *One* is only using me to better her reign." For her part, Montespan lamented to her priest that she would "never understand why God would make me suffer Madame de Maintenon."

A year after Maintenon moved to court, Montespan attempted without success to remove Maintenon from her path by marrying the widow off to the duke of Villars. Maintenon refused, clearly feeling very secure in her relationship with the king, who interacted with her as if they were "good friends." In return, the governess held unusual influence over the monarch.

One day the king witnessed Montespan yelling at Maintenon. When he asked what the trouble was, Madame de Maintenon stepped forward calmly and said, "If Your Majesty would go into the other room, I will have the honor of telling him." The king obliged, and Maintenon described Montespan's insufferable actions, worrying aloud about the king's future if he continued to be allied with a woman of such questionable morals.

Maintenon was not alone in her concerns for the king's soul. Montespan's hedonism stood in stark contrast to Louise de La Vallière, whose pathos-filled exile to the convent gained the praise of religious leaders. While the Church could overlook the king's infidelities with the unmarried La Vallière, his "*double adultère*" (double adultery) with Montespan constituted an unspeakable sin.

During Holy Week in 1675, the priest listening to Montespan's confession at Versailles refused her absolution. "Is this the Madame de Montespan who scandalizes all of France?" he asked, "Go! Go Madame, cease your scandals and afterward you should throw yourself at the feet of the ministers of Jesus Christ."

A stunned Montespan described her humiliation to Louis. The king consulted Bishop Bossuet, who surprised the couple by asserting correctness of the priest's actions and that it was not Louis's place to interfere. Bossuet counseled Louis to make an "entire [and] absolute separation" from his lover or risk being refused communion. Though torn between love and religious duty, Louis knew what he had to do. His eyes red "like a man who had been crying," he sent Montespan to Clagny and instructed her to repent of her sins.

"The king and Madame de Montespan have parted ways purely for religious reasons," wrote a court observer. "People are saying they still love each other more than life itself. They also say that she will return to court but not be lodged at the Château and will not see the king unless she is with the Queen in her quarters." The noblewoman concluded skeptically: "I have my doubts... for there is always the danger that love will have the upper hand."

Louis made frequent visits to Athénaïs's château at Clagny, but the couple remained under the watchful eyes of a group of chaperones composed of the court's most religious noblewomen. In her absence, Louis turned again to Mademoiselle des Oeillets, Athénaïs's trusted chambermaid, for physical companionship. After their encounters, Oeillets noted that the king often spent hours in front of the fire, "pensive and sighing."

Four months into the forced estrangement, the king returned to Clagny, determined to reunite with Athénaïs. He pulled her away from her chaperones into a window nook, where the couple whispered and wept with each other. With shared determination they then took leave of their matronly observers and made their way to a nearby bedroom. Shortly afterward the king reestablished Montespan's favor in the court by assigning her twenty rooms on the first floor of Versailles, which eclipsed the queen's eleven on the second. Confirming her physical as well as emotional hold on Louis, Montespan bore the king two more children whom, on the king's insistence, she once again entrusted to the care of Maintenon.

Athénaïs had always been curvaceous, but as Maintenon

announced with no small amount of pleasure, "Her girth had grown to formidable proportions." Once a stunning beauty, time and nine pregnancies—two with her husband, seven with the king—took a toll on Montespan's body. The Italian ambassador, Primi Visconti, chimed in as well, exclaiming that just one of her legs was as big as his entire body. Athénaïs knew better than anyone about the king's roving attention when it came to women. In a desperate attempt to keep him from looking elsewhere, she stockpiled corsets to appear slimmer than she actually was. It did not work. The Torrent's days were numbered; Athénaïs was desperate.

16

Offering

Voisin never told her family what she was doing, nor did she share the names of the visitors who streamed through their front door. The young Marie-Marguerite couldn't resist making up her own names. Of all the many visitors to her mother's house, the one who made Marie-Marguerite the most uncomfortable was the Prayer Man (*Le Prieur*). No one knew what the Prayer Man—elderly and missing an eye—did to make ends meet. Marie-Marguerite's father suspected he was a counterfeiter. All his daughter knew was that the man frightened her.

One day the ever-curious Marie-Marguerite followed her mother into one of the ramshackle houses nearby. Soon the girl found herself in a dark and empty room. Feeling a presence behind her, she turned and saw the Prayer Man leaning toward her. Marie-Marguerite spun around and ran.

In the months and years that followed, Marie-Marguerite slowly got used to seeing the Prayer Man not only around the neighborhood, but also in her house. One day he appeared at her doorstep, dressed in a long robe. He greeted her mother briskly, and then the two went straight to her mother's bedroom and began barking orders at Marie-Marguerite.

On her mother's command, Marie-Marguerite helped move the furniture, adjust it, and readjust it. She lifted the narrow mattress into the air and placed two footstools underneath it. She then lit the candelabras and shut the windows and door tightly.

Shadows flickered against the walls in the candlelight as the Prayer Man stood expressionless behind the mattress. At her mother's command, Marie-Marguerite ushered a woman into the room. She had a dramatic flair about her. As she strode into the room, the two trains of her dress—one in front, one in back—swayed back and forth. Marie-Marguerite nicknamed her the Woman with Two Tails. The girl watched in fascination as her mother quickly unlaced the woman's corset, marveling at the layers of undergarments once hidden under the silk dress: the puffy petticoats, the whalebone frame, the knee-length bloomers.

The woman who strode confidently into the room was now nude and stood in front of her mother and the Prayer Man. Surrendering herself to them, she stepped toward the elevated mattress and lay across the bed with her head and feet hanging over the edges. Marie-Marguerite's mother placed a cloth on the woman's abdomen, and onto the cloth laid a cross. Next to the cross, a chalice balanced precariously on the woman's stomach. Then the mysterious chanting began.

As Marie-Marguerite got older and earned her mother's trust, the girl's errands expanded beyond Montorgeuil and Les Halles. She once accompanied her mother and several of her mother's friends to a beautiful new château in a small village not far from Versailles. Marie-Marguerite stayed in the coach while her mother conducted her business. The girl did not know whom her mother met, but the trip had obviously been profitable, as she treated the group to a lovely picnic in the Bois de Boulogne with some of the money she earned.

By the time she was in her late teens, errands to châteaux and palaces became Marie-Marguerite's responsibility. On a regular basis the elder Voisin opened a cabinet in the family home to which she alone had the key. Inside, many small bottles containing powders of all colors lined the shelves: white, gray, black, and a shimmering blue-green. After mixing several of the powders together, Marie-Marguerite's mother packaged the mixture in a small envelope on which she wrote careful instructions. Voisin then gave her daughter equally detailed instructions on which palace to go to, how to gain entry, and to whom the mysterious packages should be delivered.

Marie-Marguerite took a shared coach to the palaces, which always made the girl nervous. She'd heard many stories circulated about young women being assaulted in the public carriages by opportunistic drivers or fellow passengers. After the seventh trip on her own, Marie-Marguerite refused to journey to Versailles or anywhere else, for that matter. Something had happened in the carriage. Something so terrible that she preferred to risk her mother's anger than to make the journey again. And in the months that followed, she turned to Madame Lepère—Voisin's business partner, fellow midwife, and abortionist—for help. Rather than visit her mother's shack, she chose to give birth at Lepère's home. Whatever loyalty she once felt toward her mother was now gone.

17

"The Sneakiest and Meanest
Woman in the World"

Unaware of the dark activities afoot in the Montorgeuil neighborhood, La Reynie worried about Brinvilliers's menacing last words: "Half of the nobility have done the same things, if I felt like talking, I'd ruin them all!" Yet as much as the police chief would have liked to oversee every detail of his urban empire, there was no way one man could know everything that happened in a city the size of Paris. Every day a swarm of Parisians came to his castle-like Châtelet compound to demand retribution for actions that ranged from modest insult to murder. Thousands of criminals sat in his prisons awaiting trial. Any one of them could know something about ominous activities of the sort that Brinvilliers had hinted at.

The chestnut-haired prisoner Madeleine de La Grange was one such person. She had been married to a man who trafficked goods on the black market and was hanged on the gallows. All of the family's belongings had been confiscated, and La Grange risked spending the rest of her days on the street.

In the end, however, La Grange proved to be just as enterprising as her late husband. The brown-haired beauty discovered a talent for attracting wealthy men who enjoyed taking care of her. Jean Faurye, an elderly lawyer, was one of them. It is not clear whether Faurye knew about La Grange's checkered history. Sparing no expense, Faurye treated his mistress "like a queen," providing her with dresses made of the finest silks and the most luxurious of carriages.

La Grange embraced her lover with a careful eye on his wallet and his life span. With his every sneeze or cough, she moved into a deeper state of fear and could be found weeping preemptively at his bedside like the most devoted of lovers. To La Grange's consternation, Faurye did not seem interested in marriage.

In recent months Faurye's health had declined rapidly. A calculating realist, she knew that the minute Faurye took his last breath, her good fortune would come to an abrupt end. La Grange needed to take matters into her own hands.

The previous summer La Grange had arrived at a notary's office with a "short and somewhat ugly man" with graying hair who claimed to be Faurye. The man showed the notary what looked like a legitimate marriage certificate and requested that his entire estate be transferred to La Grange in the event of his death. Conveniently enough, Faurye died just a few days later.

The man's only surviving nephews were distraught at the news of his passing, but their grief did not prevent them from staking their claim to the estate. La Grange greeted them at Faurye's palatial home. Despite the somber mourning clothes she wore, little else suggested a grieving woman. She listened impatiently to the family's demands that she vacate the house and relinquish all claims on the estate. When they finished, she triumphantly brandished not only the notarized transfer of the man's estate, but also a marriage certificate signed by one Father Léonard Nail.

Faurye's nephews were as skeptical as they were stunned. Their elderly uncle certainly would not have married a much younger woman with no noble pedigree to speak of. Moreover, a lawyer of his stature certainly would have made sure that any decision to transfer his estate to La Grange would have been solidified through a detailed will naming her as beneficiary. They filed a formal complaint at Châtelet.

It did not take long for investigators to concur with the nephews' assessment that La Grange was a con artist. The "husband" had not only been an impostor but also a priest. Forsaking his vows, the Abbé Nail had been making a living as a scam artist under the name of Launay. In the fall of 1676, La Grange was arrested and taken to the Châtelet prison to await a court hearing in the civil tribunals of the *parlement*. The priest was transferred to the Conciergerie prison to await review by ecclesiastical officials.

The legal system moved slowly in France, and many prisoners lived in squalid conditions while in detention. Space was tight, so detainees were separated by sex and held in group cells, where they slept as a pack on the floor with little more than hay for a bed. Prisoners strolled together in the courtyard several times a day as well, sharing knowledge and forming alliances.

In early February 1677, La Grange wrote a lengthy letter to the king's minister of war, the marquis of Louvois. She claimed that she had gleaned information about the ongoing conflicts in the Low Countries from a fellow prisoner, who happened to be a spy for the enemy. Louvois took the woman's claims seriously and ordered the guards at Châtelet to transfer her to his home for questioning.

The marquis of Louvois did not suffer fools. He was also convinced that social graces were a waste of time. His favorite weapon was not a rifle, a cannon, or a bomb. Instead Louvois had a gift for making others shudder with the simple violence of his words. A master of veiled threats, Louvois once quietly intimidated a neighbor whom he caught hunting on the grounds of his country estate. "I am persuaded of your honor," he wrote to the man, "but, as often happens when one shoots ducks on another's property, something else sometimes gets shot. It would give me great pleasure, then, if you would keep your children off my property."

Still, La Grange's convincing show gave the pugnacious minister of war concern. In their lengthy meeting she explained that a group of spies—led by a man named Nicolas Poncet—operated at the Châtelet prison. Poncet shared information with La Grange, allowing her to predict, long before anyone else, that the French would lift the siege on Maastricht and reclaim the town of Aire. She also said she knew an even darker secret: There was a plot afoot to poison Louis XIV.

La Grange refused to reveal anything more, insisting on an audience with the king in order to share all that she knew. For as scandalous as her accusations were, both La Reynie and Louvois demonstrated great skepticism. The woman was, after all, a proven liar, a scam artist and criminal.

Louvois left for the front the next day. In his absence he instructed La Reynie to transfer La Grange immediately from the Châtelet prison to the Bastille, where suspects could be held in greater secrecy and security. "His Majesty has commanded me to tell you that he expects you to attend to this affair with diligence and that you will do all that is necessary to enlighten him on it," Louvois told La Reynie.

La Reynie interrogated Poncet first. In order to discover the truth behind La Grange's claims, he needed to get a sense of whether Poncet was actually the spy that the woman claimed he was. If La Grange had lied about this, then she was also lying about the king.

The lieutenant of police asked Poncet about the various pseudonyms he had used over the years: Sainte-Presse, Orvilliers, Romano. La Reynie made a point of showing Poncet that he could hide nothing from the police. It worked. Poncet admitted to being a former captain in the king's army. Following a short stint in a Lille jail, he had made his way to England. There, he had a "little love affair" with the wife of an English official, but he was not a spy.

The lieutenant of police shifted tone quickly, his questions becoming more forceful: "Did you receive any letters written in code from the wife?"

"No," said Poncet.

La Reynie gave Poncet a look of incredulity and launched into a strategic accusation. "Yes, you did. And to keep anyone from knowing what you were saying to her, you also wrote them in code."

Unsettled by these unanticipated questions, Poncet denied the accusations once again. La Reynie shifted topics. Speaking in staccato bursts, the police chief peppered the man with questions, each more incriminating than the previous one: "How long did you serve in Flanders? . . . You received some letters from acquaintances there as well, no? . . . What about Holland, what acquaintances do you have there? . . . What letters did you receive from them?"

After Poncet denied knowledge of everything, La Reynie finally revealed the source of his information. "What do you know about Mademoiselle de La Grange, prisoner at Châtelet?" he asked.

Relieved to take the focus off himself, Poncet said without hesitation that the two had met four months earlier in prison. He rescued La Grange from unwanted advances by a fellow prisoner by dumping a large pot of water on the man's head. A friendship between the two quickly developed, and La Grange told him her entire story. Poncet recounted to La Reynie her efforts to dupe the late Faurye out of his fortune. La Grange had been primarily motivated by greed and also "a deadly hatred" toward Faurye for having mistreated a little dog that La Grange adored more than anything or anyone.

He was not the spy, Poncet asserted once again; La Grange was. "The woman is very dangerous," he said. Everything he knew about foreign intelligence he had learned from her. "She claims to have very beautiful secrets, some of which are about what is happening from one country to another and in one army to another. But that's all she will say, because she wants to meet the king. She wants to tell her secrets directly to His Majesty."

It was not clear whether Poncet or La Grange was telling the truth. Nor was it clear which of the two, or if both, were spies. Because of this La Reynie described his encounter with Poncet in an urgent letter to Louvois, recommending they both be kept under prison surveillance. The minister concurred and asked if "it was not impossible that La Grange is only trying to delay judgment in her criminal trial?"

Two days later La Reynie wondered the same thing after interrogating La Grange for the first time. La Reynie disliked La Grange, whom he called "the sneakiest and meanest woman in the world," from the moment he met her. In contrast to Poncet, who resisted vociferously all accusations, La Grange seemed almost too willing to talk, and what she said often seemed highly improbable. She claimed that Poncet gave her two of the letters that he had received from his contacts in England. He burned the rest of them in front of her—while they were in prison, no less. When La Reynie asked to see the letters, La Grange demurred. "I'll produce them, I don't have them on me. But I won't tell you precisely where they are."

La Reynie interrogated her again over the weeks that followed. With each session, her answers became increasingly verbose and increasingly cryptic. By April, La Reynie was losing patience. He entered her prison cell and waited impatiently for the notary to complete the standard routine requiring prisoners to state their name, age, place of birth, and to make a pledge to tell only the truth.

"Where are the letters written in code that you told us about?" he spat out the moment the notary finished with the formalities. La Grange explained that the letters were still in the Châtelet prison tucked in the sleeve of a dress that she had entrusted to the safekeeping of another prisoner.

"Where at the Châtelet? With whom did you leave them?" La Reynie demanded.

"I can't remember her name," La Grange insisted.

La Reynie quickly tired of these futile exchanges. Convinced more than ever that La Grange had no access to military secrets or knowledge of any plot to kill the king, La Reynie concluded she was merely a desperate woman trying to postpone her inevitable court trial and sentencing.

The political climate had changed substantially in the time between La Grange's arrest and La Reynie's latest interrogations, making her feigned claims of espionage less interesting. In summer 1678, Louis signed the Treaty of Nijmegen, which announced France's victory in the six-year-long Franco-Dutch Wars. Gaining control of the Franche-Comté region and claiming portions of the Spanish Netherlands, Louis could not have been more pleased. He crowed, "I fully rejoice in my clever conduct whereby I was able to extend the boundaries of my kingdom at the expense of my enemies."

After reading accounts of the interrogations, Louvois and Louis XIV concurred with the police chief's assessment. Two weeks later the king's secretary of state, Michel Le Tellier—Louvois's father—instructed La Reynie to return La Grange to the Châtelet prison, where she would again await trial so that "we can proceed against her as we would have had she not been transferred to the Bastille."

La Grange's case was now back in the formal court system, which was overseen by the *parlement* rather than by La Reynie's Châtelet. The police chief may have hoped he had seen the last of La Grange, but it was only the beginning. The next time he found himself in an interrogation room with her, the threats she foretold had become only too real.

18

"Burn after Reading"

I n fall 1678 a carriage rumbled to a halt in front of the Église
Saint-Paul-Saint-Louis in the elegant Marais quarter of Paris.
A well-dressed woman stepped out and briskly ascended the
imposing stone steps. Once inside, she made her way to one of the
confessionals. Taking a seat in the box, she waited uncomfortably
for her turn.

On the other side of the confessional, the priest steeled himself
for another sinner. In this ever-growing capital of lost souls, a
day's work in the confessional brought an overflowing river of
tales of passion and desire, of young virgins who had tested too far
the limits of their purity as they bantered with lovers in the nearby
place des Vosges. Then there were the shopkeepers whose abilities
to cheat their clientele were as limitless as their creativity. A
mismeasured gram of flour here, a counterfeited product there. No
matter how small or large the transgression, they all came to Saint-
Paul for the same reason: to be spared in the afterlife. In turn, the
priest meted out forgiveness and penances in equal measure.

The Church of Saint-Paul stood just down the street from the
Bastille prison, whose fortressed turrets had towered over the city

since the fourteenth century. Much of what took place at the Bastille remained unseen by average Parisians. However, the priests of Saint-Paul witnessed firsthand many of the activities at the fortress that were meant to take place under the cloak of secrecy, sometimes presiding over last-minute confessions or offering up last rites. Other times they watched from the main church doors as doleful prisoners were led down the rue Saint-Antoine.

The well-dressed woman in the confessional said nothing to the priest. Instead she slid a rolled and crumpled piece of parchment through the wooden lattice slats that separated them. He had barely begun to scan the document when the woman blurted out that she had found it in the public gallery of the Palais de Justice and did not know what else to do with it. Located just steps away from Notre Dame, the Palais housed the *parlement*, the criminal appeal courts, and the treasury. For hundreds of years shopkeepers hawking every type of merchandise had also set up shop under the covered galleries that wrapped the interior courtyards, serving thousands of lawyers, judges, notaries, and others who passed daily through the compound. The shops ranged from cheap to upscale, from hand-stitched clothes to artisanal clocks. The sellers and their customers also traded in gossip, both spoken and written. Lovers sent friends or household staff to the gallery to hand passionate letters and other signs of affection to their beloved. Other letters were "lost," in order to stir rumors or inflame the heart of a jealous lover.

From the first sentence of the letter, the priest understood that more than simple matters of the heart were at play. "You have made me a confidant of a secret that I wish only too well that I could forget for my own peace of mind, or at the very least I pray that what you are plotting will never come to fruition given the horror the simple idea gives to me. That white powder that you want to put on the handkerchief of *you know who* could very well have the same effect. Either you will forget such criminal plots, or you will lose me forever."

If the identity of "*you know who*" was not clear to the priest, it would soon be from the reference to treason that followed. "I fear in the extreme that our letters will be found, and that they will believe that I am the guilty one, even though I am entirely innocent. All other crimes, one has to be an accomplice to be punished, but for this one, it is enough to know only of the intent." There was no crime more serious in early France, and no form of treason more ghastly than an attempt, real or intended, on the life of the king or a member of his family. In early France treason by association—or the mere knowledge of a plot against the king's life—was enough to merit the death penalty, which the writer knew.

"Do you remember [who] we both saw in front of the Bastille? This example is still fresh enough that you should tremble." The letter writer referred to the execution of the chevalier of Rohan, a colonel of the king's corps of bodyguards, who was convicted of treason and decapitated—not at the place de Grève, where Parisian executions normally took place—but outside the gates of the Bastille prison. The gallant Rohan made the mistake of trying to court several of the king's former and current mistresses, most notably Madame de Montespan. Louis XIV dismissed Rohan from his post, leaving him penniless. In retaliation Rohan plotted with France's enemy, the Netherlands, to kidnap the king's eldest son and hold him for ransom in exchange for Quillebeuf, a strategic town in Normandy near the Dutch border. At Louvois's orders La Reynie's guards arrested Rohan on September 11, 1674. The reference to Rohan suggested a treasonous plot was afoot to poison the king.

The priest turned again to peer at the woman, the bearer of this most unwelcome letter, but she was gone. Looking down once more at the piece of paper in his hand, he read the last sentence: "Burn after reading."

A brilliant sun painted on the ceiling loomed over the priest. It signaled the omniscient presence of the Sun King. From the prisons to the holiest of spaces, the king was everywhere. All who transgressed his laws would be punished. The priest transferred the letter immediately into the care of Father François de La Chaise, archbishop of Paris and eventual namesake of the largest cemetery in the French capital. As the king's personal confessor,

Père La Chaise had a duty to inform the king, lest he also be accused of treason.

La Chaise shared the letter with Colbert, who in turn forwarded it to La Reynie. The king had been informed of the threat, Colbert explained, and instructed his police chief to spare no effort in uncovering its author.

La Reynie's first instinct was to question La Grange again. While he had dismissed her stories as pure fabrication, the timing of the letter's discovery seemed more than coincidental. Unfortunately La Grange's case had been remanded back to the *parlement*'s courts, which were the domain of the attorney general, Achille de Harlay, who was unlikely to appreciate any meddling from La Reynie. Harlay had taken the lead in the Brinvilliers case, at Colbert's orders. The police had not been invited to participate in the process then, and they certainly would not be now.

As La Grange's case wound its way through the legal labyrinth, La Reynie became increasingly agitated by the thought of the woman being executed before he could interrogate her, taking any knowledge she might have about the mysterious letter to the grave with her.

Eschewing bureaucratic protocol, La Reynie secured several opportunities to question La Grange. Showing her a copy of the letter, he questioned her about what she knew. At every turn she denied adamantly ever hearing about it or having a hand in writing it. How could she? She was in prison when it was found, she said.

The sentencing approached; La Grange's story changed. Her accusations against Poncet had bought her additional time before her sentencing. Now La Grange hoped that the gift she was about to give La Reynie would do the same. She sent La Reynie two letters, both written and signed by the Abbé Nail as Launay. She claimed they had fallen out of the pocket of one of Launay's close colleagues, a certain Chamois.

In a letter to Colbert on November 19, 1678, La Reynie requested that the *parlement* provide him with handwriting samples from Nail, in order to research the matter. Colbert agreed and informed Monsieur de Harlay to obtain his approval of the request.

The records are frustratingly silent on the results of La Reynie's handwriting analyses, but they must have given the police chief cause for concern. One week later he wrote again to Colbert asking the king's permission to torture Launay and La Grange before sentencing and have the questioning done, not by the *parlement* but by the police.

Colbert's response was prompt and unequivocal. "Monsieur," he wrote. "I have not spoken to the King about your proposition regarding La Grange and Launay. I find it extraordinary that you feel it necessary to pursue a separate investigation and to presumably apply the two to the Question." The minister was known for being humorless, but his use of the word "extraordinary" was at once wry and biting. "I feel that it is better," Colbert continued, "that the Parlement enlighten us on the letter as they review the pending case." If—and only if—the two were sentenced to death, he explained, would it be time to apply torture. La Reynie would have to be patient. "I believe strongly that there soon will be a time to begin the procedure you are proposing."

Colbert's decision was frustrating but not at all surprising. Louis's most powerful and trusted minister had a reputation for playing by the rules, for moving cautiously. La Reynie began to doubt whether he and Colbert shared the same priorities. La Reynie was not a man who was used to being told no. He also had little patience for those who stood in the way of his work—even men like Colbert. To force La Grange to reveal her secrets and expose the true depths of these poisonous plots, he needed to find a new ally.

19

Dinner Guests

In December 1678, one month after Colbert rebuffed La Reynie, winter set in. The warm glow of candlelight bathed the street in front of Marie Vigoureux's modest home on the rue Courtauvilain. Laughter and wine flowed easily as Vigoureux flirted with a Monsieur Perrin, a low-ranking lawyer at the *parlement* who frequently visited her. Perrin stopped by Vigoureux's home with the excuse of wanting her colorful friend, Marie Bosse, to read his palm. The stout, forty-eight-year-old Bosse wore a man's knee-length embroidered jacket (*justaucorps*) and earned her living as a fortune-teller. More often than not a quick visit often bled into a late evening. Perrin could always count on La Bosse and Vigoureux for uproarious stories—their tongues loosened by wine—about their adventures in duping unsuspecting nobles out of their money.

Bosse bragged about her dealings with the beautiful and poised Marguerite de Poulaillon. Madame Poulaillon had sent a friend ahead of her to describe a ruse that she wanted the fortune-teller to perform on Poulaillon's husband. When the married couple arrived, Bosse looked intently into the man's palm as prescribed

and shook her head slowly, letting out a quiet sigh. Monsieur Poulaillon would die soon, she explained. Both skeptical and shaken,
the husband turned quickly toward the door of Bosse's home and
left. Giving the fortune-teller a subtle look of thanks, Madame
Poulaillon deftly removed her expensive, blue-enameled bracelet,
encrusted with precious jewels, and handed it to Bosse.

Madame Poulaillon soon returned to ask Bosse to turn the
feigned death pronouncement into a reality, so she could have
full access to her husband's fortune. She had fallen in love with a
man named La Rivière, who—much like Brinvilliers's beloved
Sainte-Croix—preyed on wealthy women. He was swimming in
debt and threatened to leave her if the noblewoman could not
come up with a large sum of money. Madame Poulaillon vowed
to do everything necessary to keep her lover, even if it meant
murdering her husband.

Bosse did not say what happened afterward, but turning to
Vigoureux and Perrin with a knowing glance, she bragged that the
job had paid well and that Madame Poulaillon had been a very
satisfied customer. By Bosse's calculations, she needed only three
more clients like Poulaillon to be a rich woman. Perrin nervously
asked what Bosse meant by three more clients. Bosse confirmed
that she had literally made a killing by selling poison to men and
women who wished to prune their family trees.

As Perrin left Vigoureux's dinner party, his head reeled—not
from the wine, but from what he had heard. He gave his coachman
directions to the home of Desgrez. Perrin knew the man only by his
reputation as La Reynie's trusted officer who had returned Brinvilliers to France. As Desgrez listened to Perrin's account, he devised a
plan to confirm the truth behind the lawyer's accusations. He
pressed the wife of one of his guards into service. Dressed in her finest clothes, the woman made her way to Bosse's house. The guard's
wife knocked on the door of Bosse's modest home and launched
into a story about an abusive husband. She pleaded with Bosse to
make the problem disappear. Bosse agreed to help her—for a
price—and instructed the woman to come back two days later.
When she did, she left with a vial of poison.

In the early hours of January 4, 1679, archers quietly surrounded Bosse's home. On a signal they stormed the building, kicking in doors and breaking anything that got in their way in the search for Bosse. They found her sleeping in the family bed, in the company of her adult children. At the same time another group of archers arrested Madame Vigoureux.

A carriage flanked by guards on horseback rumbled along the well-traveled gravel path toward the fortressed entrance of the Château of Vincennes. The castle's keep rose in the distance. Standing over 170 feet tall, the tower had once been home to some of the most illustrious kings of France's medieval past. Three hundred years earlier, Charles V met with his grand council under high Gothic arches painted in rich hues of blue and embellished with gold-leaf fleurs-de-lis. Sculptures of prophets and the evangelists, whose robed bodies looked as if they were soaring in the air, anchored each vaulted arch. The king kept his collection of illuminated manuscripts, the finest in all of Europe, on the second floor, protected by the keep's ten-foot-thick walls.

A turret wrapped each corner of the tower. One housed the central, windowless, and winding staircase; two others held small rooms for the king, his ministers, and his staff. The fourth turret functioned as a communal latrine—among the first of its kind in medieval construction—that flowed odorously through the turret and into the tower's moat.

After the monarchy abandoned Vincennes for Paris, Charles's magnificent tower transformed into one of the darkest, most infamous dungeons in all of Europe. The small rooms in the turrets became prison cells. An interrogation room replaced the king's library. A military compound, which Louvois oversaw as minister of war, now surrounded the tower. In his choice of prison for Bosse and Vigoureux, La Reynie made his intentions and his alliances clear.

Marie Bosse looked at the tower with trepidation through the curtains of the police carriage. Armed soldiers emerged from the guardhouse. They took the prisoner's paperwork from the driver and inspected the interior of the carriage. Assured that all was well, they signaled to the troops to lower the heavy drawbridge. Several minutes later Bosse's carriage rattled across the moat and into the belly of the dungeon complex.

Once inside and in the company of more soldiers, the portly Bosse labored up a set of dark, twisting stone stairs. Her breath made white puffs in the cold air as she panted with every step. Once on the upper floors of the tower, the guards escorted her to her cell. The metal door groaned as it shut behind her. The guards slid a heavy bar across the door and locked it in place. Knowing that there was no chance of escape, she took inventory of her new surroundings.

A battered mattress sat askew on the stone floor of the small, hexagonal room. Medieval archery slits in the walls let slivers of light into the cell, illuminating swashes of indigo-blue and burgundy-red paint, traces of the royal past of the three-hundred-year-old tower. Now the walls were mostly covered in graffiti by the room's former inhabitants: hash marks counting the days, pleas to God asking for release from suffering, and obscenity-laden missives directed against the wardens.

As Bosse was being transported to the jail, La Reynie's officers collected evidence from her home. They found a small pine box containing glass flasks filled with what looked like clear water. Nearby there were several envelopes with white powder inside; one envelope had been made out of the death notice of a Marguerite Hagunet, signed March of the year before. The inspectors also discovered packets containing fingernail clippings and something that looked like dried blood, as well as six other, smaller packets filled with a luminous, bluish-green powder. After all the suspicious-looking materials had been collected, the inspectors wrapped the pine box and the packets with thick cord. They sealed both with thick red candle wax and delivered the items to a team of apothecaries for testing.

Bosse and Marie Vigoureux spent the night in different cells, shivering in the January cold. The next morning, Nicolas de La Reynie made the first of many trips from Paris to Vincennes to interrogate the prisoners. Earlier that morning he questioned

Bosse's son, François, who had been detained at the Bastille prison. François confirmed that his mother spent time with Perrin, the lawyer who reported the woman's ominous boastfulness. The son also said he heard his mother speak of a Madame de Poulaillon, who sought help in killing her husband.

The name caught La Reynie's attention. The *particule*—as the *de* (of) is called—marked high social standing, a sign of nobility. A century later, during the French Revolution, nobles would make every effort to erase the *de* from their names in the hopes of escaping the guillotine's vengeance. But now, in this era of Louis XIV and Versailles, the *particule* gave the investigation a new level of seriousness—and one that La Reynie knew he could not ignore.

La Reynie ordered the prison guards to bring Madame Vigoureux down for questioning first. The warmth of the interrogation room provided welcome relief from her frigid cell. La Reynie's chief notary, Jean Sagot, stood alongside the lieutenant general while a scribe held a quill, ready to capture every word said.

La Reynie began the interrogation. After confirming Vigoureux's name, age, and address for the record, La Reynie moved directly to questions about Bosse. The forty-year-old Vigoureux confirmed that she had met Bosse about three years earlier, when she was released from the Châtelet prison for counterfeiting. Bosse needed a place to stay until she found something more permanent, so they lived together for about five or six weeks.

"So what is Bosse up to?" he asked. "Does she tell fortunes?"

"I don't know if she tells fortunes," Vigoureux replied dismissively. "It's true that she often reads palms and tells people whatever comes to her mind...people in the neighborhood believe that she is a fortune-teller, at least that's what Bosse says."

Fixing his gaze intently on his prisoner, La Reynie asked whether Vigoureux also told fortunes herself. "To be truthful, I have a few times," Vigoureux conceded, qualifying her statement immediately afterward. "I haven't done it for years, not since I moved to Paris from the provinces."

Without prompting, Vigoureux launched into a detailed description of Bosse's dealings with Madame de Poulaillon. She confirmed that the noblewoman was having an affair with a man named Rivière and consulted Bosse regularly about how to make her husband disappear.

"Do you know who prepared the potions and drugs that Bosse distributed to people who came to her home?" La Reynie asked. Vigoureux claimed not to know. She never actually saw Bosse give her clients any poison. "Bosse told me once that if she had something to do that she didn't want anyone to know, she would never tell me anyway because I cannot keep a secret."

Vigoureux seemed uncomfortable directly accusing her associate of dispensing poison, but she had no problem making insinuations. "I did hear her say a few times that two or three women who were having problems with their husbands had come to her house to ask them if they would die soon. And Bosse, knowing what their intentions were, always answered as they wanted her to." Their husbands always died not long after, she said.

La Reynie turned his focus to the details of the dinner that led to the arrest of Bosse and Vigoureux. Vigoureux acknowledged that she knew Perrin and that he had come by her house five or six times. "Is it true that, in the warmth of the meal, Bosse said that she would be rich if she could help poison three people?" Vigoureux said she could not remember.

La Reynie reframed the question. "Have you heard rumors that Bosse was involved in three jobs? The first involved the home of a Monsieur de Valentinay, the second Monsieur de Poulaillon, and the third somewhere else?"

Without a pause, Vigoureux answered yes. From what people were saying, she explained, Valentinay was preparing to marry a young woman from the provinces. His fiancée hired Bosse to cast spells to prevent the marriage. "I saw a letter from this Demoiselle [Valentinay's unwilling fiancée] in which she demanded that the marriage be canceled, and that Bosse would not receive payment until that happened," Vigoureux explained.

La Reynie changed the subject and asked if Vigoureux visited Bosse's home in the days preceding their arrest. She confirmed that she saw both Bosse and Madame de Poulaillon there. Poulaillon had come to talk to Bosse about the possibility of finding someone who could cast a spell to protect a friend, the marquis of Feuquières, while he was on the battlefields. La Reynie ended the questioning shortly afterward.

The next day La Reynie returned to Vincennes, this time to question Bosse. Before launching into questions about Bosse's poisonous activities, La Reynie inquired about Bosse's dealings with La Grange.

"Do you know Madame de La Grange, who lived with Monsieur Faury?"

"No," Bosse replied. She must have sensed La Reynie's skepticism. Within moments she retracted her answer and launched into a detailed account of her interactions with the woman. She had met La Grange a few years earlier at the home of Catherine Voisin, a fortune-teller who lived in the Montorgueil quarter. She had since heard that La Grange was in the Conciergerie prison, awaiting trial.

"How do you know that La Grange is in prison?" La Reynie asked.

"All of Paris knows it," Bosse replied matter-of-factly.

La Reynie returned the questioning back to Bosse's own activities. He asked what she had been doing with the various powders and liquids found in her home. She explained without hesitation that she had simply been dabbling in alchemy. "I was silly, just like so many others. Voisin was the one who put the idea in my head."

When the police chief targeted his questions specifically to the wine-filled dinner with the lawyer Perrin that had led to the women's arrest, Bosse suddenly became less forthcoming in her answers.

"What did you mean the other day that you'd be rich for the rest of your life if you could have three more clients of consequence?" La Reynie asked. Attempting to hide her nervousness, Bosse replied, "I have no idea what you're talking about."

"Is it true that you intended to poison three more people?" he persisted.

"No," she replied tersely.

La Reynie did not believe her. He ended the interview and sent Bosse back to her cold cell.

The following day La Reynie sat at his desk at Châtelet and reviewed the official minutes of the interrogations. Once each session was over, a scribe reread the testimony aloud to the prisoners, who initialed each page. The shaky and uncertain handwriting of both Bosse and Vigoureux suggest that neither woman could read or write well. Bosse said as much to La Reynie when he asked if she had any alchemy or poison books in her home: "I do not know how to read," she answered.

As La Reynie reviewed the minutes, he noted the names mentioned by Vigoureux and Bosse during their interrogations. He had never heard of Madame Voisin before, but he added her to Desgrez's arrest list.

2 0

The Question

Late on a Saturday evening in February 1679, without advance warning, the *parlement* condemned La Grange and her accomplice Launay to death. Upon hearing the news, La Reynie raced to his writing desk. The police chief worried that the two criminals could be executed over the weekend before he had a chance to question her once again. He wrote two letters: one to the marquis of Seignelay, Colbert's son and assistant; the other to the marquis of Louvois.

La Reynie intended to play Colbert and Louvois against each other, betting that Louvois would win. As police chief, La Reynie reported to Colbert. Paris remained the quasi-exclusive domain of Colbert, who viewed the city as a means to enhance the glory of the king. La Reynie had long enjoyed the support of Colbert, who led the original commission to enact the lieutenancy of police and who supported the police chief unflaggingly in his efforts to change Paris from the eyesore of Europe to a jewel in Louis's crown.

Still, Colbert had proved himself reluctant when it came to the poison investigations. He put up roadblocks to La Reynie's efforts to pursue investigations outside the normal judicial process, even those that La Reynie felt strongly were for the security of the monarchy. This should have not been surprising. Colbert had oversight over the economy, the legal system, the promotion of *beaux arts* and royal architectural projects—all matters that functioned best in the context of peace, order, and a smoothly functioning bureaucracy.

Louvois, on the other hand, made war for a living. He was bold and unapologetic. Colbert still remained bitter about the king's decision to ignore his counsel and go to war against Spain and Holland in 1667 and again in 1672.

As much as the rivals vied for the king's resources and support, Colbert and Louvois were actually more similar than they were different. "Louvois has a character," remarked one court observer, "that is hard and violent with a gaze that is severe. Many say he mistreats people when he speaks, so much so that no one dares approach him. As far as Colbert, cold and dry with a sober air, he freezes out those who come to him."

During the Franco-Dutch Wars, Louis put Colbert's grand plans for Parisian construction to the side to pay for Louvois's wars. If Colbert ever needed any sign of lingering rivalries between peace and war, the massive Hôtel des Invalides now dominating the Left Bank was it. Colbert had not proposed the Invalides, far from it. To his deep frustration, the hospital and military complex was Louvois's doing. The minister of war played to the king's deepest desires. He urged Louis XIV to indulge fully in "war, glory, dominion, and self-worship." Louis's unceasing wars meant great casualties. A soaring hospital and military complex would serve, Louvois argued, the dual purpose of attending to the troops all the while reasserting the king's greatness—and Louvois's own.

Still, as La Reynie's concerns about poison plots deepened, the slow-moving legal mechanisms at the *parlement* were increasingly becoming an obstacle to his work. He needed Louvois, whom the court called the "King's Creature," on his side. In the wake of the Treaty of Nijmegen, Louvois was also looking for a way to remain prominent in the king's circle at a time of relative peace.

Less than one day after receiving La Reynie's letter, Louvois sent good news. At his urging the king put a stay on the executions in order to allow ample time for the Question. He further specified that if, during the Question, either La Grange or Launay revealed anything more than was already known, they would not be executed. Instead they would be transferred immediately to La Reynie for further investigation. This decision would be made entirely by the king, who wished to see transcripts of the Question after it was conducted.

La Reynie would not supervise or attend the Question himself; this would remain in the jurisdiction of the *parlement*. However, the decision reinforced the lieutenant of police's important status in such matters. La Reynie now had Louvois's full support, and thus the king's. Both La Reynie and Louvois delighted, no doubt, in the fact that the king ordered Colbert to communicate these wishes, born of Louvois's persuasion, to the *parlement*.

At six o'clock in the morning the following Monday, prison guards descended the narrow stairs to La Grange's cell in the Conciergerie and escorted her to the same chamber where Brinvilliers had been tortured three years earlier. Three well-dressed men looked up from a small table around which they had been standing and gathered in a line in front of La Grange. Messieurs Boultz and Girault, the court officers leading the interrogation, joined Monsieur Amyot, the principal notary for the *parlement*. The questioning began with a series of inquiries about the forged marriage contract and La Grange's role in the deception. While La Grange had been coldly calculating as a free woman and frustratingly inscrutable while in prison, her stoicism melted as Boultz and Girault took turns questioning her. "I swear on the heavens," she blurted, pleading with her captors, "I know nothing about this document. I have no idea what Monsieur de La Reynie has been told."

"So you're saying that you do not know [if] Launay wrote it?" the men asked, making no effort to hide their disbelief. La Grange swore that she knew absolutely nothing about a letter and had no idea who wrote it. "I already told Monsieur de La Reynie all of this," she insisted.

The two interrogators did not believe her. She knew very well about the existence of a letter, they said, reminding La Grange

Louis XIV, king of France (1638–1715). Charles Le Brun.
(*Château de Versailles, France/Bridgeman Images*)

Nicolas de La Reynie (1625–1709), first lieutenant general of Paris, appointed by Louis XIV in 1667. Nicolas Mignard, 1665. (*De Agostini Picture Library/Bridgeman Images*)

Jean-Baptiste Colbert (1619–1683), minister of finance under Louis XIV. Claude Lefebvre. (*Château de Versailles, France/De Agostini Picture Library/G. Dagli Orti/Bridgeman Images*)

François-Michel Le Tellier, marquis de Louvois (1641–1691), minister of war under Louis XIV. Pierre Mignard. (*Musée des Beaux-Arts, Rheims/De Agostini Picture Library/Bridgeman Images*)

Marie-Thérèse (1638–1683), queen of France. Attributed to Charles Beaubrun, after 1660. (*Château de Versailles, France/Bridgeman Images*)

Henrietta Anne, duchess of Orléans (1644–1670), holding portrait of husband, Philippe (1640–1701), duke of Orléans and Louis XIV's brother. Jean-Charles Nocret II (1670). (*Dunham Massey, Cheshire, UK/National Trust Photographic Library/ Bridgeman Images*)

Louise de La Vallière (1644–1710), Louis XIV's mistress from 1661 to 1667.
Jean Nocret. (*Château de Versailles, France/Bridgeman Images*)

Françoise-Athénaïs de Rochechouart de Mortemart (1640–1707), marquise of Montespan, Louis XIV's mistress beginning in 1667. Louis Ferdinand Elle. (*Château de Versailles, France/Flammarion/Bridgeman Images*)

Claude de Vin des Oeillets (1637–1687), attendant to the
marquise of Montespan and sometimes mistress to Louis XIV
until retiring from court in 1678. Pierre Mignard.

Marie Angelique d'Escorailles de Rousille, duchess of Fontanges (1661–1681), Louis XIV's mistress from 1678 to her death at twenty in 1681. Nicolas de l'Armessin. (*Tallandier/ Bridgeman Images*)

MARIE ANGELIQVE
DE ROVSSILLE
FONTANGE,

D'ESCORAILLES
DVCHESSE DE

LA MARQ^{SE} DE MAINTENON

Françoise d'Aubigné, marquise of Maintenon (1635–1719), Louis XIV's second wife after a secret marriage in 1683 or 1684. French School, seventeenth century. (*Private Collection/Bridgeman Images*)

Olympe Mancini, countess of Soissons (1639–1708), fled Paris after
being accused of poisoning her husband. French School, seventeenth
century. (*Musée de la Ville de Paris,
Musée du Petit-Palais, France/
Bridgeman Images*)

Marie-Anne Mancini, duch-
ess of Bouillon (1646–1714),
appeared under protest at the
Arsenal tribunal. Pierre
Mignard. (*Musée des
Beaux-Arts, Agen, France/
Bridgeman Images*)

LE MARÉCHAL
DUC
DE LUXEMBOURG

François-Henri de Montmorency, duke of Luxembourg (1628–1695),
rival of Louvois, accused of communicating with the devil with the help
of the sorcerer Lesage. (*Bibliotèque Nationale de France*)

Entry of Louis XIV and Marie-Thérèse to Arras, July 30, 1667, accompanied by the king's brother Philippe, Henrietta Anne, Louise de La Vallière, and Athénaïs de Montespan. Adam Frans van der Meulen. (*Château de Versailles, France/Bridgeman Images*)

Château of Saint-Germain-en-Laye, Louis XIV's birthplace and main palace until 1682. Perelle, France, seventeenth century. (Bibliothèque des Arts Décoratifs, France/De Agostini Picture Library/Bridgeman Images)

Construction of Versailles, which began in 1681 and continued well after the court officially moved to the palace in 1682. Adam Frans van der Meulen (ca. 1680). (*Royal Collection Trust, Her Majesty Queen Elizabeth II, 2016/Bridgeman Images*)

Château of Vincennes, where La Reynie questioned hundreds of prisoners accused of poison, witchcraft, and abortion. (*De Agostini Pictures/Gabrielle/Bridgeman Images*)

LE **PORTRAIT DE LA VOISIN.**

Source de   tant de maux maudite creature
Qui par mille poisons destruisois la Nature,
Si la parque en sillant les detestable jours
A suit regner la Mort, en prolongeant leur cours,
Vn suplice effroyable et plein d'Ignominie
A sceu trancher le fil de ton enorme Vie.

Chasteau, ex. C.P.R.

Catherine Monvoisin, La Voisin (ca. 1640–1680). French School,
seventeenth century. (*Bibliothèque Nationale, France/Bridgeman Images*)

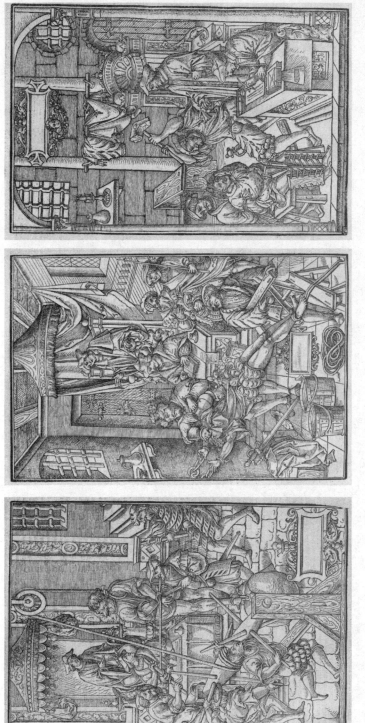

Strappado. Jean Milles de Souvigny, *Praxis criminis persequendi* (1541). (Hathitrust)

Question d'eau (water torture). Jean Milles de Souvigny, *Praxis criminis persequendi* (1541). (Hathitrust)

Brodequins. Jean Milles de Souvigny, *Praxis criminis persequendi* (1541). (Hathitrust)

Interrogation records, signed by La Reynie and Coeuret (Lesage).
(*Bibliothèque Nationale de France*)

La Reynie struggles to compose his summary of the Affair of the Poisons for
Louvois and the king. (*Bibliothèque Nationale de France*)

that she had been the one to provide La Reynie with samples of Launay's handwriting. Caught in her contradiction, La Grange remained silent.

"Have you ever meddled in poisons, Madame La Grange?" the questioners asked in a tone that confirmed their belief in her guilt. La Grange did not deny that she had, once, but never again. "Eight or nine years ago I made up a divine plaster, but never anything else, "she claimed. *Emplastrum divinum* (divine plaster) was a benign yet prohibitively expensive salve made of frankincense and myrrh, used for skin wounds and other ulcerous "corruptions."

Again Boultz and Girault made no effort to hide their disbelief. "So having talked so much before about poisons and counterpoisons, you have never once used poison or have composed them with others?" they asked.

"Never," she insisted. "Faurye used to talk a lot about poisons, he said that he had once been poisoned by Collart, his servant. But I never made poisons by myself or with anyone else for that matter, and it never even once crossed my mind."

Boultz and Girault changed the subject. "Who wrote the letter?" La Grange asserted she had nothing to do with the letter. Someone else wrote it. In fact, she was convinced that the only reason she now found herself in front of the two men was that she had fallen victim to a conspiracy intent on seeing her punished for sharing information with Louvois and La Reynie.

Shifting topics once again, the questioners pushed La Grange to admit her guilt. "Do you know Bosse; you gave her poison, didn't you? The two of you worked together to make poison, didn't you?"

La Grange insisted that she had not seen Bosse for more than ten years, contradicting what Bosse had told La Reynie in earlier interrogations. "But I never once spoke to her about poison. I don't even know what poison is."

La Grange's claim that she knew nothing about poison was so preposterous that Boultz and Girault pretended not to have heard it. "So you don't know that Bosse gave poison to many people?

"No."

Nodding to the guards, Boultz and Girault declared to La

Grange's horror that it was time to begin the torture. The guards quickly tied her wrists to a large metal ring built into the chamber's thick stone walls before noticing that the buckets of water they planned to use had frozen. At Boultz and Giraud's direction, the guards untied La Grange from the metal ring and shoved her onto a sturdy bench nearby.

Working one on each side, the guards put her legs between two thick pieces of wood, wrapped them with leather straps, and pulled the straps as tightly as they could. Hands tied behind her back, she was ready. She cried, "I swear on the heavens...!"

The notary Amyot moved the desk close to La Grange, tucked his long jacket under him, and sat upright, ready to make careful note of each word that the prisoner uttered under torture. Boultz and Girault stepped forward to begin the interrogation anew.

"Have you told us the truth in all matters?" the interrogators intoned somberly. La Grange did not respond. Girault looked up at Amyot: "Note that she refused to answer." He then turned toward the guard: "First corner." The guard took a wedge and pounded it into the corner of the torture boots, between the plank of wood and the strap. La Grange cried out in pain.

Again, "Have you told us the truth in all matters?" La Grange looked at them pleadingly and said that she had nothing more to say. "Second corner." The guard raised the heavy mallet over his head and forced a second wedge of wood into the torture boots. "Have you told us the truth in all matters?" they asked once again. La Grange howled in agony but did not speak.

Boultz and Girault waited for the notary to record the woman's refusal to speak and then signaled: "Third corner."

Shouting over her cries, the questioners demanded: "Have you told us the truth in all matters?" La Grange whimpered that she had.

"Fourth corner," Boultz and Girault ordered.

"Do you, Madame La Grange, know anything about a plot against the King's life?" She was sobbing now, praying for the pain to end. "Do you, Madame, know anything about a plot against the King?" No, no, she did not, she moaned.

Girault looked at Boultz in frustration: "Why won't you admit the truth and tell us everything that we need to know about the letter?" The guard reached for a fifth wedge, and with the thud of the mallet, forced it into her other leg. Broken and bleeding, La Grange cried desperately: "May a million devils suffocate me if I am not telling the truth. I'll tell you whatever you need me to say! If you want me to tell you I wrote the letter, I'll do it. I'll do anything you want me to. But I'm telling the truth."

"Tell us the truth!" the men yelled over La Grange's pleas: "I have nothing more to tell you." Six, seven, and then eight blows to the legs. Pale and nearly unconscious from pain, La Grange remained steadfast in her denials. Untying her, the guards carried her to her prison cell to await execution.

The following day La Grange's coconspirator Launay faced the questioners. The questioning followed more or less the same rhythm as that of the day before, as documented by the interrogation record:

First corner: "Ah! My God! May God help a poor innocent wrongly accused."

"Tell us the truth."

"You can kill me, you can do what you will with me, but I'm telling the truth."

Second corner: "If you didn't write the letter, how do you know what it says?" Launay refused to answer. Moments later his body slumped forward.

The interrogators called over Pierre Rainssant, the doctor assigned to witness the torture. Doctors were not there to prevent injury or help heal the wounds inflicted by the interrogators. Instead they let interrogators know how much more torture a prisoner could take without risking death.

Rainssant walked briskly over to Launay and lifted his limp body up, motioning to the guards to untie him. The man's pulse was racing, he was too weak to speak, and his ability to tell the truth was clouded by his weakened state. The doctor explained that if the torture continued "there would be great danger of Launay, his patient, dying from the force of the torments."

The guards immediately moved Launay in front of the fireplace without releasing him from the *brodequins* and gave him some wine to help him regain his strength. Once he began to move and speak again, they continued the interrogation as if nothing had happened.

With a loud thud they pounded the third wedge into the man's leg. "So you never wrote the letter?"

"I have no idea what you are talking about. Let me die," Launay pleaded.

Fourth corner: "I don't know anything!" Launay howled. Fifth corner: "Nothing," he moaned.

Amyot and Girault repeated the question once again, as the sixth wedge brought new screams of pain. "I will never see my Creator if I tell you that I know about the letter." Seventh corner. Eighth. "I will never know God," he mumbled in a barely audible voice, "if I tell you that I know about the letter."

The guards removed the torture boots, blood flooding the floor. "Everything I've told you," Launay moaned, "is the truth. I promise in front of God, it is the truth."

La Reynie read the transcript of the interrogation with frustration. He was convinced that they had let La Grange and Launay off too gently. The king disagreed. Two days after the interrogation, Colbert's son Seignelay informed La Reynie that the king had read the interrogation records. Louis saw no need for the criminals to be transferred to the Châtelet for further questioning by La Reynie. Remembering the frenzy Brinvilliers's death had caused, the king seemed ready to put the entire matter to rest, and quickly. La Grange and Launay, he declared, were to be executed without delay and without crowds or spectacles. As a public demonstration of his acceptance of the king's will, La Reynie was ordered to attend the execution.

Later that evening, as darkness settled in, La Grange and Launay were taken together, legs bleeding and broken, to the steps of the Sainte-Chapelle. There Amyot and Girault waited for them with torches in their hands, the light reflecting the brilliant blue of the stained-glass windows above. The magistrates asked each of them again whether they knew of "anyone else who had undertaken or planned to undertake any evil actions against the king and the royal family by powders, poisons, or similar things." After they both answered no, the criminals were transferred to a priest. Their fate was now in God's hands.

Launay and La Grange made their last prayers in the chapel and were then placed in the care of the executioner, who stood at the main gates of the Conciergerie. La Grange and Launay followed the same path Madame de Brinvilliers had taken in her last hours three years earlier. This time, however, there were no crowds. In the quiet of the night, the pair was transported in a cart to the main entrance of Notre Dame; each wore a muslin *chemise* and had a noose tied loosely around the neck as was customary for soon-to-be-executed criminals, regardless of the method actually used. The executioner shoved them to their knees for another round of prayers.

Once the prayers were finished, Launay and La Grange were pushed back into the cart, which rumbled across the narrow bridge to the Right Bank. Amyot and Girault awaited them at the place de Grève alongside La Reynie. The three men stood together on a small platform adjacent to the larger one where the execution would take place. In the flickering light of the guards' torches, Amyot read aloud the execution order and turned the rest over to the priests and the executioner. After two rounds of the *Salve Regina,* the ax fell. Launay and La Grange met their end, nooses still around their necks.

Reflecting afterward on the events, La Reynie explained that he felt no relief. In the pit of his stomach he sensed that this episode was only the beginning of something much deeper, something much darker.

21

Monsters

La Reynie had wasted no time in arresting Bosse and Vigoureux after learning that they had bragged about their
exploits to the lawyer Perrin. Still, he was more circumspect
when it came to their alleged accomplice Madame de Poulaillon. He
finally arrested her a full month after Bosse and Vigoureux and then
waited several more weeks before confronting her. Sensing that his
actions could set off another frenzy like the one surrounding the
Brinvilliers case, he wanted to make sure he had the facts straight
before questioning a member of the nobility.

He began first by interrogating Poulaillon's former servant, a
woman named Monstreux, who explained to La Reynie that Poulaillon had a strong "aversion" to her husband. That said, Poulaillon took advantage of his "strong weakness" for her. All it took
was for Madame to direct a smile or other form of feigned affection to get him to give her anything she wanted.

Madame de Poulaillon's lover, Rivière, had the same effect on
her as she did on her husband. Poulaillon sold off the couple's
belongings in order to support Rivière, who was perennially in

debt. Each time her husband bought her a new dress, she immediately sold it, claiming that it had to be sent away for alterations. Once, when Monsieur Poulaillon was on a trip to Normandy, his wife instructed Monstreux to find someone who could sell some of the couple's opulent furniture, but there were no takers.

Monstreux further explained that Poulaillon even broke into the locked room in which her husband kept his money. Poulaillon never let the key out of his sight, so she waited until he was asleep to steal it. She tiptoed down the hallway, slid the key into the lock, and raided her husband's fortune.

The next morning Poulaillon's husband noticed that the key was missing. He confronted his wife, demanding to know if she had entered the room without his permission. She insisted with disdain that she had not. As Monsieur Poulaillon searched the house for the key, his wife sneaked the key out of her pocket only to discover with a start that a portion of it had broken off. Later that evening she tiptoed again to the locked room with a pair of small scissors in her hands, and looking nervously over her shoulder, used them to remove the bits that remained in the lock. She pressed the two parts of the key into a block of soft wax and instructed Monstreux to take the imprint to a locksmith to have a duplicate made. Poulaillon later left the new key for her husband to find.

Relieved to be once again in possession of his precious key, Monsieur Poulaillon entered the room. He noticed immediately that substantial amounts of money and silverware were missing. Convinced that the servants were stealing from him, he added a second lock as well as a thick padlock.

Monstreux recalled seeing a "strong and ugly fat woman" come to the house every day. From the description, La Reynie knew it was the fortune-teller Bosse. After one of Bosse's visits, Poulaillon handed her servant a small glass bottle, no bigger than a finger. Inside there was an even smaller amount of red liquid. "Put it in my husband's wine," Poulaillon instructed her. "It will put him to sleep." Monstreux agreed to do as she was told. However, come suppertime, she took the small bottle from the folds of her dress, uncorked it, and then discreetly dumped its contents out the dining-room window and into the street below.

Visibly frustrated that the elixir did not have the intended effect, Poulaillon handed her servant another small glass bottle a few days later. This time the vial contained a clear liquid that looked like water. "Put this in my husband's wine," she instructed Monstreux once again. When Poulaillon asked later that evening whether she had completed her work, Monstreux said that she had not had the chance. Not long after, the servant retreated to her tiny quarters on the top floor of the Poulaillon's home. Before undressing for bed, she placed the vial on the mantel of the room's small fireplace.

Monstreux became sick a few days later. Her doctor prescribed a bloodletting. Arriving in her room to perform the blood letting, the barber-surgeon noticed the bottle and asked her what it was. When Monstreux explained that it belonged to her mistress, he opened the bottle inquisitively, took a sniff, and poured a few drops of its contents into the palm of his hands. "You'd better be very careful," he said somberly. "You could find yourself in trouble."

Not long after, the servant received new orders from her mistress. Madame de Poulaillon explained that, just before the dinner hour, she would distract her husband. Monstreux was to keep the doors to the dining room shut, so no one could watch her set the table. On Poulaillon's signal the servant would pour the contents of the bottle into the husband's wineglass. At the designated time Poulaillon summoned Monstreux and whispered, "Go, quickly, put it in his wine." The servant reached into the folds of her dress and removed the bottle—and again poured the contents out the window. After dinner Monstreux entered Poulaillon's bedchambers and surrendered the empty bottle, as deceptive proof that she had followed the woman's orders. Yet again, much to his wife's frustration, Monsieur de Poulaillon still failed to fall ill.

Madame de Poulaillon asked the servant for her husband's nightgown and the sheets on which he slept. Monstreux said that she had no idea what Poulaillon was doing with the items, but twice a week, on schedule, she provided her mistress with the items. Nor did the servant have any idea why Madame de Poulaillon had ordered her to catch toads in a nearby vegetable garden. All Monstreux knew was that she was to bring back as many as she could, and that she should take great care to ensure that they remained alive.

La Reynie confirmed that Bosse used frogs in her potions and got them from one Anne Chéron. Hearing that the police lieutenant was questioning anyone suspected of collaborating with Bosse, Vigoureux, or Poulaillon, Chéron did all she could to evade arrest. She feigned a broken arm and went to an indigent hospital where few would think to look for her. The ruse did not work. She found herself in a small cell at Vincennes, where La Reynie made it clear that other, more painful fates awaited if she did not cooperate. Chéron confirmed that she had once delivered a toad to Bosse's home, where she watched Bosse and a colleague named Belot perform a special ceremony to permanently poison a wineglass Poulaillon had given them. They force-fed the toad arsenic, then placed the creature in the glass, and beat it until it urinated. Thus fouled, "fifty people could drink out of the glass, even though it had been washed and rinsed, and every one of them will die."

La Reynie heard enough evidence from Monstreux, Bosse, and other witnesses to prove that the noblewoman Poulaillon had circulated among the poisoners. Recalling his frustrations with La Grange, La Reynie refused to let Bosse, Vigoureux, and Poulaillon —as well as a growing number of other suspects—slip out of his hands and into the jurisdiction of the *parlement*. To this effect he wrote a letter to Louvois, requesting that the king allow him to pursue the matter fully on his own for now, without the involvement of magistrates.

While Poulaillon and her accomplices lingered in jail, La Reynie turned his attention to gathering some hard evidence against the noblewoman. Bosse's home had been kept under seal since her arrest in early January. La Reynie knew from preliminary reports that mysterious powders, liquids, and other strange objects filled the house.

On Saturday, March 11, 1679, at three in the afternoon, La Reynie accompanied two medical doctors and two apothecaries to Bosse's home. Jean Sagot, La Reynie's trusted notary, and Claude Robert, the chief royal attorney, documented the actions and discoveries of the forensics team. The experts began with a small pine box. The paper wrappers and twine, placed by police officers around the box, were still intact. After receiving permission from La Reynie, the apothecary Guy Simon broke the seals. Inside he found a small round glass container filled with a clear liquid. Reaching into his pocket, Simon pulled out a four *sol* bill and let a small amount of the liquid drip onto the currency. He also dripped a small bit onto the tiles near the fireplace where Bosse prepared her meals. Within seconds both the paper and the tiles turned black.

One of Simon's colleagues reached for an envelope made of green paper that was similarly wrapped in official police seals, and opened it. Two smaller envelopes sat inside. Fine white powder filled the first envelope, which was crafted from the death certificate of one Marguerite Hagunet. The apothecary collected a small amount of the powder and threw it into the fire. A thick smoke smelling like garlic filled the room.

An old ripped and folded letter had been used to create a second envelope. The medical inspectors could make out a few words on the recycled paper: "Sincerely yours, Marguerite Langlois." Inside there was a much smaller quantity of white powder. It released the same thick smoke and the same rancid garlic smell when thrown into the fire. This confirmed that both envelopes were filled with arsenic, which oxidizes when heated, leaving an unmistakable odor.

Continuing their work, the team of doctors and apothecaries opened envelope after envelope. Like Russian dolls stacked inside one another, each packet contained several smaller ones that contained some form of mysterious powder. In one set of six small envelopes, they discovered a grayish-brown powder mixed with a luminous blue-and-green substance. Each member of the team agreed that they were looking at the aphrodisiac cantharis. The third envelope contained small brown clumps that looked like dried blood, likely menstrual blood. Small bits of fingernails tumbled out of the fourth envelope. The last two contained more white powder that was smelly and smoky when thrown into the fire: more arsenic.

The next day La Reynie interrogated Bosse again at Vincennes.

"Is it true that Vigoureux referred several young women to you so you could give them drinks that would end their pregnancies?" he asked.

Bosse shrugged. "She never talked about it in those terms, but yes, I went to Vigoureux's house. But I only gave a smidgen of white wine to one woman, and I never saw her again."

"What you gave her was infused with sabine, wasn't it?" La Reynie probed. Sabine, a member of the crocus family, was commonly used as an abortifacient in early Europe. Bosse did not answer.

The lieutenant of police's tone became more aggressive. La Reynie placed on the table in front of him the items that he had studied alongside the apothecaries the day before. He ordered Bosse to identify each of them. Bosse took a quick glance at the shimmering blue-green powder in the first envelope. "Cantharis," she said. She did not use it as a love potion or a poison, explaining that it helped corns on her feet.

The rust-brown powder was indeed menstrual blood. She did not intend to sell it as an aphrodisiac, as many people did. Instead she collected it from her youngest daughter, using it also for the rough spots on her feet. Again La Reynie knew better. Menstrual blood had long been a common ingredient in poisons.

Bosse stared a little longer at the white powder in the envelope. Feigning confusion, she wondered aloud whether it was shrimp powder. As for contents of the last envelope, they were just fingernail clippings.

Bosse admitted later, and only reluctantly, that several of the envelopes did contain arsenic, but that it was not hers. Chéron tried to sell it to her when she brought the toads. Surely Bosse knew someone who wished to get rid of a person, Chéron said at the time. Bosse swore that she did not, but Chéron insisted she keep the envelopes.

"So how do you know Madame Langlois? The arsenic powder that was folded into the letter was not intended for her?" asked La Reynie.

"No," Bosse replied. Langlois had given her a small amount of money in the hope that she would come to Beauvais, a small town north of Paris where the woman lived, to help her with some personal matters. Bosse ignored the request.

La Reynie shifted subjects, turning his focus to the accusations that Madame Poulaillon's servant, Monstreux, had made against Bosse. "Is it not true, however, that it was you who prepared, by yourself, a clear liquid for Madame Poulaillon?"

"It is not true."

The questioning continued for several more minutes, with Bosse refusing to concede anything else. La Reynie ended the interrogation abruptly and waited while the scribe read the transcript aloud to the prisoner. With a shaking and unpracticed hand, Marie Bosse signed an M at the bottom of each page. When the reading was done, Bosse composed her barely legible full name at the end of the text. La Reynie scrawled his name quickly across the page and ordered the guards to take Bosse back to her cell.

PART
V

"She Gave
Her Soul Gently
to the Devil"

2 2

Quanto

thénaïs spent hours at the betting tables trying to forget her troubles with Louis. In the claustrophobic world of the court, where daily life hinged entirely on the king's desires, gambling provided noblemen and -women with an illusory sense that they could control, or at least anticipate and profit from, fate. Everything could be wagered upon: from cards, dice, and roulette to dog racing; and oddsmakers took bets on everything from who would be the king's next sexual conquest to the number of bodies that would be found floating in the Seine the next morning.

Seven separate royal ordinances between 1632 and 1666 attempted to regulate the voracious appetite of the French for games of chance. In his first months as lieutenant of police in 1667, La Reynie took aim at Parisians' love of gambling, requiring all gaming to take place in public parlors, where activities could be monitored. Dictating that gambling was a manifestion of "the depravation of good morals [and] causes the ruin of families," La Reynie levied hefty punishments on private gambling parties in homes. First-time offenders paid a hefty fine of fifteen hundred *livres*, of which one-third would go to the person who reported the transgression to the police. The other two-thirds went to royal coffers as well as the main Parisian hospital, which housed debtors as well as the sick and infirm. For the second offense the gambler's hand would be cut off.

The laws against gambling clearly did not apply to Louis XIV's court. In 1671 Louis learned that the marquis of Cessac used a set of marked cards to cheat at the royal gaming table. The king punished the marquis by dismissing him from his position as superintendent of the king's robes and exiled him to French Guiana. It was, according to some, an unusually lenient punishment, given that Cessac's cheating netted him close to two million *livres* in stolen winnings.

The Cessac scandal did little to reduce gambling in the king's palaces, however. Some of the court's most prominent members, including and especially Athénaïs, spent the bulk of their days gaming. The king's mistress preferred a card game called *hocca*, or *bassette*, which dominated late-seventeenth century betting tables. Originating in Italy, *hocca* integrated both strategy and chance. A "banker" distributed a single card to each player and laid it face up. Using a deck of fifty-two cards, each player worked to complete a full run of a single suit, making a wager or deciding to fold on each turn. In a fast-paced game where one could win or lose "fifty or sixty times in a quarter hour," the potential for remarkably high winnings as well as devastating losses was stunning.

Athénaïs often did not leave her seat for hours, playing until the sun came up. After one long day and night of gaming with the king's brother Philippe at her table, the banker wanted to retire. Athénaïs refused to let him leave. She needed to recoup her exorbitant losses. By the time she gave up, it was eight in the morning. Philippe was past due for his brother's morning rising rituals. When he arrived late and looking rumpled, Louis decided once and for all to ban *hocca* from the court.

Louis's resolve did not last for long. At Athénaïs's begging, Louis allowed her to set up a private gaming table in her quarters a few months later, making her promise she would show some restraint. If anything, however, Athénaïs's predilection for gaming only increased. She organized and participated in lotteries and even went so far as to organize one in a nearby Carmelite convent.

Athénaïs's behavior enraged pious members of court, especially Madame de Maintenon. "Never has the sovereign influence of *Quanto* been so well established. She believes herself to be above all things," Maintenon wrote to her priest.

Though Louis may have been less than approving of Montespan's gambling predilection, it did provide a convenient cover for his own extracurricular activities. The forty-six-year-old king still craved the thrill of sexual conquest. Mademoiselle des Oeillets had been an excellent surrogate for Athénaïs when passion still remained between the couple. Oeillets had quietly held out hope that the king would make her his official mistress. However, Louis had quickly tired of her once she became pregnant. Either by choice or at the king's encouragement, Oeillets left the court in 1677, disappointed and bitter.

In late 1678 Louis set eyes on the seventeen-year-old chestnut-haired Marie-Angélique de Scorailles. He met the teenage girl—twenty-three years his junior—at his brother's home, where she served as maid of honor to Philippe's second wife, the princess of Palatine. Marie-Angélique was originally from the Auvergne province, and the court mocked her rustic ways, considering her "as stupid as a basket." The princess of Palatine concurred: "[She is] a stupid little creature, but she [has] a very good heart."

On a crisp fall night Athénaïs settled in at the gaming table. The king called for his carriage to transport him to the Palais-Royal, which sat directly behind the Louvre. As instructed, Marie-Angélique waited in private quarters there. The king left shortly after his desires were satisfied, taking care not to be seen. Over the following months he continued his affair with Marie-Angélique, who dutifully awaited Louis in a remote wing of the palace.

In public the king pretended not to know her. Privately he moved Marie-Angélique to quarters closer to his and ordered a closet on the floor above his to be transformed into a small bedroom that both he and Marie-Angélique could access through a shared staircase.

It did not take long for Louis to tire of such machinations and begin openly flaunting his new dalliance. For her eighteenth birthday the king gave Marie-Angélique a house in the country and appointed her duchess of Fontanges. The play on the girl's first name, Marie-Angélique, which evoked the word *ange* (angel), in her new title did not go unnoted by the court. Nor did the pearlgray carriage drawn by eight horses, also a gift from the king.

The court watched, and commented on, Fontanges's every move. One evening she accompanied the king on a hunt. A strong wind blew her hat off, leaving Fontanges to tie up her curly locks with a ribbon. The new look pleased Louis so much that he forbade her to change her hairstyle. Much to the consternation of Athénaïs, the "Fontanges" hairstyle was christened, and soon noblewomen spent hours as their servants heated iron rods in the fireplace to replicate Fontanges's trademark curls.

Between Montespan, Oeillets, and now Fontanges, Madame de Maintenon continued to pray for the king's soul. On January 18, 1679, she wrote to her priest, the Abbé Gobelin: "I ask you to pray and to have others pray for the king, who is on the edge of a high precipice."

While Maintenon prayed, Athénaïs did all she could not only to regain her place in the king's heart but also to solidify her political status just in case he abandoned her altogether. Since her early days at court, she had found clever ways to place family members and supporters in positions of authority. She succeeded in having her father named governor of Paris, her sister as abbess of Fontevrault, her cousin d'Albret as governor of French Guiana, among others.

Athénaïs's insistence that her elder brother, Louis-Victor de Vivonne, be named as general of the galley prisons pitted Louis's mistress against his most powerful minister, Louvois. In concert with Louvois, the king had drafted a list of candidates for the galley post. After Louvois mentioned in passing that they had completed their task, Montespan demanded to see the list. When

Louvois refused, she dug through the minister's pockets to retrieve it. She flew into a rage when she did not see her brother, a celebrated military commander, on the list and went immediately to Louis to complain. To pacify her, the king blamed the error on Louvois.

"Call him immediately," Athénaïs ordered. When Louvois arrived, the king compelled him to take responsibility for the mistake, which he did. Vivonne was added to the list and, shortly after, officially named general.

Louvois did not suffer this humiliation well. Moreover, the fact that Athénaïs seemed forever "at knives" (*aux couteaux*) with him was all the more enraging given what he had done to help Montespan silence her extravagant husband. At the height of Monsieur de Montespan's theatrics at court, Louvois had threatened him with a military trial, causing him to flee to Spain. His "abandonment" of his wife later facilitated the formal separation of the couple's assets, allowing Athénaïs to continue her adulterous affair with the king.

The animosity between Montespan and Louvois intensified later, in 1678, when the minister announced he was seeking a husband for his eldest daughter, Madeleine-Charlotte. Athénaïs boldly proposed her nephew Louis de Rochechouart, Vivonne's son, to the minister. Louvois did not refuse the offer; he ignored it altogether. Enraged by the slight, Montespan turned immediately to Louvois's rival, Colbert, who readily agreed. Montespan's nephew and Marie-Anne Colbert married a few months later, in February 1679.

Montespan's renewed alliances with Colbert proved useful only months later following a series of ongoing public spats between Athénaïs and the king. In an attempt to regain her beauty, Athénaïs often spent entire afternoons stretched out nude on her bed as servants rubbed her with pomades and perfumes. One day as the king and queen stepped into their carriage at Saint-Germain, Louis made a face and turned toward Athénaïs. He complained that she smelled too strongly of perfume, saying it made him feel sick. The embattled mistress flew into an argument with the king, who matched her anger with profanity. Another explosive fight followed less than a week later. In return the king announced that he would no longer make private visits to Athénaïs's quarters, which had once been filled with passion and were now little more than brief and dispassionate greetings.

Once again coming to Montespan's rescue, Colbert helped the king calm down and dissuaded him from his decision. Louis agreed, but insisted that other court members be present so he would not have to spend time alone with her. To add to the insult, he stripped Athénaïs of her title as head of Marie-Thérèse's entourage and the privilege of the *tabouret*, which had allowed her to be among those to remain seated in the presence of the queen—and offered both to Fontanges, who was now pregnant with their first child. "And so, the king's violent passion for Madame de Montespan is no longer," wrote one contemporary observer. "She cries bitterly after conversations with the king. I've heard she would have fallen even farther without Monsieur Colbert."

Quietly gloating about Montespan's fall from grace while nonetheless bristling at the marriage of Colbert's daughter before his own, Louvois continued his ongoing efforts to broker a strategic pairing for his daughter. His rival, the duke of Luxembourg, also approached him, hoping that a marriage between their two children would bolster the duke's military aspirations. Louvois flatly refused.

Instead Louvois fixed his sights on one of the country's most renowned noble families, the house of Soissons. The late count of Soissons hailed from a cadet branch of the royal Bourbon family. His widow, the former Olympe Mancini, also shared close ties to the monarchy through her uncle, the late prime minister Jules Mazarin, and now served as the queen's highest-ranking lady-in-waiting. Louvois's hopes ended, however, when his wife overheard rumors of the countess's public reaction to the idea: "What an odd thing it would be to see a bourgeoise girl marry a prince!" The minister of war was outraged at the slight.

The countess of Soisson's dismissal of Louvois touched a sore point for the minister. Despite his privileged place in the king's entourage, Louvois's family did not have noble origins. Louvois hailed from the bourgeois Le Tellier family of Parisian merchants, which over the course of a century slowly entered public service. Louvois had done well financially and politically, but he did not suffer gladly any reminder of his family's humble origins.

Undeterred, Louvois shifted his paternal matchmaking efforts to the Rochefoucauld family. While the family is now best known for the *Maxims* of François de La Rochefoucauld, in the late seventeenth century the Rochefoucauld name signaled above all power and proximity to kings. Louis's father, the late Louis XIII, solidified his close relationship to François's own father by addressing his letters to "our dear and beloved *cousin*." Like Soissons, François balked. Louvois reached out to La Rochefoucauld's close friend, Madame de La Fayette, to argue his case. When that proved not enough, the king interceded.

While still nursing his pride following the difficult marriage negotiations, Louvois was thrown from his horse and broke his leg. After over two months immobilized in bed, he wrote to his brother: "I [am] focused right now on learning how to walk…because I am working very hard, I am hoping that I will [soon] be very knowledgeable in it." Although his leg would eventually heal, the minister proved less able to recover from the injuries imposed by the transgressions of Soissons, Montespan, and Vivonne. He would soon focus all his energies on finding ways to punish them. As his contemporary the abbé of Choisy once remarked, Louvois was "a dangerous enemy [who] looked for chances to strike anyone who offended him, always striking them in secret."

23

Search and Seizure

On the morning of March 12, 1679, François Desgrez arrived at the Châtelet headquarters. He held a warrant for Voisin's arrest and an order to seize her property. Desgrez handed the search warrant to Camuset, the Châtelet commissioner on duty. Shortly after, La Reynie's trusted sergeant left on horseback with three other officers for the Church of Notre-Dame-de-Bonne-Nouvelle, where Voisin attended mass. The officers waited outside until she emerged and arrested her on the spot.

While guards escorted Voisin to the Vincennes prison, Camuset and his men made their way to the sorceress's home. Voisin's husband, Antoine, and their now twenty-one-year-old daughter, Marie-Marguerite, met them at the door.

It did not take Camuset long to search the home, which was mostly empty save for a few pieces of furniture. It seemed that Voisin knew ahead of time that she would be arrested. The commissioner rummaged through an old and battered armoire in the first room, finding only linens and needlepoint inside. In the drawer of a table, he uncovered a few papers stuffed in a nightcap.

He collected the papers, wrapped them in twine, and pressed a heavy wax seal onto the package.

As Camuset approached a large wooden box, an expressionless Marie-Marguerite walked toward him and held out a key. He took the key and inserted it in the lock, opening the box just wide enough to see that it also contained papers. He placed those, too, under seal.

In the second room, distillation equipment surrounded the space around the fireplace. Traces of a powderlike substance dusted the space on the floor where a large alembic rested. An unlocked wooden box sat next to it. Opening the box with caution, Camuset noted that it contained only baby clothes and a few blankets.

If Camuset wandered into Voisin's courtyard, he did not mention it. Had the commissioner entered the garden and the remnants of Voisin's activities remained, he would have been unable to forget what he saw: the shack, the stove, the cauldron, tiny charred bones. But signs of the worst of Voisin's crimes there had, no doubt, been already cleared away.

After sealing the items and documents, Camuset delivered them to La Reynie. La Reynie examined the cache. Most of the documents looked to be little more than simple beauty recipes or were filled with astrological drawings and signs. A few more troubling ones consisted of letters to Voisin from women begging for her help in gaining "full power over the heart and mind" of their husbands or lovers. Promissory notes accompanied their pleas, indicating the payment Voisin would receive for her initial services and additional bonuses to be earned if her potions, elixirs, and spells produced the desired effect.

Five days after Voisin's arrest, La Reynie ordered the guards to bring the woman down from her cell for questioning. She looked at the police chief coldly. In a profession where intimidation and coercion were tools of the trade, if she felt anxious at all, she certainly had no intention of showing it to the police chief.

La Reynie began by asking about Voisin's husband. With characteristic pride, Voisin explained that Antoine was a failure who had been unable to support their family. In happier days he had made a modest living selling hats, fabric, and sewing supplies in one of the small stores along the Pont Marie. In 1658, around the time of their daughter Marie-Marguerite's birth, a flood swept the bridge and its stores into the Seine. The Voisins lost everything. The family had no option but to rely on Catherine's "chiromancy" skills.

"This is why," she boasted, "I insisted on cultivating the knowledge that God gave me. I learned about chiromancy and physiognomy when I was nine." The law did not forbid palm reading, she reminded La Reynie, and she made no apology for earning a living from her talents.

Quickly shifting topics, La Reynie asked Voisin if she knew Bosse. She did. Bosse had gone through a rough patch several years earlier, she explained. Being a charitable woman, Voisin invited Bosse to live at her home for a little while. "But I have no idea what she has been up to since." Insisting she had nothing more to say about Bosse, Voisin told La Reynie, "I certainly would not wish to do any harm to anyone, no matter what harm others are doing to me."

La Reynie asked next about Vigoureux. Voisin claimed she had heard about the woman but had never met her personally. La Reynie remained skeptical. He knew from Bosse and Vigoureux that the three women traveled in the same circles. Picking his battles, he changed the subject. The lieutenant of police trusted his abilities to sense—through a suspect's movement, breathing, or a subtle shift in tone of voice—where the most productive lines of questioning lay.

He asked Voisin about rumors that she had been paid to make novenas in church on behalf of several women. In Catholic tradition, novenas were, and still are, prayers repeated for nine consecutive days either as part of mourning rituals, a personal petition to God, or as penance for sins. La Reynie suspected that Voisin performed novenas for less devout purposes.

"You've never performed any novenas for women with husband problems, or for husbands who had problems with their wives?" he inquired. Voisin claimed she had not, saying that she always told them to do it themselves at Montmartre.

In the late seventeenth century the rural village of Montmartre sat high above Paris and outside the city walls. A small chapel capped the top of the hill, which was a pilgrimage site dedicated to Saint Ursula, who had refused marriage to a pagan prince and was later killed by the Huns. In Voisin's time unhappily married women swarmed Montmartre carrying their husband's *chemises* so they could be blessed by the chapel's priest under a painting of Ursula—no doubt in hopes that the saint would see fit to change their fates.

The more La Reynie pressed Voisin with questions about her own actions, the more she talked about Bosse. Passing blame to her rival, she revealed that Bosse performed the novenas that Voisin refused to do. Bosse did them for Madame Philbert, the widow of Jean Brunet, whose death freed her to marry a court musician. Then there was Madame Ferry, whose husband languished for weeks before dying. Bosse, Voisin hinted, had infused his shirt with poison.

La Reynie added Ferry and Philbert to his arrest rolls. However, he was most troubled by the rumors of two noblewomen whose names he could not compel Voisin to reveal. From what he could tell, one of the women had offered Bosse a large sum of money to perform incantations over a small fire. Another had asked Voisin to poison a bouquet of flowers, which she adamantly swore she refused to do—but insinuated that Bosse had been less principled and been paid a handsome price for her services. While the police chief felt far from knowing the full story, one fear grew: Madame de Poulaillon was not the only court member tangled up in this network of poisoners, sorceresses, and thieves.

He continued to forge ahead, homing in on the little evidence he had of Voisin's own potential crimes: "What were you doing with the distillation equipment we found at your house?"

Shrugging off the question, Voisin responded that it was just an ordinary alembic; she used it to make face-whitening waters. "And you never used arsenic for any reason," La Reynie said curtly, phrasing it less as a question and more as an accusation. Never, she answered.

"And you never sent any women who thought they might be pregnant to the midwife Lepère." Never, she replied again, shaking her head.

Sensing there was little more to learn for now, La Reynie ended the interrogation. In the days that followed, he ordered his guards to bring Bosse and Voisin down to the interrogation room together. He wanted to pit the two rivals against each other to see if that would help loosen their tongues.

The hostility between the two women was palpable as they stood before the lieutenant of police and listened to a reading of the transcript from Voisin's interrogation a day earlier. La Reynie let Bosse speak first. Bosse snortled that if she earned as much money as Voisin did, "I would be a very wealthy woman." Without wasting time, the stout woman turned her focus on each of Voisin's accusations against her, knocking them down one by one. Voisin, not she, sold poison to Madame Philbert. Bosse said she witnessed Voisin give diamond powder to the woman inside Notre-Dame Cathedral. Reputed to be one of the deadliest and most expensive forms of poison available, the sharp shards of diamond crystal entered the digestive system, where they supposedly made tiny deadly, yet imperceptible, perforations in the intestines.

Madame Philbert, the daughter of a jeweler, knew better. She could tell it was not real diamond powder. According to Bosse, Voisin protested that whatever it was, she could count on it working. Bosse said Voisin had first tested a small amount of the powder on her husband, Antoine, making him violently ill. Voisin denied all accusations.

Bosse also claimed that Madame Leféron, the widow of a wealthy judge at the *parlement*, had visited Voisin years earlier for help in killing her husband. Defending herself, Voisin did not deny that she knew Madame Leféron but had played no part in the husband's death. Instead Leféron confessed to Voisin that she intended to kill her husband. The noblewoman had already purchased diamond powder for her husband and bought tainted perfumes and gloves from someone in Italy. On hearing Leféron's plans, Voisin said she prepared two vials of opium water to calm the woman's nerves and tried to persuade her not to make good on her macabre plot. Obviously Leféron did not listen, she said.

"Surely," Bosse interrupted, "Voisin can't forget another woman of quality who brought flowers to the house to be poisoned." Bosse recalled that a noblewoman named Madame de Dreux offered Voisin six thousand *livres* to rid her of her husband. Once the deed was accomplished, Madame Dreux met Voisin at Notre-Dame to pay her.

Over the two weeks that followed, La Reynie set in motion orders for the arrest of more than thirty new suspects, whose names had surfaced during the interrogations. Among them were the abortionist Madame Lepère and the widow Philbert. He had little hard evidence against either. But their involvement in poison was the only thing on which Voisin, Bosse, and Vigoureux seemed to agree. For now it was evidence enough.

To offset the herculean amount of work associated with the increased number of arrests, Louvois agreed to compensate Desgrez for coordinating so many arrest warrants over such a short period. The warden at Vincennes, Monsieur de La Ferronnaye, also received additional resources and guards to ensure the security of the prison as it filled. Meanwhile La Reynie's resolve intensified: He would not stop until he had uncovered every truth.

24

A Noble Pair

As detailed as La Reynie tended to be in his communications to Louvois and the king, he proved nonetheless cautious when it came to the noblewoman Dreux. Instead he offered a very brief summary of the accusations that Bosse and Voisin made against Leféron and an unnamed "woman of quality." Like Leféron, Dreux's husband was a judge at the *parlement*. However, unlike Leféron, Dreux's family and personal connections linked her to some of the most prominent and powerful men in the royal court, including the king.

Frustrated by La Reynie's unusual circumspection, Louvois wrote back that the king demanded to know the woman's name. The next day La Reynie divulged his suspicions that Madame de Dreux had poisoned her husband. Louis expressed "shock" in learning that a woman of such high standing was allegedly part of the cabal of poisoners. On the king's orders the minister of war instructed La Reynie to continue his investigations but to be sure of all accusations before bringing Dreux and Leféron in for questioning.

The latest set of arrests, along with rumors of suspects among the nobility, triggered a wave of panic among Parisians across all social ranks. "The smallest of accidents are being attributed to poison," wrote an Englishman visiting Paris at the time, "so many people remain in a stupor over the fear [the arrests] are causing." A seventeenth-century equivalent of a tabloid newspaper reported that "fathers are suspecting their sons [of poison] and are observing closely all of their movements; and mothers are cautious around their daughters. Children are taking precautions against their parents; brothers and sisters don't dare to eat or drink anything one of their siblings gives them."

Where La Reynie was once able to move without notice, his departures from his home headquarters now drew mobs seeking a glimpse of him and guessing whom he would arrest next. Hearing of the chaotic crowds, Louvois increased the number of guards accompanying the police chief.

Between March 20 and April 7, La Reynie conducted scores of interrogations. He centered his efforts on Voisin, whom he questioned seven times, and her coconspirator, the eccentric Adam Coeuret, otherwise known as Lesage. When La Reynie's chief officer took Lesage into custody, Desgrez discovered a small quantity of gray powder folded inside a paper bill while frisking the suspect. By all indications it was diamond powder.

Twelve years earlier Lesage had been sentenced to the galleys for life for tricking customers into believing that he could communicate with the devil. He was freed just five years later, after a "lady of quality" successfully petitioned the king for his release. Lesage would never learn the identity of his benefactor, nor does history leave any indication of whom it might have been. She was likely one of his grateful female clients, of whom there were many.

Rumors swirled that he and Voisin had once been lovers—rumors that, during interrogations, neither denied. Although Voisin was married and lived with her husband, Lesage had moved into Voisin's house and remained there until just before her arrest. But whatever affection there might have been between the two of them was gone now.

"Voisin is a nasty woman. May God punish her," Lesage told

La Reynie. "Bosse is even worse," he continued. "That one is a *very* nasty woman."

La Reynie asked Lesage about Voisin's dealings with Madame Philbert, the window of the court musician Brunet. Lesage explained without hesitation that Voisin and Bosse started working with Philbert about three or four years earlier, in 1675 or 1676, selling whitening powders and other beauty elixirs to noblewomen at Saint-Germain.

"Did you ever hear either Voisin or Bosse say anything about the death of Brunet?" La Reynie inquired, trying to understand the pair's links to Madame Philbert.

"I'll have to think about that," replied Lesage with flair, "I will ponder it. The question takes me a little by surprise. Yes, I'll have to think about it."

It looked as if Lesage's cooperation was going to be short-lived. La Reynie leaned in toward Lesage and told him to work harder to remember.

"Don't ask me any more about it right now. Ask me about something else," he said, waving La Reynie away.

Undeterred, La Reynie asked Lesage about La Grange. Lesage replied curtly that, of course, he had heard about the "cabal" from Voisin. "But I know little else about it." La Reynie asked about Leféron. Lesage replied, "I know very little." La Reynie asked if he had ever heard Voisin talk about how Leféron's husband died. "I have not."

Clearly the interrogation was going nowhere. La Reynie announced that he planned to leave Lesage in his cell for several days to see if the discomforts of Vincennes might prompt a change of heart. The police chief's notary then read the transcript of the interrogation aloud. Lesage initialed each page with bravado.

Five days later La Reynie tried again. A disheveled and gaunt man had replaced the confident and cocky one. Cold nights spent on a stone floor with only bowls of thin broth and stale bread to eat had had the desired effect. Lesage proved more forthcoming this time. He admitted providing amateur alchemists with supplies to turn base metals—metal sulfate, ammonia, lye, talc, and rock salt—into pure silver. He said he knew how to transform them into gold as well, but wanted to keep the secret to himself. In truth his "secret process" was little more than what we know today as metal plating.

The police chief next laid two pieces of paper on the table. Each was filled with numbers and symbols carefully written inside geometrical shapes. "Those are astrological charts. They chart the movement of the sun and the planets," Lesage explained. He used those, for a price, to counsel clients about ideal times to enter into business dealings or to court a love interest.

Multiple interrogations of Lesage, Voisin, and Bosse eventually brought forward more names of nobles who had "commerce" with the poisoners, astrologists, and magicians of the Montorgeuil neighborhood. Additional arrests followed, leaving the warden Ferronnaye once again scrambling to find places for the new prisoners in the Vincennes tower. While the questioning netted few new revelations about Dreux and Leféron, the stories Lesage, Voisin, and Bosse shared about the noblewomen's activities also overlapped enough for La Reynie to make a convincing case to the king that the two noblewomen should be arrested. Madame Leféron was taken to the Vincennes prison on April 9, 1679, with Madame Dreux following her there two days later.

Involved as always in every aspect of the investigations, Louvois wrote privately to the Ferronnaye to ensure that Madame Dreux be kept safe and comfortable in the tower. It was not appropriate for ladies "of quality" to be treated like the rest of the prisoners, who slept on dirty mattresses or piles of hay and were given little to eat and drink. Like Madame Poulaillon and Madame Leféron, Dreux received a modest but clean bed, a small desk, a few candles, and warm meals. Louvois also instructed the warden to take particular care to protect the noblewomen from the other prisoners, who might try to hurt them out of jealousy or in an attempt to keep them from revealing their secrets.

In the week after their arrests, La Reynie questioned Leféron and Dreux. Unusually deferential, he listened instead of probing, asking just one or two questions. The elegant and poised sixty-nine-year-old Leféron admitted to La Reynie that she went often to Voisin for palm readings. She was unhappy in her marriage, so much so that she and Monsieur Leféron had slept in separate beds for more than fifteen years. Nonetheless Leféron insisted that her husband did not die of poison, claiming instead that his death had been "up to nature." Older and weaker than she, he had fallen victim to smallpox. With this La Reynie politely dispatched the woman back to her cell.

La Reynie's interactions with Madame Dreux were similarly nonconfrontational and short. The police chief asked if she knew Voisin. Dreux answered without apology that Voisin read her fortune for years, saying sheepishly that she knew it was all a ruse to get otherwise smart people to part with their money. Still, she had gone to her all the same.

Now with three noblewomen in prison for consorting with accused poisoners from Paris's den of crime, the public's interest became insatiable. To minimize the impact of the scandal on his court, the king established a special tribunal to try the ever-increasing numbers of prisoners at Vincennes accused of dispensing poisons. Louis justified his decision to move the trials out of the public eye by claiming that the *Parlement* had so many duties already, it would be overwhelmed and not able to expedite these extra trials. This met with consternation in the *parlement*, but the king did not yield. Justice would be done quickly and on his own terms.

The hearings took place at the sprawling Arsenal fortress, which stood between the Bastille prison and the Seine on the Right Bank of the city. Fortified in the sixteenth century, the Arsenal served as the primary arms depot for France. Inside its thick stone walls, soldiers melted iron to create cannons and manufactured gunpowder. In the heart of the Arsenal were also several large rooms where military leaders held court-martial hearings for intransigent soldiers. The Arsenal tribunal was called, in more familiar terms, the Chambre Ardente (Burning Chamber). It harkened back to similar ad hoc courts of much earlier eras, where black curtains lined the walls, blocking all light, while judges tried criminals by torch- and candlelight. Now those rooms would be used to try charlatans, poisoners, and witches.

Although he had ministerial oversight of the French judiciary, Colbert also had no choice but to accede to the king's wishes to establish the special court in Louvois's territority. He had lost again to the minister of war.

Louvois left no doubts about his influence on the court. Louis Boucherat, a close friend of Louvois's father, chaired it. The king's chief attorney, Robert, also shared family connections to Louvois. Then there was La Reynie, who had amply demonstrated his allegiance to Louvois. In addition to serving as judge, La Reynie served as *rapporteur*. In this role he presented the evidence gathered against each of the defendants and made a case for their conviction—which meant he served at once as detective, prosecutor, and judge. Joining him as assistant *rapporteur* was Louis Bazin de Bezons, who similarly had close ties to Louvois and who had been interrogating prisoners alongside La Reynie.

Several times a week the police chief traveled by carriage to the Arsenal complex. There he and Bezons guided the twelve other judges through the stacks of evidence that they had collected. The judges made note of their questions during the review, requesting additional arrests and encouraging La Reynie and Bezons to conduct further interrogations to fill in missing information. By early May, with well over fifty people in prison to be judged by them, the court completed its review of evidence and settled in for the trials.

25

The Burning Chamber

arie Bosse was among the first to meet her fate in the secret court. Once large and prideful, she now looked weak and fearful. She sat on a small *sellette,* a wooden stool traditionally used to question the accused in early French court proceedings. For two days, the judges loomed over her from a high, long table and took turns peppering her with questions. The court also put Vigoureux and a woman named Madame Ferry, another resident of the impoverished Montorgeuil neighborhood and one of Vigoureux's clients, on the stand.

When the judges finished questioning the three women, they confirmed one by one, with "due diligence and conviction," their agreement that Bosse, Vigoureux, and Ferry were guilty of murder. Ferry was sentenced to death on the gallows, after first having one of her hands cut off. Bosse and Vigoureux were to be burned alive and their "ashes thrown to the wind"—but not before they each received the Question.

On May 9, three days later after the conviction, Vigoureux was dealt the first of what was intended to be two rounds of torture at the nearby Bastille prison. Few details remain about what method was used or what was said. The fragmented report acknowledges only Vigoureux's death at the hands of her torturers: "Dead at four o'clock in the morning, from a head wound."

Moments after guards dragged Vigoureux's lifeless body out of the torture chamber, they brought Bosse in to face the same tormentors. Several large buckets of water sat at the foot of a long, sturdy table. A guard filled the pitcher he would use to pour the water down the woman's throat. However, after taking a look at the corpulent Bosse, the torturer recommended *brodequins* instead. Vigoureux's unexpected death had clearly given rise to caution. It also likely inspired Bosse to confess to every charge against her, including poisoning the husbands of Poulaillon, Philbert, Dreux, and Leféron.

On May 10 Desgrez transported Bosse and her former client Madame Ferry from the Bastille prison to Notre-Dame. Accompanying them was Bosse's daughter, who was forced by decree to witness her mother's death. The two women recited prayers for forgiveness and made an *amende honorable,* which included paying a fine to the church before execution. The executioner then escorted Ferry a short distance away from the main door of the cathedral. With an efficient blow of the sword, he lopped off one of the woman's hands. Desgrez helped load the bleeding Ferry back into the cart and toward the place de Grève, where she was hanged. The executioner and his assistants then set to work preparing a towering pile of hay and firewood. When they were done, they placed a chair in the middle and tied Bosse to it. With one touch of a torch, the hay burst into flames—taking Bosse screaming along with it.

Anxieties ran high in Vincennes as news of the deaths were whispered by inmates passing one another in twisting staircases or on their way to the latrines. These rumors, intensified by the stress of captivity, proved unbearable to the noblewoman Madame Leféron. She pounded her head repeatedly against her cell wall.

Showing concern for Leféron's well-being, La Reynie sent a request to Louvois for permission to send a doctor to Vincennes. Unlike at the Bastille, where nobles were generally held, there was no regular medical care at Vincennes. Louvois responded without delay by assigning one to the prison to take care of any sick prisoners.

Eager to get to the heart of what Lesage and Voisin knew about the activities of Leféron and the other noblewomen, La Reynie arranged for the two to meet in person for the first time since their arrests. Standing in front of the police chief, they eyed each other angrily. After being asked for the record whether they knew each other, Voisin snarled that she knew him too well, saying he was an unfaithful ingrate. Lesage spewed his own insults, protesting that Voisin was the one who had been unfaithful. Eager to settle scores, the two volleyed accusations. The confrontation confirmed La Reynie's suspicions that the two had once been romantically involved. But other than that, the joint interrogation yielded no new insights.

The atmosphere was much calmer on June 5, 1679 when the tribunal met to question Madame de Poulaillon. Although she had spent the last several months in prison, she held her coiffed head high as she was escorted into the chamber. Monsieur Robert, the lead prosecutor, announced their finding that she had attempted to kill her husband in order to marry Monsieur de La Rivière. Initially, the report asserted, she had tried to end his life with small doses of poison with the help of her servant, Monstreux, so that his death would appear to have been caused by illness. Unsuccessful in her efforts, she then hired two "assassins"—Bosse and Vigoureux—to do the job for her.

La Reynie spoke next, explaining to Poulaillon that Bosse had been condemned to death, and Vigoureux was already dead. Instead of showing fear, Madame de Poulaillon sat quietly, with "great self-containment," as she waited for her own judgment to come. In fact, her demeanor so impressed the notary that he wrote at the bottom of the court transcript: "During the entire interrogation, this woman had an extraordinary and admirable presence of mind." Still, the lead judge, Robert, ruled that Poulaillon would be put to the Question and then beheaded.

As gruesome and violent as beheading may seem, the decision to behead Madame de Poulaillon was an act of deference. Beheading was thought more fitting to noble ranks than hanging or being burned alive. Nonetheless, one of the committee members, Monsieur de Fieubet, disagreed vehemently with the sentence. During the committee's deliberations, he had made a vocal show of support for clemency for Poulaillon. It was inconceivable, he argued, that a woman as well mannered and well bred could be guilty of attempted murder. La Reynie argued forcefully against leniency, but the majority of the judges changed their minds. Instead Poulaillon would spend the rest of her life in a jail outside of Angers, in western France.

Despite La Reynie's dissatisfaction with the outcome of the proceedings, the police chief could not disagree that she had carried herself in a manner befitting of her status. Recalling the event years later, he wrote: "Madame Poulaillon is from a very good and honorable family...and was even more well put together when she was judged and sentenced. She was very polite."

Though Poulaillon had been spared, most were not. In a matter of a few months, dozens of men and women faced trial for having collaborated with Bosse, Vigoureux, Voisin, Lesage, and others. They questioned Madame Chéron, the fruit vendor who provided Voisin with toads and who feigned a broken arm to avoid prison. Bosse had claimed that a small package of powder confiscated in a raid on her home belonged to Chéron and had been bought at the Château of Saint-Germain. Chéron conceded that she traveled frequently to Saint-Germain, where she rented a small fruit and vegetable stand, but she rejected all accusations of buying and selling poison at the king's palace, insisting that the powder was little more than finely crushed horse dander that she used in plasters to soothe her injured arm. "I never committed any crimes...and that is all I can tell you for my defense," Chéron asserted. Convinced otherwise, the judges sentenced her to the Question by *brodequins* and then to be burned alive.

Chéron was transferred immediately into the hands of the torturer, who was accompanied by Monsieur Vezou, a physician, and Monsieur Terode, a surgeon. Vezou wore the long black velvet gown of a university-trained doctor and strode in quietly before taking his place among the magistrates in the room. Wearing a bloodstained apron, Monsieur Terode carried a wooden box filled with bandages and sutures. The doctor was there to provide counsel to the torturers about how far they could go without killing Chéron, while the surgeon stood at the ready with bandages and sutures to make sure the woman lasted long enough afterward to face execution.

Before the *brodequins* the interrogators asked Chéron once again whether she sold poisons at the Château of Saint-Germain. "I swear to the heavens," she pleaded. "I don't know anything about poison at Saint-Germain. I will tell you whatever you want, but I will not lie."

The torturer shoved Chéron onto the nearby bench and placed her legs into the boots. Lifting her eyes toward the ceiling, she cried: "My Jesus! Have pity on me." Three bone-breaking blows later, she screamed: "Ah! My God! I am dying." Her face ashen, Chéron slipped toward unconsciousness.

Doctor Vezou ordered the guards to untie her and lay her on a nearby mattress, worrying aloud about the possibility of a "deadly accident" should the torture continue. He brought a bottle of wine to Chéron's mouth. After a few sips, she turned her head slowly toward her tormentors: "Ah, messieurs. I die innocent. If by the grace of God, I remember anything else, I will tell you at my execution." She revealed nothing more before being burned alive on the place de Grève.

The judges sentenced the elderly midwife Lepère to death as well, despite her claims that every abortion she performed was at the orders of Voisin. She also swore that she never knew the names of her clients and that Voisin handled all transactions. Although Lepère received the Question following the trial, Vezou decided that no torture should be applied given her advanced age. Leniency proved short-lived, however. Lepère was hanged the following day.

The court also tried François Belot, who helped Bosse poison the chalice with toad venom that she later gave to Poulaillon. Without lengthy debate or deliberation, the court sentenced him to death by hanging followed by a public burning of his corpse at the place de Grève.

Before his execution, guards transferred Belot to the nearby Bastille prison. At precisely seven the next morning, they escorted him into a small room in one of the prison towers. In the presence of La Reynie, Bezons, and the notary Sagot, Belot was placed in *brodequins* and questioned under torture for the next four hours. With each painful hammer to his legs, he denied all wrongdoing. After much torment, he was released from the heavy ropes restraining him and carried to a nearby mattress. As Belot lay bloody and writhing in pain in the hours before his death, he repeated the words: "Saint-Germain. Saint-Germain."

Where La Reynie's Arsenal tribunal once served as a circuslike distraction for the populace, it now struck concern in the hearts of Parisians of all social ranks. "Everyone is scared," wrote Madame de Sévigné. "Thank God, I never bought any makeup or had my fortune read." Others like the court doctor Pierre Bourdelot noted drily that "if they are going to punish [everyone involved in magic and poison], all of the valets and servants of Paris are at risk."

Stories circulated about horrific activities that were taking place under the cloak of secrecy in the Arsenal's military compound. For some prisoners the mere possibility of facing the committee seemed a fate worse than any death penalty that might be served. Not long after Poulaillon's sentencing, a guard entered the cell of one Madame Dodée to deliver breakfast, which consisted of little more than a few scraps of bread and a small tumbler of water. The thirty-five-year-old woman, who had been in prison for several months, had been accused of poisoning her husband as well as running a business selling charms. Her initial questioning in the Chambre Ardente had been "light"; La Reynie and his colleagues were not convinced that she meddled in poisons, concluding the accusations to be neighborhood hearsay. The committee chose not to hold her for questioning by the larger tribunal, but had not yet released her.

The next morning Dodée did not stir from her straw bed on the floor when the guard turned the key in the lock. Suspecting something amiss, the guard kicked Dodée with his foot. She did not move. He then flipped the motionless woman onto her back. Thick rust-brown blood covered the woman's ashen face. She had slit her neck with a small knife hidden in the folds of her dress. Present at Vincennes when the guards discovered Dodée's body, La Reynie ordered it buried immediately.

26

"Beginning to Talk"

"Voisin is beginning to talk," Louvois wrote to Louis on September 16, the day of Dodée's death. Voisin met with La Reynie at least three times as the news of Dodée's suicide and other executions spread through the prison. "I don't want to hide anything any longer," Voisin said after requesting an audience with La Reynie. "I want to declare everything I know in order to unburden my conscience, leaving it in the care of God, and hoping that the King will have pity on me and my family."

For the first time Voisin admitted having dealings with Madame Leféron and Madame Dreux. Voisin explained that Leféron came to her for a palm reading and asked hopefully whether it looked as if her husband might die. Leféron explained how unhappy she was in her marriage and that she desperately needed a way out. Voisin then consulted with her associate, Madame Leroux, who gave her a small vial of what she said was arsenic. Voisin said that she transferred the vial to Madame Leféron, insisting that she was only a courier for Leroux's poison business. Madame Leféron returned one last time to Voisin's home to thank her. Dressed in black, the woman said, smiling, "It's done, thank God."

Voisin told a similar story about Madame Dreux. It was true, Voisin claimed, that Madame Dreux wished to see her husband dead so she might marry her lover. Dreux even gave her a diamond-encrusted cross to encourage Voisin to take the job. She kept the gift, swearing that she did nothing in return. All Voisin could speculate was that either Bosse or Leroux had been responsible. In fact she heard that Madame Dreux offered Leroux two thousand *écus* and, soon afterward, she learned of the husband's death.

Voisin implicated herself as an accomplice in Leféron's death and an acquaintance of Dreux, but she stopped short of admitting she had played a direct role in either of the poisonings. Still, Voisin knew that the longer La Reynie believed she had yet more secrets to share, the longer it would be before she found herself in front of the Arsenal judges and a certain death sentence.

To put Voisin's assertions to the test, La Reynie arranged for Madame Dreux and Madame Leféron to be brought for questioning in the presence of Voisin. The difference between the treatment that the noblewomen received at the prison compared with that of Voisin was evident. Whereas Voisin looked dirty and bedraggled, both Leféron and Dreux were still well dressed and rested.

La Reynie allowed Voisin to have the first word. Stepping forward, she explained calmly that Madame Dreux had come to her home to discuss the woman's desire to do away with her husband. They also met at the church on the city's Île Saint-Louis.

"You know you remember," said Voisin, turning to Dreux with a stare. Dreux denied everything. Before she had a chance to say anything else, Leféron launched into her own accusations against Voisin.

"Voisin is insulting me in my time of grief," the noblewoman said pleadingly to La Reynie. "My husband died from a bone-wasting disease."

"I have no desire to insult you," Voisin chided Dreux. "Even if you yourself are the main cause of your grief." Turning toward the police chief, she added, "She knows I'm not saying anything that is not true."

The stress of the encounter proved more than Leferon could bear. "This woman has duped so many people," she retorted, bursting into tears.

Scoffing at her, Voisin said, "She's not crying because I'm insulting her. She's crying because she is guilty."

If Voisin was beginning to talk, so was Lesage. Much of what he had to say during La Reynie's interrogations did little more than reinforce his disdain for his former business partner and lover. Lesage claimed that Voisin was at the heart of nearly every crime by poison in Paris, especially among the nobility. He said she was lying about her role in Leféron's death. She did not obtain the poison from Leroux but distilled it herself from the seeds of rye grass, poppies, and mandrake root. She was also lying about having nothing to do with Monsieur Dreux's death. She had gladly poisoned a bouquet of flowers that Madame Dreux brought her.

One detail proved to be the most troubling to date and, once again, placed the king's palace of Saint-Germain at the center of La Reynie's investigation. Lesage recalled that four years earlier, in 1675, Voisin made regular trips to Saint-Germain to deliver cantharis to Mademoiselle des Oeillets, Montespan's attendant and the king's lover when Montespan was pregnant and "indisposed." Money seemed to be flowing at about the same time. Voisin bragged of making more than one hundred thousand *écus* and had plans to leave the country. "I warned her husband that something bad would happen to his wife" from whatever she was meddling in.

La Reynie communicated the details of Lesage's most recent interrogations to the king, via Louvois. Louis received the news with "grave concern," instructing La Reynie to continue his investigations but to keep all documents confidential, "to be used only and according to how I order them to be used."

The following day La Reynie questioned Voisin about Mademoiselle des Oeillets. Voisin denied knowing her. Again Lesage contradicted Voisin's account. He said that she had been in regular commerce with Oeillets as recently as three years earlier. He believed that Voisin's goal was to help one of her clients, Madame Vertemart, find employment as a servant in the household of Madame de Montespan. All the negotiations were handled by Mademoiselle des Oeillets.

Without delay La Reynie arrested Madame Vertemart and interrogated her. Where his tone with Lesage and Voisin remained calm and measured in the hopes of teasing as much information from them as possible, he flew into Vertemart when she denied knowing Oeillets, Montespan's lady-in-waiting and Louis's former mistress: "You are lying.... you even offered her a pearl necklace so you could get a job with Madame de Montespan." Though shaken, Vertemart stood firm in her assertion.

As the intensity of La Reynie's investigation into the possible involvement of Oeillets increased, Louvois did his best to calm the king. He explained that Mademoiselle Oeillets's intentions were good. If she were involved in some way with the accused criminals, it was surely nothing more than a *sottise* (a trifle, something for fun).

Louvois did little to downplay other accusations, however. When he learned that Bosse, Lesage, and Voisin had all implicated the duke of Luxembourg, the minister of war could barely contain his delight. According to Lesage, Luxembourg had hoped desperately for Louvois to reconsider his rejection of a marriage between his son to the minister's daughter. With this in mind, the duke sought Lesage's help. As usual, Lesage pretended to communicate to the devil by casting Luxembourg's written request into the fire. Lesage later read the duke's list of wishes, which included the death of his difficult wife, hardships to befall his rivals, and his son's marriage into Louvois's family. On learning this, Louvois wasted no time in reporting Luxembourg's alleged transgressions to the king: "Everything that Your Majesty has against Monsieur de Luxembourg up to now is nothing compared to [evidence acquired] in this interrogation."

Though still recovering from his riding accident, Louvois made plans to travel to Vincennes to interrogate Luxembourg personally.

It was an odd move. While Louvois involved himself in every detail of the investigations, he had not once set foot in the Tower of Vincennes since the interrogations began—preferring instead to leave them to La Reynie. But on October 7, 1679, Louvois slowly limped toward a private holding area on the ground floor of the dungeon. Prior to his meeting with Lesage, Louvois and La Reynie had agreed that the minister would feign a deal with the prisoner. Whatever Louvois said to Lesage must have been convincing: Lesage promised to cooperate fully with La Reynie.

To ensure that Lesage made good on his oath, Louvois sent La Reynie a letter to show the prisoner. In it the minister of war pretended to be responding to a report by La Reynie that Lesage was not sufficiently forthcoming: "It seems the hope that I gave to Lesage for his release served only to reinforce his opinion to say nothing of what he knows.... You may nullify all that I told him and begin his trial when you wish, if he does not change his behavior."

Their strategy worked. A few days later Lesage asked to meet with La Reynie to discuss something he had "forgotten" about the duchess of Vivonne. Sister-in-law to Madame de Montespan and mother of Colbert's son-in-law, the duchess had been directly embroiled in Louvois's frustrations as he tried to marry off his daughter. Moreover, Louvois was still smarting after having been obliged to "apologize" in front of Athénaïs for his "error" in leaving Vivonne's husband off the list for the post of galley general.

Following his meeting with Louvois, Lesage claimed for the first time that Montespan's sister-in-law the duchess of Vivonne had come to him three years earlier in a panic to request his help to retrieve a letter from Françoise Filastre, her servant. She did not say what it was about, but the tears in her eyes confirmed that it was something "dreadful." Lesage understood from "certain words" that it had something to do with the king. Despite the duchess of Vivonne's pleas and promises to pay him well for his services, Lesage was unable to persuade Filastre to part with the paper. When La Reynie pressed Lesage for additional information, he refused to offer anything more than: "Arrest Madame la Filastre. You will learn many strange things."

The king received the details of Lesage and Voisin's most recent accusations of connections to Montespan's family "with horror" and once again ordered La Reynie to "acquire every possible proof against those named."

Over the weeks that followed, Voisin, too, shared several other shocking details about "persons of quality." In particular Voisin implicated Olympe Mancini, now the countess of Soissons and the target of Louvois's ongoing ire. In her youth Olympe had been one of Louis's first mistresses. She never fully recovered from his decision to abandon her in favor of her younger sister and, later, for Louise de La Vallière. Voisin claimed that the countess had come to her house years earlier, when Louis and Louise were still together. She wanted Voisin to read her palm and tell her whether the king's love for her might return. Before Voisin could tell her fortune, however, Olympe spat out that she wanted to see Louise de La Vallière dead for having stolen the king from her and, if that was not possible, she would take her vengeance "even farther up."

The story rang true. Olympe had a reputation for outrageous behavior. Upon learning of the king's love for La Vallière, she once concocted a plan to expose the king's infidelities to his wife. While attending to the queen, the countess quietly slipped a letter that Marie-Thérèse received from Spain into the folds of her dress and replaced it with another that she had written (in Spanish to be sure the queen understood), describing the king's love for La Vallière. Olympe arranged for the letter to be delivered to Marie-Thérèse's chambermaid, but the servant became suspicious and brought the letter to the king. When Louis learned several years later that Olympe was behind it, he exiled her to the provinces.

In the end the countess of Soissons inadvertently rendered Louis a service, which the king acknowledged when he allowed her to return to court a few years later. In the wake of rumors, the king decided to reveal his affair to Marie-Thérèse—and began seeing La Vallière openly, often in the company of his wife. Soissons returned to her position as superintendent of Marie-Thérèse's household until she was replaced by Athénaïs and later by Fontanges.

As early as 1673, there had also been whispers that the death of the count of Soissons, Olympe's husband, had been caused by poison. The count had been found dead in his carriage on the Westphalian battlefield. Noting that Olympe had vowed at the time of her wedding that she would feel only an "inconceivable aversion" to whatever man she eventually married, the count's mother demanded an autopsy. Unable to prove that poison was at play, surgeons simply recorded "internal abscess" as the cause of death.

Voisin swore that she met with Olympe only once and this only to read the woman's palm. She insisted however that Olympe's sister was one of Lesage's regular clients. Unlike Olympe, her sister Marie Anne shared no past romantic history with the king and harbored no interest in gaining his affections. Instead she wished simply to discard a husband she did not love.

The plump and lively thirty-one-year-old duchess of Bouillon was no stranger to scandal. A passionate woman, the married Bouillon often found herself attracted to men who should have been off limits. She created a stir after flirting openly with her husband's brother, a cardinal. For this the family exiled her to a convent to reflect on her sins.

She clearly did not reflect enough. Not long after her return, she set her eyes on her nephew, the duke of Vendôme, five years her junior.

Over the past several months, Bouillon's name had come up often in La Reynie's investigations. Trying to understand the depths of the accusations against her, he reviewed the interrogation records. While Bosse and Vigoureux rarely agreed on much, they both stated that Bouillon had to come to them hoping that they could help her get rid of her husband. Voisin also claimed that Bouillon and the duke of Vendôme accompanied Lesage and her in the courtyard of her home on the rue du Beauregard. Voisin said she watched Bouillon write something on a slip of paper and hand it to Lesage.

In a description that corroborated Voisin's, Lesage confessed having performed services for the duchess in Voisin's courtyard, while her lover, Vendôme, watched. Lesage also said Bouillon's intent was clear: She wanted her husband to die.

Lesage burned the paper in front of the woman and told her to return in a few days. However, according to Lesage, the duchess insisted on repeating the ritual at her home as well. Lesage accompanied the woman to her estate, where they burned a second request. As he left, Bouillon handed him a sack of money. He said he refused to take it, but accepted a few coins for his trouble.

As the evidence mounted against the duke of Luxembourg, the king convened La Reynie and other members of the Arsenal tribunal to Saint-Germain. Two days after Christmas, La Reynie's carriage arrived at the palace gates. Fellow tribunal members Messieurs Boucherat, Bezons, and Robert accompanied him. All came on the orders of the king, who had read the latest interrogation records and wished to speak to the men after supper.

It was well past ten o'clock, and the halls of Saint-Germain buzzed with activity. Louis rarely took his meals alone, preferring instead to be surrounded by members of his court as they stood in deference and fascination, watching the monarch's every bite. As the court dispersed, the king's servants ushered La Reynie and the other men into the king's private counsel room. The meeting did not last long. Louis expressed his wishes succinctly: "For the good of the public, I want you to penetrate as quickly as possible this unfortunate business of poison in order to cut it off at its roots."

Louis empowered La Reynie and his colleagues to impose justice, "without any personal distinction, of social status or of gender." With this the men were dismissed. Reflecting on his brief audience with the king, La Reynie wrote, "It is impossible to doubt his intentions in this regard and not to understand his commitment to justice."

27

Fortune-Teller

On the evening of January 9, 1680, the duchess of Bouillon arrived at the Guégénaud Theater on the Left Bank of Paris to attend a sold-out performance of *The Fortune-Teller*. An enthusiastic supporter of the arts, Bouillon regularly gathered poets and playwrights at her home, where she provided them resources and a ready audience. The duchess pressed Jean de La Fontaine to create a steady stream of fables, which he read aloud to her delight. Molière, too, made regular appearances at her home. When Jean Racine staged his masterpiece, *Phèdre*, Bouillon bought every available ticket for six different performances, distributing them to friends as well as strangers who promised to whistle appreciatively during the play.

The talk of Paris, *The Fortune-Teller* was something that neither Bouillon nor any other self-respecting theater lover could afford to miss. The society gossip and enterprising journalist Jean Donneau de Visé had partnered with playwright Thomas Corneille, younger brother of the legendary Pierre, to craft a play that capitalized on public interest swirling around the Arsenal trials. Loosely based on the Voisin case, the comedy starred the male actor André Hubert playing Madame Jobin, a fortune-teller. She preys on the gullibility of a marquis by pretending to conjure up spirits and cast spells to attract lovers. In contrast to Voisin's macabre world of abortions and poison, Jobin turns out to be little more than a ridiculous charlatan.

The "machine play" included elaborate special effects requiring scores of stagehands to operate the noisy cranks, wheels, pulleys, and levers that allowed humans to fly in the air and that animated creatures with glowing eyes and gaping mouths. In the final scene Jobin waves her arms wildly to cast a spell. The stage filling with smoke, a monster-size Lucifer appears and attacks the marquis. Extracting a pistol from his pocket, the marquis stands his ground against the otherworldly force and exposes the devil as Jobin's brother in disguise.

On the floor closest to the stage, it was standing room only. Spectators elbowed one another as they tried to dodge splatters and sparks emanating from the oil lanterns on stage as well as the pickpockets and prostitutes who wove through the crowd looking for their next targets. In upper loges the elite watched the shows both onstage and in the crowd with both disgust and fascination.

As part of his ongoing efforts to reform the moral failings of Parisians, La Reynie kept a careful eye on public theaters, which had long been associated with disorder and vice. Lackeys attending during their off-hours from their noble masters proved most troublesome. While La Reynie's earlier ban on weapons and firearms kept the streets somewhat safer during their drunken brawls, it did little to keep the men from fighting with one another during showtime. Eventually they were prohibited altogether from theaters and the Opéra.

While there is no record of La Reynie having attended *The Fortune-Teller,* he was no stranger to the Guénégaud Theater. A year earlier the owners had offered him a box to see Jacques Pradon's *Phèdre et Hippolyte.* Some historians have suggested that La Reynie had a role in the development of the play for propaganda purposes, which is doubtful. The play reassured spectators that there was nothing to fear, and that otherworldly powers and poisons required too much imagination to be true. For the moment, however, the lieutenant of police felt anything but lighthearted about the prospect of charlatans, fortune-tellers, poisoners, and murderers in his city.

Bouillon had no way of knowing as she laughed at Jobin's gullible clients from her comfortable seat in the theater's loge that she too would soon be sitting uncomfortably in front of the Arsenal judges.

Two weeks after Bouillon attended the play, Louvois addressed a letter to one of the judges of the Chambre Ardent, Monsieur Robert. Frustrated that no arrests had yet been made, the minister of war reminded Robert that the king wanted justice imposed without concern regarding the social rank of the accused and gave the court full "liberty to make conclusions on the facts and proof presented."

Soon after receiving Louvois's letter, the chamber requested the king's approval to question the duchess of Bouillon and her sister Olympe, the countess of Soissons. In contrast to his minister's disdain for the two women, the king had long had a fondness for the lively Mancini sisters. He appreciated the duchess of Bouillon's feistiness and unwavering support of the arts. He also shared childhood memories of playing in the corridors with her sister Olympe, who was exactly his age, as well as their youthful explorations for a short time as lovers. As with most of his former mistresses, the king continued to hold a place, if small, for Olympe in his affections— despite her outrageous attempts to undermine his other affairs.

The king reluctantly gave the tribunal permission to question the two women while also finding a way to inform Bouillon's husband ahead of time of the sisters' impending arrests. Both fearless by nature and newly emboldened by the king's show of concern, the duchess arrived arm in arm with her husband and her nephew Vendôme on January 29, 1680, in the Arsenal chamber. Before answering any of the judges' questions, she stated for the record that she was at court only as a gesture of "respect and obedience to the king." However, she made clear her refusal to acknowledge the jurisdiction of the special tribunal, claiming that only the courts of the *parlement* had the right to judge her. After the judges assured her that her objections would be duly recorded, Bouillon settled onto the *sellette* and, without letting the judges ask questions, launched into a narrative that told a very different story than the one Lesage shared with La Reynie.

The duchess claimed that she had long heard of Lesage and Voisin's talent for producing "marvels." Acting on impulse as she often did, she ordered her horsemen to hitch up her carriage and take her to Voisin's home, where she was joined by her nephew Vendôme and Lesage. Lesage explained that he had the power to burn a piece of paper and have it reappear wherever she wished to see it. The duchess claimed that she had refused to participate. Instead she watched Vendôme write two or three wishes on the paper. Lesage filled the paper with sulfur and wrapped it tightly with silk thread. They then watched the ball burst into flames in Voisin's bedroom fireplace. Lesage insisted that she would find Vendôme's paper inside one of her vases at home. Once there, she looked in every piece of porcelain she owned. To little surprise she found nothing.

Continuing her story, Bouillon claimed that Lesage arrived uninvited at her home a few days after her visit to Voisin. He stretched out his open hand to reveal the original piece of paper, intact and still wrapped in silk thread. Lesage asserted that the spirits had refused to cooperate because they had not been sufficiently paid. Bouillon did not believe the man, but she saw no harm in playing along. She gave Lesage several coins. He then set the ball on fire once again and left, telling her it would soon rematerialize. It never did, nor did she ever see Lesage again.

Once she was done telling her story, she looked arrogantly at the judges, her eyes daring them to ask questions. The men shifted uncomfortably in their seats as they pondered silently how to approach the difficult witness. La Reynie, however, had heard enough. Making no attempt to hide his annoyance with Bouillon, he launched into a series of leading questions.

"Is it not true that you are the one who wrote the message with a request for your husband's death and put it in Lesage's hands?" he asked.

"No," she responded defiantly. "The question is so strange that it answers itself."

Undeterred, La Reynie probed further, "Is it not true that you offered Lesage a considerable sum to hire him to do what you wished?"

"No, I only gave him two coins," Bouillon said curtly. La Reynie's face betrayed his disbelief. Without pausing, he asked: "Why did you want to kill your husband?"

"Kill my husband! Ask him what he thinks. He held my hand all the way to the door," she answered. Turning to address all the judges, Bouillon declared with a voice full of haughty disdain: "Messieurs, is this all you have to say to me?"

It was not. La Reynie leaned toward the woman and asked, "Madame, have you ever seen the devil?" he asked.

"Monsieur," she replied, glaring squarely at La Reynie. "I see him right now. He is ugly and old, and disguised as a judge."

Bouillon's show of defiance left the judges speechless. Even the normally well-composed La Reynie found himself at a loss for words. After quickly calculating they had little to gain from a battle with the duchess, the judges dismissed her.

The noblewoman rose from the *sellette* in belligerent triumph. Exiting the courtroom, she groused: "Truly, I would have never believed such smart men could ask such dumb questions," making sure the judges heard every word. As she walked out of the Arsenal again arm in arm with her husband and Vendôme, the crowd waiting outside let out a cheer.

Bouillon's elder sister, the countess of Soissons, did not fight. Instead she fled. After learning of the impending arrests, the duke of Bouillon had rushed to his sister-in-law's home. Finding Olympe among friends at a gaming table, Bouillon nodded his head toward a nearby room. She stood and followed him. Her brother-in-law wasted no time in explaining the situation: If she did not leave France immediately, she would soon be on her way to the Bastille. Without further discussion Olympe returned to the gaming room and excused herself, taking along her close friend, the marquise d'Alluye. The two quickly plotted their escape.

After shooing their guests away on the pretext of having other dinner plans, Olympe and d'Alluye filled suitcases full of clothes, money, and jewels. The two women fled for the border at three in the morning, accompanied by two of Soissons's children and her household staff.

Upon hearing the news of her flight, the chamber proceeded with her trial in absentia. From a distance Olympe attempted to negotiate, offering to return to France as long as she would not be imprisoned in either the Bastille or Vincennes during the deliberations. The judges rejected the request.

Some speculated that Louvois had been behind the countess's arrest. Olympe herself was reported to have said before she fled, "[Louvois] is my mortal enemy because I refused to marry my son to his daughter.... He will have me die on the gallows or, at the very least, put me in prison." The prolific court gossip Primi Visconti also described Louvois's actions toward Soissons after her flight from France, claiming that Louvois arranged to have scores of black cats released outside a church in Brussels where Soissons was attending mass. Panicked by what they took as a sign of Soissons's connection to the devil, the locals chased her from their city. The show had reportedly been arranged by spies from Louvois's armies.

Publicly the king remained unapologetic in his decision to alert the Mancini sisters, especially Olympe, of their impending arrests. Some said that he told his niece, the princess of Carignan, "Madame, I wanted the Countess to flee. Perhaps I will have to make amends one day to God and to my people."

The king also signaled a seeming change of heart when it came to pursuing crimes of poisoning among preferred nobility when he ordered La Reynie to Saint-Germain for his morning rising not long after Bouillon's trial. A single balustrade divided the narrow space between the king's bed from the crush of courtiers who peered over one another's shoulders, nudging and jostling, as they watched carefully selected nobles help the monarch perform his most intimate actions. Louis signaled to La Reynie as the police chief approached the balustrade. The two men chatted briefly about a variety of small matters. The king then turned to La Reynie, saying firmly, and likely loud enough for the court to hear, "It is necessary to make war on another crime." Louis then dismissed him.

Privately, however, the king sent firm orders to the tribunal that they should continue their work. Writing to the head judge, Boucherat, a week after Bouillon's trial, Louvois explained that the king was more than aware of Parisian pushback against the tribunal. However, Boucherat should assure his colleagues of his majesty's protection and remind them of their responsibility to impose justice with the same strength of resolve as they always had.

The king issued a disclaimer, however, when it came to Mademoiselle des Oeillets. "His Majesty is assured that it is impossible that Lesage is telling the truth about her." Louvois explained. He instructed the court to delay arresting Oeillets until La Reynie had investigated matters further. As for the others, they were urged to push ahead. "I have no doubt that you will find His Majesty ready to do what is proposed to him for the sake of justice."

The duke of Luxembourg, too, soon found himself before the court. Louvois had used the information he had coerced from Lesage to persuade the king to arrest the duke for blasphemy and witchcraft. In the days preceding the arrest, Louvois offered his own show of "support" by informing Luxembourg personally of the accusations against him. The minister encouraged his nemesis to flee to avoid the humiliation of prison. Rightly, Luxembourg did not know what to make of their conversation. He worried whether Louvois was making a genuine effort to extend an olive branch or instead setting a trap by encouraging him to flee, thus signaling his guilt.

Every Wednesday the king gave an audience to nobles at the Château of Saint-Germain. Over the years Luxembourg came to count on a warm greeting from Louis. This time, however, the monarch's face showed little more than quiet disdain. Luxembourg had not been the only person to notice the king's change of heart. Murmurs soon filled the hall, as courtiers looked sideways toward Luxembourg, then toward one another, and back at the duke.

Luxembourg gathered his composure and walked toward the king. "I would like to talk to Your Majesty," he said with more deference than he was known for.

Turning his head with royal nonchalance, Louis XIV dismissed the man drily: "If you are innocent, you have only to turn yourself in for questioning at the prison. I have made sure that there are good judges in place to examine these affairs, and I have given them my full confidence."

Luxembourg begged the king not to have him arrested. The plea fell on deaf ears. Luxembourg called for his carriage and ordered the driver to take him first to see his confessor, Père La Chaise, and then to the Bastille. Moments after Luxembourg's departure, Louvois sent a letter by express courier to Boucherat, the head inquisitor at the Arsenal. "Monsieur de Luxembourg will arrive at the Bastille prison tonight. Please continue the proceedings against him." The warden of the Bastille, Besmaux, also received instructions to show no mercy to Luxembourg, who was swiftly transferred to a tiny dank cell deep in the bowels of the prison.

When news circulated that the duke, a respected "officer of the Crown," was being kept in solitary confinement in the depths of the Bastille, the cries of protest among the nobility reached a deafening pitch. Madame de Sévigné noted: "Everyone is questioning a little the wisdom of the judges, who are creating a stir by scandalously targeting such big names for such little things." To test just how reactionary La Reynie's investigation had become, an anonymous correspondent sent the police chief a letter in code as if taunting him to take the bait. La Reynie took one look at the letter and decided it was a hoax.

Luxembourg's family protested his arrest. The duchess of Luxembourg threw herself at the king's feet on three occasions, begging for her husband's release. When this did not work, she presented a formal request to the tribunal judges that evoked formal provisions in the criminal ordinance of 1670 allowing for family visits and the right to an attorney. Once again she was rebuffed. By virtue of its special status, the court claimed it had no obligation to follow established procedures.

On May 2, 1680, a full five months after his arrest, Luxembourg had a chance to view the only piece of physical evidence against him. The duke stood about four feet in front of the judges, who sat at a long table. The notary Sagot slid a slip of paper in front of him and asked Luxembourg if he recognized the signature. The duke confirmed it was his. It was a letter dating from 1665 that gave his assistant, Pierre Bonnart, permission to do all that was necessary to recover lost documents related to a sale of forest property. In it Luxembourg offered a handsome reward to anyone who helped find them.

The duke explained that, without his knowledge, Bonnart took the letter to Lesage and hired him to perform rituals to find the papers, which materialized soon afterward. Late one night a few days later, Bonnart woke Luxembourg from a deep sleep and asked him to sign the original request for assistance to acknowledge that the services had been rendered and payment should be made to Lesage. It was still dark in the room, and the duke, who could not read what he signed, trusted his assistant.

Bonnart later used the signed letter as extortion, threatening to spread rumors about the nobleman's commerce with the devil. At the time Luxembourg believed he was still on fine terms with Louvois and turned to him for help. The minister declined to get involved.

Luxembourg strained to see the incriminating document and asked the judges to let him examine it more closely. When they refused, the duke dived toward the table and grabbed the paper. In indignant desperation, Luxembourg waved the letter in front of the judges' faces. Between the last line of the original order and his signature someone had inserted another sentence. The handwriting was different, and the ink much lighter. It gave instructions to make all spells necessary to recover the business documents. Luxembourg said he had been framed by Bonnart. He also suspected that Louvois had had a hand in resurrecting the matter, but chose not to voice his concerns given the minister's clear influence over the proceedings.

The court ruled that Luxembourg had indeed dabbled in fortune-telling and likely allowed himself to be duped by Lesage's paper tricks. However, they concurred with Luxembourg that the physical evidence had been forged. In lieu of any substantial punishment, the judges exiled Luxembourg from Paris. Bonnart spent the remainder of his life doing hard labor in the galleys.

The fate of Bouillon, Soissons, and Luxembourg intensified the nobility's mistrust of the process. Perceptive as ever, Madame de Sévigné lamented, "Today the talk is all about the innocence of the accused and the horrors of defamation. Maybe tomorrow it will be the exact opposite...no one speaks of anything else. Truly, there is hardly another example of such a scandal in a Christian court." Later the court chronicler also made her thoughts on La Reynie still clearer: "[The reputation] of Monsieur de La Reynie is abominable." One contemporary offered a solution: "All we need to do is burn the witches, the witnesses, and the judges and all will be taken care of."

2 8

"From One Fire to Another"

Voisin appeared in front of the judges on February 17, 1680, a full eleven months after she was arrested, to hear the charges against her. The following day the court condemned her to death by fire. Monsieur Robert made the case for having her tongue pierced and a hand cut off before the execution, but after much discussion, the chamber decided against it. Remembering the spectacle of Brinvilliers's death, the judges were concerned that the added punishments could overexcite the crowd or, worse, lead spectators to feel sympathy for her.

At one thirty in the afternoon on February 19, guards ushered Voisin into the torture room at the Bastille. The questioners, led by La Reynie, asked Voisin to review, one by one, her relationships with La Grange, Bosse, and Vigoureux, the noblewomen Leféron and Dreux, and a host of others. Voisin appeared calm and forthcoming during the interactions, though she revealed little new information. After five straight hours, the remainder of the Question—and the torture yet to come—was put off until the next morning.

The sun had not yet begun to rise when Voisin was returned for questioning. This time the focus centered on the woman's interactions with the countess of Soissons and the marquise of Alluye. Once again Voisin appeared forthcoming but revealed no new information. She admitted to having gone to Saint-Germain on two occasions to plead for the release of her former lover the alchemist Blessis. However, she denied ever having brought "powders" to either Saint-Germain or Versailles.

The clock tower outside struck one. The questioners broke for lunch. An hour later they reconvened in the interrogation cell to question Voisin about the abortions she had performed. "I feel an obligation, for the relief of my conscience, to declare that Lepère performed a large number of abortions," she said emotionlessly, never admitting that she also performed them at her home with the elderly midwife's help.

After several more hours and questions regarding scores of accused poisoners and their clients, Doctor Vezou and the surgeon Monsieur Morel entered the room. As before, their job was to witness Voisin's impending torture to ensure that she would survive just long enough for the public execution to take place afterward.

Guards led Voisin to a bench and placed each of her legs in *brodequins*. "You can impose whatever torments on me that you'd like, I will tell you nothing more than what I have already declared," Voisin said. She looked to the heavens, asking aloud for God to grant her the strength to endure the suffering. The questioner began by urging her to tell the truth, to which Voisin responded: "God have mercy, I have told everything I know. I know nothing else."

The questioner signaled the first blow to the leg, then the second. Voisin's emotionless resolve was replaced by screams: "Oh! My God! Ah! The Virgin! I will not tell anything more." With the third strike she cried more loudly: "Have pity on me! I have told the truth. I did not bring powders to Saint-Germain and I know nothing else about Madame Soissons and Madame Alluye."

After another strike the questioning continued. The same questions were repeated over again with only brief pauses between each fall of the hammer. Did she know Madamoiselle des Oeillets? On the fifth strike: Did she bring powders to Saint-Germain? On the sixth: Was what she said about Mesdames Dreux and Leféron true? Between howls of pain she denied everything, swearing she had already told them all that she knew. After the seventh blow she pleaded for the pain to end.

As the torturer held the mallet in the air ready for the next strike, the questioners asked: "You have nothing more to declare to us to relieve your conscience, then?" La Voisin moaned that she did not. Seconds later the hammer fell for the eighth and final time. The questioning was over.

In the early morning of February 22, three days after her interrogation began, Voisin rested on a dirty mattress in the middle of the stone floor. Her body caked in dried blood, she mumbled something to the interrogators as they entered the room. They leaned in to listen. Her words were barely decipherable, but they understood that she wanted to share several more things before she was sent to her death: She had cheated Lepère and her daughter of much of their earnings due from abortions performed at Voisin's house. She had provided poison to a neighbor who had fallen in love with a woodworker and wanted to rid herself of her husband. The details of these and other sins were plentiful, complete with addresses and descriptions of the accused. The revelations were hardly earth-shattering in comparison to the rest. But through cracked lips and with her voice fading, she said: "For the sake of my conscience, I must tell you everyone who came to me seeking death. Debauchery was always at the heart of it all."

After three days of brutal questioning, perhaps Voisin was indeed attempting to unburden her soul. Or perhaps she was attempting to postpone her inevitable death. In any case the investigators believed that she had nothing more of interest left to tell. If this was the best that Voisin could give, it was time for the execution.

At noon that same day Voisin was transferred from the torture room to a small chapel inside the Bastille prison. She was forced to her knees and was once again read the death sentence that had been pronounced against her. A priest arrived to offer her a final chance for confession; she refused. She wanted to talk instead to the notary Sagot. A full accounting of her activities was more important, it seemed, than to make amends to God. Resigned to her fate, Voisin asked Sagot to record for posterity that she had never given Madame Leféron any sort of vial, nor had Leroux. It was true that, after the death of Leféron's husband, a glowing and joyous-looking widow had come to see her. However, she swore adamantly that she had nothing to do with the husband's death. With this Voisin was loaded into an open cart and taken out the gates of the Bastille prison.

Despite the cold, Parisians who lived in homes along the rue Saint-Antoine leaned out their windows to catch a glimpse of the most notorious poisoner in Paris since the marquise de Brinvilliers. The horse-drawn procession stopped first at the doors of Notre-Dame, where Voisin was required to make her *amende honorable*. Intractable to the end, Voisin refused to kneel. The executioner shoved her to her knees. Still, she refused to give any sign of contrition.

Crowds gathered in front of Notre-Dame watched Voisin loaded back into the cart and then taken out at the place de Grève. Offering no sympathy, the executioner chained her, seated, to a large pile of logs as she spat and swore. Howling, she tried six or seven times to duck away from the massive mounds of hay the guards dumped on top of her. But it was too late; the fire had been lit. Soon after, Voisin's body was consumed in a ball of heat and smoke. Watching the execution, Madame de Sévigné commented wryly: "She gave her soul gently to the devil right in the middle of the fire. All she did was pass from one fire to another."

Voisin's death did not bring closure. Instead it brought a sense of dread among many that this was only the beginning. Watching the execution, the painter Antoine Coypel predicted correctly that "many things are still yet to come that will surprise us all."

PART VI

Wicked Truths

2 9

The Poisoner's Daughter

As crowds watched the flames consume Voisin, her daughter
awaited questioning at Vincennes. Having spent months
interrogating the elder Voisin, La Reynie knew all too
well what a mean-spirited and abusive woman she was. He could
hardly imagine what it must have been like for the quiet and some
what skittish Marie-Marguerite to have been raised by such a vile
mother.

On March 28, 1680, Marie-Marguerite sat with La Reynie in
the interrogation room, unaware of her mother's execution. As she
warmed herself in front of the fireplace, the police chief eased his
way into the questions, asking what it was like to grow up in the
Montorgeuil neighborhood. She said that she welcomed the opportunity to "unburden herself" of her memories.

What she remembered most was the smell of incense hovering
in the air and the quiet chanting in the courtyard at odd hours of
the day and night. She had once plucked up the courage to spy
between the boards of the small shed in the courtyard. She saw a
man in priest's clothing uttering a prayer in front of a large cross
as he held a communion host in his open palms. She watched in

fear and fascination as her mother and a red-wigged man stood next to him, chanting in an odd language. Placing the host on an altarlike stand, the priest next raised a strange wax figure above his head, wrapped it in a cotton cloth, and put it in a metal box.

Overcome by curiosity, Marie-Marguerite went back later that night to retrieve the figure and brought it to her father. He explained, unconvincingly even to a child, that it had been a harmless religious ceremony. Then he grabbed the wax figure from Marie-Marguerite, threw it to the ground, crushed it under his feet, and tossed the pieces into the fire. Marie-Marguerite stood transfixed as she watched the wax melt and disappear.

Another memory—one of the rare good ones—was a visit she made to a rich family's house with her mother and a burly woman who wore a man's overcoat. A servant brought Marie-Marguerite fresh apricots on a porcelain plate while her mother and her companion met with the noblewoman out in the garden. As she ate her apricots, she watched the women chant as they walked around a fire and then buried a wax figure in the ground.

As more childhood memories floated toward her, Marie-Marguerite told La Reynie about the elderly woman named Madame Pelletier who often came to the house. She usually carried a basket heavy with glass flasks, many containing a ruby-colored liquid, as well as small pouches made of taffeta, each filled with mysterious powders. Marie-Marguerite once asked her mother what they were for. "They bring happiness," her mother said dismissively. Marie-Marguerite asked if she could have some of the happiness powder. "It will do nothing for you," Madame Pelletier snapped. A few days later, however, Pelletier poured her a small glass of white wine, into which the old woman added some of the powder. Not long after drinking the wine, Marie-Marguerite became "sick in extremity." Her mother later told her she got what she deserved.

Of all of the visitors to her mother's home, she liked the Woman with Two Tails the most. Marie-Marguerite had given her this nickname for the long, elaborate dress fabric that draped in front and trailed behind her, swishing with each step she took. The dark-haired woman was kind when so many of her mother's other clients and business partners barked orders or, worse, took advantage of her in ways she had tried to forget.

La Reynie surmised from the details that the girl had witnessed the colorful charlatan Lesage and the priest Mariette casting spells in the shack. It had also been Bosse and the noblewoman Leféron whom Marie-Marguerite had visited with her mother while she snacked on apricots.

However, La Reynie could not place the Woman with Two Tails. The girl told La Reynie that she once made the mistake of uttering the woman's real name aloud: Mademoiselle des Oeillets. Marie-Marguerite told him that she received a beating from her mother for her indiscretion.

Marie-Marguerite's memories moved closer to the present. She remembered a man named Romani, whom she had seen at her mother's house around Christmastime a year earlier. Fond of disguises, Romani changed his appearance with every visit. One thing, however, remained constant: the way he eyed her greedily, telling her at every opportunity that he wanted to make her his bride. Marie-Marguerite wisely kept her distance.

Despite her wariness of Romani, Marie-Marguerite could not help eavesdropping on her mother and her business partner. From what she could make out, the pair was plotting to have Romani dress up as a foreign clothier and sell gloves and silks for a tidy profit to women at court. As part of their plans, Romani and Voisin also talked at length about a *placet,* a note, that her mother would deliver to the king. Once a week the king allowed subjects to present their *placets* to him in person at a table set up at the entrance of his palace. The petitioners waited long hours for a chance to submit their entreaties.

While Romani wandered Saint-Germain with his wares, her mother joined the crowds in hopes of getting their note into the king's hands. Neither Marie-Marguerite nor her father had any idea of what the note contained. All they knew was that it was urgent: "My father asked my mother what kind of business was so important. She told him over and over that she would either accomplish the task or die trying. He said, 'What, die? That's a lot to say all for a piece of paper.'"

After two months and many trips, her mother returned from Saint-Germain. Having failed in her mission to deliver the *placet*, she was in a foul mood. La Reynie asked Marie-Marguerite if she knew what the note contained. She said she did not, nor did she ever find out because her mother was arrested two days later.

With this La Reynie returned the girl to her cell. There would be another time for more questions, and he had other, more important prisoners to focus on. Louvois had just sent word that the king wanted to put the noblewoman Leféron, Dreux, and Philbert on trial. The trials, which took place on April 7 and 8, concluded swiftly. Reinforcing the importance of class status in the proceedings, the court spared the women from the fiery fate of Voisin. Instead Madame Leféron was banished from Paris for nine years and fined fifteen hundred *livres* for having plotted the death of her husband. Dreux and Philbert's cases were dismissed entirely.

In the course of the days and weeks that followed, Marie-Marguerite learned about her mother's death through furtive whispers from other prisoners. The next time she met with La Reynie, the reticent young woman had been replaced by an outspoken and agitated one. Finally released from her mother's hold, Marie-Marguerite appeared eager to talk openly for the first time. Apologizing for withholding the truth from the police chief, she launched into a lengthy inventory of her mother's sins.

Marie-Marguerite explained that Romani and her mother had actually been employed to kill Mademoiselle de Fontanges, and to do it they planned to sell the king's mistress a pair of poisoned gloves. The *placet* intended for the king was also laced with poison. Her mother boasted to her that no one would be suspicious if they timed the deaths well. Everyone would assume the king's mistress had died of a broken heart following the death of the king, or vice versa.

After the elder Voisin learned of her impending arrest, she handed Marie-Marguerite the note for safekeeping. She then set to work emptying the house of all traces of her criminal activities, including the courtyard furnace filled with tiny charred bones. Just before Inspector Camuset arrived at the house, Marie-Marguerite had burned the note without opening it, lest she accidentally poison herself.

Before La Reynie had a chance to ask who had hired her mother to poison Fontanges, the young woman volunteered the name without hesitation: Athénaïs de Montespan. "Every time something new happened to Madame de Montespan that left her to worry about the king's diminishing good graces toward her, she came to my mother for some remedy," Marie-Marguerite explained. Over the years, however, Montespan had become frustrated that the spells had seemed to diminish in their effect. "My mother told me that Madame de Montespan wanted to take everything to the extreme. She hired my mother to do disgusting things."

According to Marie-Marguerite, Voisin had shared the details of the plot with Catherine Trianon, a close friend and fellow fortuneteller. "Disappointment in love is a beautiful thing," Marie-Marguerite heard her mother say to Trianon, listing aloud all she had done for Montespan over the last five or six years. Voisin told her friend she had concocted love potions, cast spells, and arranged for the services of Lesage, Mariette, and the Prayer Man, Guibourg. Marie-Marguerite also recalled that, when Montespan's wishes did not come true, her mother prepared a wax effigy of the king, which Montespan stabbed with angry delight.

At the request of the king's mistress, she had also once scribbled Montespan's name on a slip of paper and tossed it into a fire. Reciting for Trianon the accompanying incantation, her mother intoned: "Burn, fire. This is the body, the soul, the spirit, the heart, the understanding of Louis of Bourbon. May he neither go nor come, rest nor sleep until he fulfills the wishes of the woman whom I name."

La Reynie's head reeled as he listened to Marie-Marguerite weave her tales. In earlier interrogations Voisin and Romani had acknowledged the existence of a *placet*. However, neither had indicated in such clear terms what its true purpose was, preferring instead to claim it contained only a plea to release a colleague from jail. Lesage had hinted, but only obliquely, that the letter was dangerous. Voisin's daughter now provided the missing pieces of the story.

"Why didn't you say [all of this earlier]? That you knew about plots against the king?" La Reynie asked. Marie-Marguerite paused for a moment and then replied: "I couldn't put Trianon or my mother at risk based just on hearsay." True, the bulk of what she had told La Reynie was grounded on furtive snippets of conversations overheard by a child years earlier. The police chief wondered for a moment if perhaps Marie-Marguerite's story had been made up. But La Reynie found himself inclined to trust the girl, who seemed so earnest and convincing. "It is difficult to conceive how Voisin's daughter, who appears to be smart and who understands the dangers to which she exposes herself, would want to invent and to put forward such strange and unbelievable things," he wrote following their meeting.

La Reynie reminded Marie-Marguerite that it was a crime to add even the smallest unproved detail to what she claimed to be facts. "I have understated rather than overstated," Marie-Marguerite replied. "Having no reason to fear anything anymore in regard to my mother, I have no thought other than to declare the truth."

Taken together, the testimonies of Lesage, Guibourg, Marie-Marguerite, and Filastre provided ample reason to believe that Athénaïs had been in contact with the poisoners, witches, and priests of Montorgeuil at some point during her long affair with the king. However, the extent of her direct involvement remained unclear. La Reynie felt certain that a trial was not only the best way to uncover the truth, it was also the right thing to do.

The king disagreed, refusing adamantly to believe the accusations against his former mistress. Louis had always remained loyal to those women who had figured importantly in his life. Even the elderly one-eyed woman to whom he lost his virginity lived comfortably until her death in the château he had built for her. Despite his marital infidelities, he also rarely missed a night in bed with his wife, Marie-Thérèse. Contradicting everything he said publicly in regard to justice without concern for rank, he had even given the countess of Soissons, whom he also bedded, advance notice so she could flee to safety. When her sister, the duchess of Bouillon, chose to stay and fight, he allowed her to push back against the tribunal without retribution.

Louis's decision to keep details about Athénaïs out of the public eye, however, did not mean that his relations with his former mistress had thawed. In fact they had gotten worse long before the king first became aware of the accusations against her. "Madame de Montespan has fallen...to an unbelievable point," wrote the court observer Roger de Bussy-Rabutin. "The king does not look at her, and you can bet the court follows his example."

As Montespan's favor at court diminished, the reputation of Madame de Maintenon was on the rise. Eager for a break from the Torrent, the king found refuge in the calm friendship of the devout governess, whom he visited in her chambers every evening before dinner. "She is showing the king a completely new country, by that I mean, the exchange of friendship and conversation, without chicanery or contrariety," wrote Madame de Sévigné. "He seems charmed by her." Playing on the homophony of her name, courtiers whispered their confirmation that Maintenon had become "Madame Now" (Madame de Maintenant").

Fate had also not been kind to Angélique Fontanges, Louis's teenage mistress. In early January 1680 she suffered severe hemorrhaging while giving birth to Louis's child, which arrived stillborn. "Injured in the service of the king," Sévigné had put it. Over the three months that followed, Fontanges had still not recovered and remained bedridden, was feverish, and had a swollen face. Rumors had circulated briefly at court that poison was involved, but they had been quickly dismissed. Still, the prognosis for the once beautiful Fontanges looked as uncertain as the future of her relationship with Louis. The king had signaled as much when he gave her a generous pension, his standard parting gift.

Fontanges died on June 28, 1681, at the age of twenty, after being bedridden for more than a year. Convinced to the end of the king's continuing love for her, she whispered her final words: "I die happy because my eyes have seen the king cry."

Angélique's death further fueled suspicions of foul play among the king's mistresses. Louis's sister-in-law, the princess of Palatine, speculated that Athénaïs had a hand in her death: "Montespan is the devil incarnate, but Fontanges was good and simple; both were beautiful. The latter is dead, they say, because the former poisoned her milk," she wrote.

Whether it was because he did not believe the accusations or he simply did not want to know, the king resisted cries for an autopsy. He wrote to the duke of Noailles on the day of his mistress's death: "As for those who desire to open her body, if it is possible to avoid it, I believe this to be the best decision." The autopsy took place anyway, with all six surgeons in attendance agreeing that Fontanges had died of natural causes.

30

Sacrifices

Working to uncover whether there was truth behind the accusations against Athénaïs, La Reynie now turned his focus on the former servant of Montespan's sister-in-law, the duchess of Vivonne. "Arrest Filastre. You will learn many strange things," Lesage had said. The elder Voisin had also warned that Filastre had a "maliciousness of spirit...and is as dangerous with a sword as she is with poison."

In her first interrogation by La Reynie, Filastre confessed to having attended Father Guibourg's black masses at his Saint-Denis church and having been a regular participant in séances led by Father Cotton, a priest at Saint-Paul. She claimed to have seen both Cotton and Guibourg bless snakes and heard them utter prayers backwards in their churches.

The unmarried Filastre explained that, several years earlier, she became pregnant after being "debauched" by Chaboissière, the servant of François Vanens. La Reynie was more than familiar with Vanens and Chaboissière who, along with close to fifty of their accomplices, were sitting in the Châtelet prison awaiting trial for counterfeiting, alchemy and, La Reynie suspected, poisonings.

A group of men had abducted Filastre while she was in the throes of labor and delivered her to the home of a witch named Madame Simon. Shoving her onto the floor, the witch lit candles and placed them in the form of a pentagram around her. She then gave Filastre a black candle in honor of Lucifer to hold and chanted "execrable" spells. After the birth Simon placed the placenta in a small sack and took it away, along with the newborn. Filastre claimed she never saw her child again.

Simon denied Filastre's charges when La Reynie questioned her two days later, saying that she was a midwife, not a witch, and certainly had not performed a black Sabbath. To the contrary, she had feared for the child's soul when Filastre insisted that she did not want the baby baptized and insinuated to her that she had other plans for it. Simon claimed instead that she took the child from Filastre, placing it with another family to protect it from its evil mother.

One of Guibourg's colleagues, Father Leroyer, had yet another version of the story to tell. Simon and Filastre were both doing the work of the devil for profit. Following the birth, the women delivered the sack containing the placenta to Guibourg, who placed it on the altar of his church and performed a mass. According to Leroyer, Filastre and Simon then sold the placenta as an aphrodisic. They put the newborn child up for sale as well, splitting the money. Leroyer could not say what happened next to the child.

La Reynie immediately interrogated the elderly Guibourg, who stood unsteadily before the police chief. La Reynie minced no words, asking right away if the cross-eyed and ruddy-faced priest knew Filastre and whether he had performed a ceremony on the afterbirth. Guibourg nodded. La Reynie questioned the priest about the masses that Voisin's daughter had claimed he had performed on the bellies of women and girls. Nodding again, he said: "I submit myself to the mercy of God and the King. It is true. I allowed them to take advantage of my weaknesses."

The priest described the first mass he performed, which took place near Montlhéry, a small village not far from Paris. He did not recognize the woman who offered herself on the mattress; her long hair had obscured her face. Voisin had told him it was the king's mistress Madame de Montespan. His words echoing off the high ceilings of the Vincennes's interrogation room, he recited the spell he had cast on behalf of the woman whom he believed to be Athénaïs: "Astroth, Asmodée, princes of darkness, I conjure you to accept the sacrifice that I now offer you in the form of this child. I request that the king's love as well...be continued to be bestowed upon me, as well as the favor of the court, and that the king deny me nothing that I should ask of him, both for myself, my family, and my servants." Guibourg performed the spell again at a second mass on the same woman, which took place not long after the first at the base of the ramparts of the city, just steps away from Voisin's home. The woman's hair once again covered her face.

In later interrogations Guibourg also confessed to La Reynie that he performed a different kind of ceremony for Mademoiselle des Oeillets. Wearing a priestly robe, he met Oeillets and an unknown man at Voisin's home. He understood at the time that the man was serving as a proxy for the king, for whom the effects of the mass were intended. Holding a chalice, Guibourg instructed the couple to fill the vessel with their sexual fluids. Oeillets, who was menstruating, asked if she might make an offering of her blood instead. Guibourg agreed. The man slipped behind the bed and masturbated, ejaculating into the chalice. Then the priest stirred powder of dried bat into the semen to form a thick paste. After Guibourg blessed the concoction, he put the paste in a small dish and gave it to the couple to administer inconspicuously to the king as a love potion. Guibourg did not offer any suggestions about how this might be done, nor did the couple mention how they intended to do it, nor did Oeillets share her plans in this regard.

Louis exploded in "indignation" when he heard of the "blasphemies" and demanded that La Reynie continue his investigations, emphasizing again that the police chief should not share any records with the tribunal judges that made reference to his mistresses, both former and present. La Reynie urged the king to reconsider the decision to withhold evidence, feeling strongly that the tribunal needed to be allowed to hear the burgeoning evidence against Oeillets and Montespan. Louis promptly denied the request.

In an unusual show of resistance against the king's wishes, the police chief wrote Louvois the same day, putting forth once again his conviction that the tribunal should reconvene. Rather than stress the need to try Oeillets, Montespan, or their accusers, La Reynie explained that the prisoners at Vincennes, who now numbered more than 150, were on edge while they waited in their dank cells, not knowing when, if ever, their trials would take place. The king denied Louvois's request as well, explaining he had plans to travel through the northern provinces and wanted to be nearby, just in case matters got out of hand. He counseled the police chief to let the prisoners know he would be back in a few months and would reopen the tribunal on his return. The following day Louvois also sent word to the warden, Ferronnaye, to provide more and better wine to the inmates.

As promised, the king reconvened the court three months later. The tribunal swiftly sentenced the priest Cotton and Filastre to death, to be preceded by the Extraordinary Question. On September 30 La Reynie joined the notary Sagot, Doctor Vezou, and the executioner in the Bastille torture room to question Filastre. Standing in full view of bloodstained *brodequins,* hammers, and various straps and pulleys, Filastre answered La Reynie's initial questions nervously. She explained that only the welfare of her family lay behind her efforts to secure a position in Fontanges's well-paying household, adding in indignation that Cotton and Guibourg had not been tried. They had performed spells on behalf of Madame de Montespan, as well as for a nobleman who had designs against Colbert. "Those people will not be brought to justice," she asserted. "Yet you punish me for having attended just one mass."

If the initial questioning on September 30 proved short and painless, the session that followed the next day made up for it. By the time guards strapped Filastre into the torture boots, her belligerence had disappeared. La Reynie ordered her to reveal everything she knew. The woman nodded with trepidation. On the police chief's signal, the torturer raised the hammer above his head. The dull sound of the weapon meeting flesh reverberated against the stone walls, intersecting with Filastre's high-pitched cries. A second strike followed, then a third.

"It's true," she howled. "I offered my child to the devil. I gave it to [the witch] Simon." A fourth blow, then a fifth. Between moans of pain, Filastre said Montespan wanted Madamoiselle de Fontanges poisoned and also needed stronger magical powders to make the king love her again. This was why, Filastre confessed, she had tried to secure a place in Fontanges's household, and it was also why she made a pact with the devil while she was in labor.

La Reynie signaled to the torturer to rest for a moment as he let what Filastre told him sink in. He then leaned in toward Filastre, urging her to confirm that what she had said about Montespan was the truth. It was absolutely true, she said. Then she dropped her head and fell silent. On La Reynie's signal, the torturer swung the mallet for the fourth time. Throwing back her head in agony, she screamed, "Oh God!" Mustering every bit of strength she had left, Filastre told La Reynie that Guibourg also worked with Madame de Montespan. "But except for what I just told [about] Madamoiselle de Fontanges, I never heard anything else about [a plot] against the king," she stammered through the pain.

Blood spilled from her legs as guards released her from the *brodequins* and carried her to a dirty mattress on the floor nearby. Moaning, she promised that everything she just said was true. La Reynie allowed Doctor Vezou and his surgeon to dress the women's wounds and administer sips of wine to help her regain her strength.

When they were done, La Reynie looked down at the half-dead woman and asked calmly, "Is what you said about the plot against Madamoiselle de Fontanges true?" He took a breath, then added, "Look deeply into your conscience." If she was not telling the truth, he said, she would find herself in an even more miserable state when she had to justify her actions to God. Voice fading, she vowed once again that she had told the truth.

Recovering in her cell before her execution later that afternoon,

Filastre must have conversed again with her conscience. She begged the guards to let her talk to La Reynie. The broken woman told the police chief that everything she had said during the Question had been a lie. She had done it to "liberate herself from the pain and suffering of torments," fearing that if she did not say what she thought he wanted to hear, he would impose another round of torture. "I don't want to die with charges against [Madame de Montespan] on my conscience," she admitted.

Her avowals did not change her fate. Over the next hours, Filastre followed the standard, well-traveled route to her death: a confession in the prison's chapel, then to Notre-Dame for the *amende honorable*, with a final stop at the place de Grève. There, the executioner led the woman onto a hay-filled pyre, tied her to a chair on top of it, and lit the pyre with a torch.

Filastre's child had not been the only one to go missing. Under torture the poisoner Debray, an acquaintance of Guibourg, claimed that at least one of Jeanne Chanfrain's children had also disappeared under suspicious circumstances. Chanfrain, an aging prostitute whom Guibourg frequented for more than twenty years, later confirmed it was true when La Reynie interrogated her.

She had been pregnant seven times, she said, explaining that she had given birth to one child just outside the village of Montlhéry. Guibourg accompanied her and her newborn to the village, where she rested at the priest's home while he tended to the baby girl. When Chanfrain awoke, there was no sign of the child. Guibourg told her he had entrusted the baby to the care of an acquaintance, Monsieur Froquié, a local gardener. When she saw the man several weeks later, she inquired about her baby. He claimed that the infant had fallen ill and died five days after the birth, but he would not tell her where he had buried the baby's body. Suspicious, Chanfrain confronted Guibourg, asking what he knew. When the priest refused to answer, she screamed: "You killed my child!" The priest merely replied, "It is none of your business."

La Reynie shuddered at the thought of what likely happened to the baby. His concerns intensified after learning from Marie-

Marguerite that her mother and the midwife Lepère kept a side business selling powders and potions made from the placentas, intestines, and mangled limbs of babies they had either aborted or abducted. La Reynie also recalled Marie-Marguerite's story of the day her mother came in from the courtyard and shoved a newborn child into her hands. Marie-Marguerite put the child in a basket and waited for her mother to tell her what to do.

Later that evening Voisin instructed her daughter to come into the room where she and Guibourg held their masses. There, Marie-Marguerite said she saw a woman stretched out nude on a mattress, the same one she had seen them use for Mademoiselle des Oeillets. Chalice in hand, the elderly Guibourg hovered over the woman in his priestly robe, chanting.

Moments later the wild-eyed priest looked over at Marie-Marguerite, who lifted the newborn from the basket and brought it over to Guibourg. Handing the chalice to Voisin to hold, Guibourg took the child in one hand. Marie-Marguerite described how the priest reached into his cassock and pulled out a small knife with his other hand. Ignoring its cries, he swiftly cut open the child's neck. Marie-Marguerite's mother held the chalice under the baby, collecting its blood. They all watched dispassionately as the life drained from the child. In a hellish imitation of the Eucharist, he blessed the blood and dipped a host in it. Marie-Marguerite told La Reynie that "during the consecration, he said the King's name as well as that of Madame de Montespan."

In the wake of Filastre's trial, the police chief had been eager to deliver swift justice against this deadly cabal of poisoners, witches, and priests. Several days earlier La Reynie agreed to provide a redacted record to the court at Louvois's request. This last interrogation with Marie-Marguerite, however, made him change his mind.

La Reynie wrote to Louvois, voicing his hesitations about the best path forward. On one hand, the king had been right in his decision to suspend the court. "I am far from believing that we should allow the public to be aware of [the crimes]," he wrote. La Reynie worried that exposing "all of the horrors" would serve as an admission that the king could not control even his own mistresses, which could inspire even more crime among his subjects, who would begin to doubt the king's strength. On the other, abandoning his investigations did not seem be a viable option either. "If the course of justice is stopped, the majority of these wicked people will go unpunished," he worried. "The greatest cause of evil and excess comes from justice's failures."

Concluding his letter, La Reynie lamented, "My mind is confused.... I cannot pierce the thick darkness that surrounds me." He asked Louvois and the king for more time to continue his investigations, hoping that "God will help [me] make sense of this criminal abyss and will show me ways to find a way through it, as well as inspire the king to do everything that he must do at such an important time." The king agreed, urging La Reynie to do whatever he felt necessary.

31

"A Strange Agitation"

In order to gauge the truth behind Marie-Marguerite's horrific accusations, La Reynie made her repeat in front of Guibourg what she had told him about the child sacrifice. The old man stood quietly as he listened to Marie-Marguerite's story, interrupting only to make quiet grunts of agreement. When she was done, Guibourg told La Reynie that everything she had said was true. The only point up for debate between the two prisoners was who had eviscerated the child's body after the ceremony. Wishing to keep his robes from getting dirty, Guibourg claimed, he had had nothing to do with it. Marie-Marguerite countered, saying she had watched him do it. In the end Guibourg conceded he cut the child's heart open and put it into a crystal vase that Madame de Montespan took with her, after the priest had blessed it. Voisin later delivered the child's entrails, which Guibourg also blessed, to Lepère to be dried, powdered, and delivered later to the king's mistress.

When La Reynie pressed Guibourg to tell him how he knew the woman had been Montespan, the priest conceded he could not be sure it was her. The woman's hair covered her face at all times during the séances, he maintained. He only knew it was the king's mistress because it was what others had told him. Marie-Marguerite insisted it was Montespan. She knew because she had met her in person twice: once when she delivered powders to her during mass at a church near the Palais-Royal and again on the road to Versailles.

La Reynie knew he needed to hear the other side of the story if he had any hopes of uncovering the truth about Montespan. Interviewing her even informally was out of the question: She was still unaware of the charges against her. Approaching her too soon could put her on guard, or worse, make her desperate. The risk was too great.

Oeillets was a safer choice. She had left the court three years earlier, in 1677, after the king had made it clear he had no further need of her services as a sexual surrogate for Athénaïs. Out of the public eye, Oeillets could be questioned more discreetly. After discussing the matter with Louvois, the men conspired for the minister to arrange a meeting with the woman at his home in Paris.

La Reynie prepared a detailed memo for Louvois describing the approach he should take and the questions he should ask Oeillets, whom he referred to simply as "you know who." The police chief suggested that the minister should put Oeillets at ease by asking her how life had been since her departure from court. Midway through the conversation Louvois should catch her off guard by telling her that Voisin's daughter and others at Vincennes had accused her of buying powders from them, and then watch her reaction. "But it is critical," he warned, "not to say a word about the masses, the sacrifices, or other abominations." Doing so could put the investigation in jeopardy if Oeillets shared what they knew with anyone at court.

Two weeks later Louvois reported to La Reynie that he had met with Oeillets and that she showed "inconceivable steadfastness" in asserting her innocence. She had admitted to having passed Voisin's daughter on the street once during a visit to her mother, who also lived in the Montorgeuil neighborhood. Other than that, she vowed she never had any direct contact with the girl. To prove her innocence she challenged Louvois to take her to Vincennes so her accusers could have a look at her. Oeillets "swore on her life" that her accusers would not recognize her, provided they were not informed in advance who she was.

La Reynie met Louvois and Oeillets in a small room off the entry to the dungeon. They had the guards bring Marie-Marguerite, Lesage, and Guibourg down, one by one, from their cells. Both Lesage and Guibourg identified Oeillets immediately. However, Marie-Marguerite told Louvois and La Reynie she did not recognize the woman standing in front of her. Later she retracted what she said, telling La Reynie she knew very well who the woman was and had just felt uncomfortable saying her name aloud.

When Oeillets left the prison, she was terrified at the thought that she might soon be back. The next day she asked to meet again with Louvois at his home in Paris. She attempted to convince the minister that a marquise at court had a servant who resembled her "like two drops of water." Oeillets later reiterated her innocence in a letter to the minister, this time expanding her claims to suggest she had been the victim of a conspiracy. Of the twenty women who gravitated toward Montespan, she said, eighteen of them made no secret of their loathing for her. She would not put it past any one of them to send the marquise's servant to Voisin's home, pretending to be her. For that matter, she could think of a handful of other servants at court who also had long chestnut hair and were about her height and build. Louvois told La Reynie he did not believe Oeillets one bit.

Following Oeillets's visit to Vincennes and with Louvois, both the king and La Reynie struggled anew with the decision about what to do next. Louis ordered La Reynie to provide him with a report detailing who he believed was telling the truth and who was not, along with his personal recommendations.

The endeavor was enormous, given the mountain of documents before La Reynie. Undertaking the Sisyphean task, he began by grouping the interrogations chronologically by witness and by those whom they had accused, sorting them into piles that filled his desk, chairs, and every other surface in his study. Taking copious notes as he read and reread each one, La Reynie tried to make sense of the contradictory testimonies. On a regular basis he stopped and began moving his notes around like puzzle pieces on the floor, cross-referencing each claim in the hopes of knitting together even the smallest bit of truth.

As he reviewed his interrogations of Bosse, he noticed that on two different occasions the poisoner told him the king would do well to "exterminate" all those who dabbled in the business. By Bosse's estimate there were upwards of four hundred people helping Parisians of all walks of life make good on their murderous intentions. Vigoureux agreed with Bosse's assessment during a joint interrogation. Their count had not been off by much; by the time La Reynie was done, his own list of suspects totaled 442 people.

La Reynie tried to push forward, yet he despaired that the king was asking the impossible. On January 23, 1681, he began drafting a letter to Louvois explaining the difficulties he was facing. The letter did not come easily. His draft was full of crossed-out words and rewritten sentences. Eventually he settled on the following message: "I know that, as on the other occasions that I tried to [provide a summary], this was beyond my ability. Considering myself alone in the middle of 150 prisoners, all charged with extraordinary crimes…it is impossible to present all of the facts and to have them be understood in the most general of terms."

Reaching for a new piece of paper, he continued his letter. After he filled the page, he reread what he had written and then drew a long vertical line through the middle, crossing nearly everything out. La Reynie conceded in one of the few sentences that remained: "I can only admit my own weakness in trying to describe the state of these sad affairs." He then edited the sentence to say, "the state and the *consequences* of these sad affairs."

Three pages later, his hand aching, the police chief paused to turn each messy page over to review: "The number of crimes mentioned here stuns the mind…. Monsieur, this is as far as I am able to go. All the rest is outside of my abilities and depends solely on God's inspiration on the king for his glory and the public good." Ending his letter, La Reynie offered the only suggestion he could think to make: Reconvene the tribunal. Once again the king refused.

Over the course of the weeks that followed, La Reynie scribbled three questions onto a piece of paper: Was Montespan behind the *placet*? Was she part of the efforts to provide Fontanges with poisoned gloves? And what about the black masses, the child sacrifices, and the other sacrileges that Filastre, Guibourg, and Voisin's daughter described?

"It is difficult even to presume that these crimes are possible," he wrote. "They seem…so strange that I can hardly make myself consider them." Still, he forced himself to review the evidence once again, making note of all information that would support each question in the affirmative as well as in the negative. Filling sixty pages, La Reynie lamented: "It puts the mind in a strange agitation."

La Reynie consoled himself with the thought that the final decision of guilt did not reside in his hands alone. His responsibility was to present the facts and let others do with them what they would: "This same responsibility obliges me to ask God to continue to protect His Majesty and to show him what should be done with these conjectures for his glory, his safety, and for justice."

Having finally accepted that the king was not interested in reopening the tribunal, La Reynie devised the next-best strategy. Louis's "most faithful" advisers, Louvois and Colbert, could review the most incriminating documents and decide, in consultation with the king, whether the women were guilty. In effect La Reynie was proposing a secret court within a secret court.

This time the king agreed. Over the days that followed, La Reynie sifted through the piles of papers he had sorted months earlier, pulling out all references to Oeillets and Montespan. The records from Trianon and Filastre alone totaled nearly two hundred pages. By the time he was done, he had filled an enormous black leather box with manuscript records. To secure the sensitive documents, he locked the box, keeping the key. He then ordered Desgrez and his men to take it to the Château of Saint-Germain, with La Reynie sending the key by armed guards in a separate delivery. Louvois and Colbert took turns reviewing the documents over the months that followed.

From the first investigations, the king had made it clear that he preferred Louvois and La Reynie at the helm of the inquiries rather than Colbert. Though frustrated, Colbert largely kept his distance. However, after reviewing the accusations against Athénaïs, Colbert could not remain complacent. Montespan had recently become a member of his family by marriage: Her disgrace would also mean his own. The fact that his nemesis Louvois played a leading role in the process also made it all the more urgent that he intervene.

With the assistance of his legal adviser, Claude Duplessis, Colbert denounced the evidence against Athénaïs as "execrable calumnies." While he did not deny that Athénaïs likely did visit Voisin years earlier, it had been long before any "small jealous worries that her affection [for the king] produced in Madame de Montespan's mind." Colbert argued indignantly that the idea that Athénaïs would seek to kill the king was preposterous, given everything she would have stood to lose. "What! To believe there was a plot to poison her master, her benefactor, her king, a person that she loves more than life! To know that she would lose everything in losing him...! These are things that one cannot conceive of, and His Majesty knows Madame de Montespan deep in her soul and will never be convinced that she could be capable of such abominations."

Colbert took aim at Athénaïs's primary accusers. Morally corrupt, not a single one of them could be a reliable witness, he said. Focusing most especially on Voisin's daughter, Colbert insisted that everything she had said was a lie, made up as a way to avoid being put to death. This explained the inconsistencies in her stories and why she did not say anything until her mother was dead. Her mother would have exposed her as a liar.

The minister also chastised La Reynie and Louvois for the way they handled Oeillets's visit to Vincennes. They should have presented Oeillets with four or five other people. By bringing her in individually, it had been too easy for Lesage and Guibourg to guess whom they were about to meet, given what they had heard from other prisoners. Colbert was convinced that Voisin's daughter had never seen the woman, which is why she was unable to identify Oeillets.

In a cunning move, Colbert asked whether there could be a

witness more reliable than the monarch himself. "His Majesty...saw all of [Montespan's] behavior, knows her mind, everything she does all the time and in every occasion. [His] mind is so penetrating and all-knowing and [he] never noticed a single thing or had even the slightest suspicion." He urged the king to trust his God-given wisdom in this matter.

At Colbert's request, the lawyer Duplessis followed the minister's letter with an analysis of the legal basis for the special tribunal. Duplessis explained that while the original charge of the court was to try only crimes of poison, the scope of the tribunal had expanded to include a host of other crimes, including witchcraft. "This is contrary to the spirit of all [existing] ordinances...which regulate the jurisdictions and the powers of judges in criminal matters." Whether or not the continued existence of the court could be justified legally, Duplessis noted that the amount of time that accused prisoners had remained in jail also went against the spirit of the king's original ordinance, which stressed expediency as a reason for moving the cases out of the *parlement*. Walking a fine line, Duplessis added: "But, of course, all of this depends on the desires of the king."

To find a way out of the "embarrassment," Duplessis offered four suggestions. First, the king could disband the tribunal entirely and exile all those in prison or otherwise under suspicion. He dismissed this option immediately, saying, "The chamber would be terminated, but the Affair would not end." Some criminals, like Guibourg, were too dangerous to let back into the public. Moreover, their return to society could inspire more crime once they shared their stories of imprisonment.

A second option would be to disband the tribunal and return the cases to the *parlement*, which was not practical. It would be too much work for the judges to get caught up on all that had already taken place in regard to each case. The third possibility would be for the court to determine which of the inmates had committed the most egregious crimes and sentence them to life in prison. Duplessis explained that the disadvantage of this approach would be that it also did not bring closure to the Affair.

Finally, the king could remand all the inmates to the tribunal and sentence each swiftly, based on the extent of the accusations made against them to date, conducting no additional investigations. Under no circumstances should the Question be administered, in order to make sure no new accusations surfaced that would require investigation. Whatever the king decided to do, both Colbert and Duplessis recommended strongly that he destroy the contents of the black box given "all of the execrable impiety and abominable trash in [it], it is important that no memory of it remains."

Louis, Colbert, Louvois, and La Reynie met for four four-hour sessions to discuss next steps. It had been a long time since the rivals Colbert and Louvois had been forced to spend so much time together. For both men the stakes were high. Should Louis decide to continue the investigations and trials, it would be a sign of his confidence in Louvois. If the king took one of Duplessis's recommendations, he would reaffirm Colbert's role as head of the *parlement* and his control over legal matters more generally in Louis's administration.

Siding with Colbert, the king reopened the tribunal on May 18, 1681. He also ordered the black box containing all sensitive documents to be returned to La Reynie for safekeeping until further notice. The police chief resealed the box and entrusted it to Sagot, who stored it in his home just steps away from La Reynie's headquarters.

The tribunal reconvened on May 19, 1681. The court was instructed to try only those cases that could be disposed of easily without jeopardizing public safety. Working with redacted records, the judges remained unaware of accusations against Oeillets and Montespan. By the early spring of 1682, 88 of the 194 people who had been arrested had been tried. In the final days of the hearings, the court selected a handful of prisoners—most of whom were charged with relatively minor crimes and unknown to the public—for execution to serve as a lesson to those who might consider following in their path.

Once the docket was "cleared," Louis disbanded the tribunal

for good in May 1682 and ordered La Reynie to begin emptying Vincennes and the Bastille of their remaining prisoners arrested in the Affair. Of the 106 inmates remaining, La Reynie and Louvois determined that 61 were benign enough to be released and exiled for life from France. The remaining 35—including Lesage, Guibourg, and Marie-Marguerite—were too dangerous to be let out of sight.

On La Reynie and Louvois's recommendation, the king ordered them to be sent in clusters to far-flung citadels, castles, and work camps, where they would spend the rest of their lives in isolation. Voisin's best friend and business partner, Trianon, killed herself in prison before the transfer. Others may have later wished they had done the same.

Voisin's daughter, Marie-Marguerite, was taken with eleven other women, including Bosse's daughter, to an abandoned abbey on Belle-Isle-sur-Mer, a remote island off the coast of Brittany. Writing to the governor of the island, Louvois insisted that no one should ever know their names. The women should also be spared no mercy: "His Majesty orders you to...treat them very severely." Condemned to harsh labor on the desolate and windswept island, they struggled to survive on meager rations of bread and water. Clad in threadbare sack dresses and denied access to firewood or even blankets, two of the women died not long after their transfer. The fate of the others, including Marie-Marguerite, remains unknown.

Lesage, Guibourg, and Romani spent their final days in the citadel of Besançon, near the Swiss border, where their hands and feet were shackled together by chains just long enough to allow them to sleep uncomfortably on the floor. "[These men] have said crazy things about Madame de Montespan that are without foundation," Louvois informed the governor of the citadel. "Threaten them with the cruelest punishment if they dare make the smallest noise." Guibourg died four years later, in January 1686. The dates of Lesage's and Romani's deaths are lost to history.

32

Lock and Key

La Reynie's trusted notary Sagot died in the early fall of 1682, just months after the tribunal was disbanded. Immediately after hearing the news, the police chief sent Desgrez and his officers to place a seal on Sagot's study to protect the documents stored there until arrangements for a transfer could be made with the notary's successor, François Gaudion.

Shortly after Sagot's death, his widow arrived at the police chief's home, asking that the seals be removed. It was less a question of convenience and more one of financial urgency. Sagot had left his wife penniless, which meant she had no choice but to move from the home the couple rented on the rue Quincampoix, just a few houses down from La Reynie's. She begged La Reynie to arrange for the transportation of the mountains of documents and boxes that lingered at her home so she could transfer the lease.

A few days later Gaudion met La Reynie and Desgrez in front of Sagot's home. Madame Sagot escorted the group to her husband's study. The door was locked, the keyhole sealed with wax. After confirming that the wax had remained undisturbed, La Reynie ordered Desgrez to unlock the door.

Stepping into the room, La Reynie took a visual inventory. His eyes scanned the bookcases with shelves bowed under the weight of Sagot's letters and notes; his gaze moved across Sagot's desk, blackened with ink, and paused at the mantel of the chimney, where a number of spare quills lay. Finally he spotted the precious black box containing the king's secrets.

La Reynie instructed Desgrez to deliver the black box to Gaudion's home in the Marais, as well as the many other boxes and parcels in the home of the deceased notary. There were eighty-five boxes in all: twenty-nine from his study and another fifty-six from a room on the second floor. Each was wrapped tightly with cord, and a large mass of melted wax imprinted with La Reynie's official police seal encased the places where the cord had been cut and tied.

La Reynie made it clear to Gaudian that he was not to touch any of the materials unless the police chief was there. As for the black box, it was also off-limits. In any case La Reynie was the sole owner of the key needed to open it.

Several months later, La Reynie arrived at the new notary's home. Gaudion had been waiting for him. He led the police chief to what had once been servants' quarters on the fourth floor. The staircase was narrow, the ceilings low, and the rooms drafty and cold from the January air. La Reynie's only concern was whether there were any signs of human activity—past or potential—in or near the rooms. He saw nothing worrisome.

Repeating what he had done at Sagot's home, La Reynie looked around the space for the large box. With relief, he located it sitting inconspicuously in the corner of the room.

For his part Louis made it clear that the Crown considered the matter officially closed. "We do not speak at all of poison. The word is banned at Versailles and all of France," declared Madame de Sévigné. In July 1682 the king had issued an edict vowing to punish severely all "fortune-tellers, magicians, witches, and poisoners." In it he reflected publicly on the last three years: "We have employed all appropriate means possible to stop these detestable abominations in their track." This experience "showed us how dangerous it is to accept the smallest transgression regarding such crimes, and how difficult it is to pull out their roots."

The edict ordered anyone who persisted on engaging in fortune-telling or magic to leave the kingdom immediately. For those who did not heed his warning, the king promised that their punishment would be death. As for poisoners, it did not matter whether their crime killed their victim. Even in the absence of definitive evidence, all would-be poisoners would receive the death penalty. The king also outlawed the sale of any ingredient that could be used in poisonous mixtures, as well as the sale of any poisonous insects or reptiles, promising severe corporal punishment for those who refused to heed his orders. Formal approval would be required for formulations such as arsenic or mercury chloride, necessary ingredients for certain trades such as goldsmiths and jewelers. A royal register would track all such sales.

In 1682 Louis announced that Versailles would become his permanent home. The architect Mansard had almost finished the construction of the Hall of Mirrors and would soon leave it to the painter Le Brun to fill the ceilings with enormous murals lauding the king's triumphs, both at home and abroad: from the War of Devolution in 1667, in which Louis gained new territories for France in the Spanish Netherlands, to the lighting of Paris with La Reynie at the helm. Colbert died less than a year later from a bladder stone, after spending years coordinating the construction of the château and worrying about its exorbitant price tag. Louvois remained minister of war until his death in 1691.

In June 1683 Marie-Thérèse fell suddenly ill, the result of an abscess under her arm. When she died not long after, Louis's words of mourning were characteristic of the couple's unexciting life together: "This is the first trouble she has ever given me."

Following tradition, the king and close family members left the royal palace to mourn at the Château of Fontainebleau. Louis asked Madame de Maintenon to join them. When she hesitated, the duke of Rochefoucauld urged her to go. "This is not the time to leave the king," he said. "He needs you."

Three years older than Louis, she "was not young," wrote one court observer. "But she had lively and bright eyes [and] a bubbly spirit." While the increasingly devout Louis undoubtedly found her attractive, Maintenon believed that at their age piousness mattered more than passion. Whether he felt the weight of his age or the fatigue of spending the last two decades under the spell of Montespan, the king agreed. In a secret ceremony at Versailles in late October 1683, Louis and Françoise de Maintenon married.

Between her departure from court in 1677 and her death in 1687, Mademoiselle des Oeillets lived out her days comfortably in a large home not far from where her mother once lived in the Montorgeuil neighborhood. Athénaïs, too, continued with her life at court after the king's marriage, though at the margins. To make room for Louis's new wife, she was forced to move from her quarters near the king's to the ground floor of the palace. The king continued to visit her on a regular basis, but the chaste visits served only as a bitter reminder that nothing remained of the passion, the love, or even the friendship that the couple once shared.

After eight more years at Versailles, Montespan asked Father Bossuet, the same priest who had chastised her for her moral failings sixteen years earlier, to inform the king that she would be leaving Versailles for good. Louis made no effort to dissuade her. Instead he ordered his servants to remove all traces of his former mistress from the palace the minute she walked out the door.

Athénaïs stepped into her carriage and left Versailles for the last time in 1691. Several days later she arrived at the Abbey of Fontevrault in the Loire Valley, where her sister was abbess, and thereafter divided her time between the austere abbey and her country home in southwestern France. Though the home was modest, she sumptuously outfitted one room, christening it the "king's bedroom." Until the end of her days Athénaïs never lost hope that the king would someday return to her. He never did.

On the morning of May 28, 1707, as he prepared for a hunt in the royal forest of Marly, Louis was told of Athénaïs's death. Nodding in acknowledgment, the elderly Louis climbed into his carriage

and set off for the day with the usual crowd of nobles and courtiers following behind. Upon the group's return early that evening,
the king held a public dinner with Maintenon at his side. After the
meal he rose with his guests and headed toward the gardens. Waving everyone away, the king wandered alone among the carefully
tended hedges, trees, and parterres of late spring flowers until the
early hours of the morning.

As for La Reynie, the four long years he spent during the Affair of
the Poisons investigating the darkest facets of human nature had
taken a toll. As early as 1689, Colbert's successor, Pontchartrain,
argued that La Reynie should be replaced and that he was too old
and too "used up" to continue in his post. La Reynie offered his
resignation to the king without protest. Louis refused it, insisting
that La Reynie continue in his work.

Over the decades between the end of the Affair of the Poisons
and his death in 1709, La Reynie kept watch over the king's most
precious secrets. Long before his last breath, he arranged to have
the key to the black box and a letter delivered to the king on his
death. There would have been every justification for him to have
an elaborate funeral followed by a sepulcher burial inside a church,
given his long service to the king and his steadfast faith. Instead he
made sure in his will to specify that every effort be made to keep
his "rotting cadaver" from corrupting the air. La Reynie was buried in a simple grave just outside the walls of Paris, as attentive in
death to keeping his city clean as he had been in life.

Epilogue

The numbers are staggering: Between April 1679 and July 1682, the Arsenal tribunal met 210 times, questioned 442 people, put 218 of them in prison, executed 34, and sentenced another 28 to life in prison or the galleys.

We have La Reynie to thank for this final accounting. When Louis XIV burned the records of the Affair of the Poisons on that hot summer day in 1709, he hoped to keep one of the greatest scandals in French history from posterity. The very fact that I was able to write this book is a testament to the king's miscalculation.

Unknown to the king, the police chief kept a separate set of documents—more than eight hundred manuscript pages in all—containing his personal notes, summaries of interrogations, drafts of written reports, and even his personal to-do lists. In addition to La Reynie's writings, there are several thousand extant manuscripts of judicial records, police interrogations, signed confessions, death notices, inventories of seized property, drawings, doodles, astrological charts, magic spells, and poison recipes—all of relevance to the Affair of the Poisons.

How these documents survived is almost as fascinating as the story they tell. It begins nearly fifty years before that fateful day in front of the fireplace. In 1660, a few months before Louis began his personal reign, a small archive at the Bastille was created to house the ever-growing number of *lettres de cachet* and other documents related to the general administration of the prison and its inmates. It was located in a large room deep in the prison, just off a well-protected courtyard.

After Louis declared the end of the Affair of the Poisons in 1682, La Reynie placed the most incriminating records under seal, storing them at Sagot's and then Gaudion's homes. These were the documents that Louis destroyed twenty-six years later, following the police chief's death. Fortunately for historians, La Reynie did not include his personal notes in those boxes, keeping them instead at his home and headquarters on the rue de Bouloi.

In his will La Reynie entrusted all his papers and correspondence to his wife, Gabrielle de Garibal. It is likely that, as had Sagot's widow, Gabrielle kept the bulk of his belongings at the couple's Paris estate. When she died in 1714, La Reynie's successor, Marc René de Voyer de Paulmy d'Argenson, would have taken responsibility for them.

In 1716, the year following the king's death, his grandson Louis XV expanded the archive to include all police correspondence, notaries' papers, commissioners' reports, and administrative documents, as well as any personal papers found in the headquarters and private home of all lieutenants of police, past and future, at the time of their death. The edict came just two years before Argenson retired from his post in 1718, which suggests that concerns were brewing about the fate of confidential police records in anticipation of a leadership change. Located deep in one of France's most secure prisons and protected by two guards who stood watch at all times, the Bastille archive proved a most logical choice to store these sensitive documents.

Following Argenson's death in 1721, still more records flooded into the archive. In 1725 and 1755 the prison warden at Vincennes requested that all prisoner records be stored at the Bastille in order to free up more space for inmates. Ten years later Argenson's successor transferred all the documents, including those from the secret trials, to the Bastille from the Arsenal, which was slated for demolition.

By the 1770s, however, the Bastille archive had outgrown its space. In 1775 prison administrators began plans to enclose the courtyard to make room for a large library worthy of the Enlightenment. But any such thoughts of construction came to a halt July 14, 1789, when revolutionaries ransacked the prison and set it on fire, using bundled papers as kindling and tossing what remained into the dry moat surrounding the prison.

Once the violence quieted and the flames were extinguished, Hubert-Pascal Ameilhon, a prominent librarian and bibliophile, went to the Bastille to survey the damage. Fearing the worst as he made his way deep into the prison and toward the archive, he was relieved to find everything intact once he arrived. Only the documents stockpiled after 1775, the ones cluttering more accessible spaces, had been destroyed. Nearly everything before that, including the records from the Affair of the Poisons, had survived. Ameilhon placed them in the basement of the nearby Saint-Paul Church.

In 1799 Ameilhon was appointed director of the newly constructed Bibliothèque de l'Arsenal, built on the very same site where the Chambre Ardente held its secret trials. The librarian transferred the documents to the new library, where they sat for another forty years in the corner of an abandoned storage area until Ameilhon's successor, the lawyer-turned-librarian François Mollien-Ravaisson, rediscovered them.

Over the next thirty years Ravaisson undertook the massive task of sorting, cataloguing, binding, and transcribing the more than five hundred thousand manuscripts contained in the archive. He stopped working only once, shifting his focus from cataloguing to keeping both the archive and the Arsenal library safe from uprisings during the four-month siege of the Paris Commune in 1871.

Before his death in 1884, Ravaisson organized the manuscript collection into 2,271 bound volumes, each at least six inches thick. He also transcribed and published sixteen books, integrating selections from the archive with primary texts from other library collections. Four of the books focus specifically on the Affair of the Poisons and include excerpts from sixteen of the manuscript volumes (Archives de la Bastille, mss. 10338–10354). In 1892 the historian Frantz Funck-Brentano continued Ravaisson's work and published an inventory of the collection in 1892, without which it would be nearly impossible to make one's way at all through the massive Bastille collection.

Ravaisson's transcripts are invaluable to any researcher investigating the Affair of the Poisons. However, his volumes are in no way exhaustive and are, at times, riddled with mistakes. Especially unnerving is Ravaisson's tendency to truncate interrogations without noting that he has done so, or to leave out key documents altogether. As Funck-Bretano had no trouble pointing out, "Ravaisson was not a learned man by trade." For this reason I worked as much as I could with the original manuscripts from the Bastille archives. This was especially important in regard to La Reynie's personal notes, which Ravaisson cut and pasted to give a sense of coherence and clarity to the police chief's writings that undermines their actual complexity.

Over the course of the four years I spent researching this book, I often found myself identifying with La Reynie in his quixotic search for the truth. I had access to a corpus of primary documents that was so copious as to be at times overwhelming. Each eyewitness report, interrogation record, and torture "confession" corroborates or contradicts another document—or, frustratingly, does both at the same time. At one point I filled a long wall in my office with index cards secured by masking tape, which I moved around for hours at a time, much as La Reynie did with his own notes, trying to make sense of the testimonies and to create a timeline of events.

To retrace the paths of the prisoners, I made several trips to the Château of Vincennes. There I climbed the tower's cold and twisting staircases and counted the hours with each loud chime of the eleventh-century church outside. I spent months at the Arsenal library reading thick manuscript pages, my eyes straining to decipher the often illegible handwriting of magistrates, prison guards,

and notaries. Studying these volumes felt like being on an exhila-
rating treasure hunt, exploring pages with astrological drawings,
poison recipes, instructions for magic spells, appeals from desperate clients to the witches and poisoners, the shaky signatures of
frightened prisoners, and the doodles of bored scribes.

Then there were the times when history became all too real. I
will never forget the moment when I stumbled on the medical
report of Dodée's suicide, which I describe in chapter 25. Reading
the detailed and heart-wrenching description, I let out a gasp loud
enough to startle the librarian in the quiet reading room of the
Arsenal library. It gave me shivers when I realized that, just days
earlier, I had been in her cell. As I lingered in the tiny room to
study the graffiti that filled its walls, I had no idea that I was standing in the very spot where she had killed herself in desperation.

My book would have been impossible to write had it not been
for the work of the researchers who have gone before me: Pierre
Clément, Antonia Fraser, Arlette Lebigre, Lynn Mollenauer,
Georges Mongrédien, Jean-Christian Petitfils, Julia Prest, Jacques
Saint-Germain, and Anne Somerset, among others. These and
other scholars have not always agreed on the events, characters,
and motivations behind what was arguably the greatest social and
political scandal in early French history. I have indicated in the
notes where my interpretation of events differs from theirs, without
intending to diminish in any way the rigor and significance of
their work.

I share the belief of Somerset, Mollenauer, and Prest that we
will likely never be able to resolve with certainty all that took
place in the dark years between 1667 and 1682—particularly in
regard to extent of Athénaïs's participation in the horrific, almost
unimaginable, crimes of which she was accused. Taking a cue
from Natalie Zemon Davis's groundbreaking work *Fiction in the
Archives,* I have chosen, however, not to tell this story from the
goal of uncovering indisputable "truths." My sense is that no historian can provide a definitive account of a scandal so complex
using a historical corpus that is at once vast and dense, and yet so
oddly limited.

Still, there are a few things we *can* know with reasonable certainty. I share La Reynie's conviction that Montespan, like so
many of her contemporaries, employed Voisin and her colleagues
at least to some degree. In a letter to Louvois in 1680, La Reynie
affirmed his belief that Montespan was "in the hands of Voisin"
beginning in 1667. However, La Reynie could not be sure of the
exact nature of Voisin's contact with the king's mistress, particularly in later years (1671, 1673, 1675, 1676, and 1679). After much
research I am also confident that the events that I describe in parts
1 and 2 did take place as Marie-Marguerite witnessed them. I base
my trust on multiple sources of corroborating testimony by other
witnesses.

To facilitate my analysis of interrogations and other primary
texts, I coded the documents using qualitative data-analysis soft-
ware (NVivo). Coding allowed me to locate and place side-by-
side overlapping testimonies. From there I performed a second
level of coding to determine not only where accounts confirmed,
or deviated from, one another, but also where there were potential lexical and syntactic similarities. When in doubt, I also
looked for instances of self-incriminating testimony, with the
thought that few witnesses would offer details of their crimes if
they did not actually commit them, even if they embellished some
details in the telling. However, I did look skeptically at confessions made under torture. Filastre's post-torture retraction pro-
vides an excellent example of the perils of interpreting claims
made in these contexts.

Unlike La Reynie, I have a hard time indulging many of the
horrific claims made by Voisin's daughter, Lesage, and Guibourg
regarding Montespan's participation in child sacrifices and
attempts to kill the king. I am inclined to agree with Colbert and
Duplessis that Athénaïs had nothing to gain and everything to lose
if the king were to die, especially since her status was already in
peril at the time the worst of her alleged crimes happened. As
Antonia Fraser reminds us in her history of Louis XIV's loves,

Montespan herself once said in regard to her marital infidelities and other moral lapses: "Just because I commit one sin [that is, adultery] it does not mean that I commit them all."

From the first days of my research, I found Voisin's daughter Marie-Marguerite to be a fascinating enigma. My sense is that she was a troubled young woman, the product of a difficult childhood in which secrets, lies, and violence formed the fabric of her daily life. Yet I think it would be a mistake to see her only as a pathos-inspiring victim, which is what I did during much of my early research. When in the course of my research I learned that she admitted to La Reynie that she had given the infant to Guibourg for sacrifice, my sense of her character as a young woman shifted. In her own way I believe she proved herself to be as cruel and heartless as her mother.

As for Marie-Marguerite's father, it is both interesting and odd that La Reynie never interrogated Antoine, given the information that the man could have provided the police chief about the activities that took place. For as much as every moment of La Reynie's waking hours focused on rooting out the poisonous plots, this surprising show of restraint demonstrates that the rule of law tempered—in this moment, at least—his otherwise vigilant enthusiasm. In all of the interrogations he conducted, no one suggested that Voisin's husband was a willing participant in his wife's dark business. In the end, however, Antoine may actually have known too much. It is interesting to speculate that his death two months after his wife's arrest was not due to natural circumstances.

It also seems more than a coincidence that the worst of the accusations were made *after* Louvois's visit to Lesage in his prison cell and that, from this point forward, the stories of Lesage, Guibourg, Filastre, and Marie-Marguerite all align in remarkably similar ways. Nor does it seem just a coincidence that, around this time, Louvois and La Reynie began having great difficulties maintaining order in the prison.

To both La Reynie and Louvois's frustration, the warden Ferronnaye had done an abysmal job keeping the prisoners from communicating among themselves and with the outside world. The minister of war even heard complaints of Ferronnaye's children running unsupervised around the prison and spending time with the prisoners in their cells. "You must send your children back to school, or wherever you want, as long as they are out of Vincennes," Louvois ordered Ferronnaye. To ensure that the warden followed the orders, Louvois moved his own guards into the prison and demanded that Ferronnaye surrender the keys to the cells to them. With his own guards in place at the prison, Louvois could have communicated surreptitiously with the prisoners. Moreoever, these ex parte communications could very well have taken place without La Reynie's knowledge.

So much has been written about Louis XIV. Yet one question remains: Why would a monarch as unyielding in his personal and political life decide not to punish his mistresses for participating in the dark arts? To my mind the Affair of the Poisons demonstrates the extent to which the women in his life mattered to him, as well as the inconsistencies evident throughout his reign. If the king had truly considered Athénaïs guilty of the worst of the crimes, it is difficult to believe he would have let her remain at court for another ten years. For this reason I feel confident that the king's decision to end the affair for good following Colbert's refutation of the evidence against Montespan offers us as clear an explanation as we are going to find in regard to Louis's thoughts on the matter: The king simply chose to believe she was not guilty.

Both principled hero and cruel enforcer, La Reynie was undoubtedly extremely loyal to his king. He tried to impose order on a world of desperate passion and greedy access to power, making difficult choices along the way. Far from perfect, he was a singular man of his time. Even after living with the police chief for so many years, I still find him fascinating. I hope my readers do too.

Acknowledgments

This book could not have been written without the support and generosity of colleagues, friends, and family both in the US and abroad. I benefitted from the expertise of librarians at the Bibliothèque Nationale de France and Bibliothèque de l'Arsenal in Paris, the special collections of the Bibliothèque Méjanes in Aix-en-Provence, the Wellcome Library and British Library in London, the Huntington Library in San Marino, the Newberry Library in Chicago, and of course, our own Jean and Alexander Heard and Eskind Biomedical Libraries at Vanderbilt University. I am forever grateful to my daughter Audrey Hamilton for her understanding and encouragement during my many research trips away from home, as well as to Jon Hamilton for offering a loving hand during my absences. There is not a day that I look at my daughter, a talented artist in her own right, without awe and admiration.

I would like to thank the entire team at W. W. Norton for all of their hard work on this book. Angela von der Lippe saw the story's potential from the beginning. When Angela retired, Amy Cherry made her enthusiasm for this book and my work in general clear from the beginning and has been a steadfast partner throughout.

Few editors have such an uncanny ability to know how to encourage without indulging and when to push without discouraging. I have become a better writer for it. Thank you, Amy.

Remy Cawley worked patiently with me as we navigated copyedits, page proofs, and permissions across time zones. I also have Sue Llewellyn to thank for her excellent copyediting work on this book, as well as on the last. Nancy Palmquist and Susan Sanfrey heroically made sure all the necessary corrections and edits found their way into the finished pages, and Beth Steidle and Anna Oler guided the bound galleys and final books, respectively, through production. And *mille mercis* go out to Erin Sinesky Lovett, Louise Brockett, Meredith McGinnis, Steve Colca, Golda Radmacher, Yurina Ko, and the whole *macaron*-loving marketing and publicity team at W. W. Norton for helping get this book into readers' hands.

At Sanford J. Greenburger, there are also not enough ways to thank Faith Hamlin for her clear-eyed wisdom in all things publishing (and life) and also Ed Maxwell for all of his help.

Vanderbilt University provided much-appreciated resources in the form of a sabbatical and travel funding. From my earliest days at the university, Chancellor Nick Zeppos's enthusiastic support of my work has also helped keep me going. I thank as well my colleagues in the Department of French & Italian, the Center for Biomedical Ethics & Society, and the Robert Penn Warren Center for the Humanities. I am especially grateful to Joel Harrington and Dan Sharfstein for sharing their own writing journeys with me, as well as to Mona Frederick and the Warren Center Fellows Program on Public Scholarship in the Humanities (Marshall Eakin, Aimi Hamraie, Joel Harrington, Ifeoma Nwankwo, Laura Stein Pardo, Lynn Ramey, Dan Sharfstein, and Paul Stob). I am similarly fortunate to have been able to work with and learn from several fantastic undergraduate and graduate research assistants (Elizabeth D'Angelo, April Stevens, Jake Abell, Abby Broughton, Roxane Pajoul, Lindsey Kelt, and Raquelle Bostow).

Heartfelt gratitude goes out to Meredith Hindley, whose generosity and good sense mark every page of this book. The week we spent writing together on the Street at the End of the World (now the rue Léopold Bellan) and following Voisin's footsteps through Paris will forever remain precious to me. My friend and colleague Lynn Ramey has also contributed so much to my writing, career, and sanity over these many years. Sincere thanks also to Karen Abbott, Vanessa Beasley, Christine Jones, Eric Larsen, Cheryl Kreuger, Pamela Toler, Margaret Littman, Chris Gunter, Kayt Sukel, Helen Glew, Hannah Lewis-Bill, Erin Blakemore, Holly Dugan, Cindy Horton Doran, Jennifer Howard, Rebecca Noel, Robin Flincham, Laura Laing, and Anne Boyd-Rioux—as well as the posse of wickedly smart and raucously boisterous science writers who adopted this history writer into their fold: Simon Frantz, Alok Jha, Maryn McKenna, David Dobbs, Jennifer Ouellette, Ed Yong, and Deborah Blum.

My apologies, and great thanks, go out to friends and colleagues who suffered through early versions of the manuscript: Steve Wylie, Joel Harrington, Meredith Hindley, Vanessa Beasley, Lynn Ramey, Faith Beasley, Joyce Wiggington, and my mother, Carolyn Tucker. Thanks again, Mom, for sending the lucky bamboo plant with the note from "Nick" telling me to get busy and finish his story. And Dad, you mean the world to me too. I feel indeed lucky to have both of you on my side.

Through it all, I've been supported and loved by dear friends both in Nashville and Aix-en-Provence: Martine Giumelli-Solet, Sandrine Philippon, Mike Rodgers, Harold Solet, Magali and Jean-Christophe Stratigéas, Colette and Gilbert Gailliègue, Todd Peterson, Roberta Bell, Lauren Schmitzer, Larry Taylor, Hunter Kay, and Karen Brown. You are more than friends, you are family. *Je vous aime tous.*

Finally, to Steve Wylie, my Southern Gentleman: you had me at waffles. There are no words to describe all that you, Audrey, Emma, and the whole Tucker-Wylie family mean to me. What a beautiful adventure this is.

Affair of the Poisons:
A Chronology

1665
August 24: Murder of Jacques Tardieu, criminal lieutenant of Paris.

1666
September 7: Death of Dreux d'Aubray, civil lieutenant of Paris.

1667
March 20: Nicolas de La Reynie appointed lieutenant general of Police.
June: Louis XIV visits the front with his wife, Marie-Thérèse; brother Philippe; sister-in-law. Henrietta Anne; Louise de La Vallière, and Athénaïs de Montespan.

1670
May 20: Nicolas de La Reynie witnesses and certifies production of theriac, an antidote against poison.
June 17: Antoine d'Aubray, civil lieutenant of Paris, dies of poison.
June 29: Henrietta Anne, Louis XIV's sister-in-law, dies.
September: François d'Aubray dies of poison.

1672
January: Gaudin de Sainte-Croix found dead.
September 4: Jean Hamelin, dit La Chaussée, arrested.

1673
March 3: La Chaussée executed; Marie-Madeleine de Brinvilliers tried in absentia.

1676
March 26: Arrest and trial of Marie-Madeleine de Brinvilliers.
July 17: Marie-Madeleine de Brinvilliers executed.

1677
Mid- to-end January: Madeleine de La Grange arrested.

1678
End September: Anonymous letter found in a church.
Early December: Dinner party hosted by Marie Vigoureux.

1679
January 4: Marie Bosse and Marie Vigoureux arrested.
February 8: Madeleine de La Grange and the Abbé Nail, *dit* Launay, executed.
March 1: Madame Philbert arrested.
March 12: Catherine Voisin arrested.
March 22: Adam Coeuret, *dit* Lesage, arrested.
April 7: King creates secret tribunal (Chambre Ardente).
April 9: Marguerite Leféron arrested.
April 11: Françoise de Dreux arrested.
May 9: Marie Vigoureux dies during the Question.
May 10: Marie Bosse executed.
June: Marguerite de Poulaillon tried in Chambre Ardente.
June 17: Anne Chéron executed.
September 16: Dodée commits suicide.
September: Lesage implicates Athénaïs de Montespan.
November 19: La Devineresse (The Fortune-Teller) at the Hôtel Guégénaud Theater.

1680
January 20: Marie-Marguerite Voisin arrested.
February 22: Catherine Voisin executed.
March 28: Marie-Marguerite Voisin implicates Claude de Vin des Oeillets.
June 23: Etienne Guibourg arrested.
August 20: Marie-Marguerite implicates Montespan.
September 30: Chambre Ardente suspended.
November 22: Claude de Vin des Oeillets questioned by Louvois.

1681
May 19: Chambre Ardente reconvenes.
June 28: Angélique de Fontanges dies.

1682

   May 1682: King dissolves Chambre Ardente, begins releasing prisoners, requests list of prisoners who are too dangerous to be released.

1709

   June 14: La Reynie dies.
   June 15: King receives letter from La Reynie.
   Mid-July: King burns documents related to the Affair of the Poisons.

Notes

Unless otherwise indicated, La Reynie's correspondence and interrogations are drawn from the Archives de la Bastille (Bibliothèque de l'Arsenal, mss. 10338–10354) and his personal notes (BNF, mss. *français* 7608). Where there are substantial differences between the manuscript original and Ravaisson's transcription (*Archives de la Bastille*, vols. 4–7), I cite both texts. Where there is no reference to Ravaisson, which occurs most often in the case of BNF, mss. *français* 7608, the text is not included among the Archives de la Bastille transcription references.

xvii **A Note on Currency:** For equivalences see A. N. Hamscher, *The Royal Financial Administration and the Prosecution of Crime in France, 1670–1789* (Newark: University of Delaware Press, copublished with Lanham, MD: Rowman and Littlefield, 2012), xv; and George S. Cuhaj and Thomas Michael, *Standard Catalog of World Gold Coins*, 6th Ed. (Wisconsin: Krause Publications, 2009), 712. Period prices from Jacques Saint-Germain, *La Reynie et la police au grand siècle d'après de nombreux doucuments inédits* (Paris: Hachette, 1962), 49, 62, 127–128, 203, 207; and François Ravaisson-Mollien, *Archives de la Bastille*, Vols. 4–7 (Paris: A. Durand et Pedone-Lauriel, 1870), 5: 165, 217, 225, 241, 468 and 6: 194.

Burn Notice

xx **never to trust:** P. Visconti, *Mémoires sur la cour de Louis XIV, 1673–1681*, ed. Jean-François Solnon (Paris: Perrin, 1988), 73. As one contemporary observer noted, all it took was for "the king to open his mouth and

speak about someone" and, depending on his tone, the person would forever be seen as "a saint or avoided like a soul damned."
xx **more dynamic officer:** Marc-René de Voyer de Paulmy d'Argenson succeeded Nicolas de La Reynie as lieutenant criminel de police in 1697. He
was forty-five years old; La Reynie was seventy-two.
xxi **constant traffic:** T. Spawforth, *Versailles: A Biography of a Palace* (New
York: Macmillan, 2010), 110.
xxii **support and confidence:** Versailles: *La Galérie des Glaces, Catalogue
Iconographique,* http://www.galeriedesglaces-versailles.fr/html/11/collection/
c29.html, accessed May 1, 2016.

CHAPTER 1
Crime Capital of the World

3 **soaked into the earth:** *France Observed in the Seventeenth Century by
British Travellers* Stocksfield, England: Oriel Press, 1985, 54. "Paris is
always dirty," a British visitor observed. "By perpetual motion dirt is
beaten into such a thick black unctuous oil, that where it sticks, no art can
wash it off."
4 **"to kill the living":** "A world of coaches, carts, and horses of sorts go to and
fro perpetually, so that sometimes one shall meet with a stop half a mile
long of those coaches, carts, and horses [and] can move neither forward nor
backward," ibid., 54; C. Jones, *Paris: The Biography of a City* (New York:
Penguin, 2006), 168; quote from Jean-Paul Marana, cited in Eric Le
Nabour, *La Reynie: Le policier de Louis XIV* (Paris: Perrin, 1990), 22.
4 **leaving him dead:** L. Bernard, *The Emerging City: Paris in the Age of
Louis XIV* (Durham, NC: Duke University Press, 1970), 159; on the murder of the watchmaker, see J. Saint-Germain, *La Reynie*, 98.
4 **making the city all the more unsafe:** S. Carroll, *Blood and Violence in
Early Modern France* (Oxford, England: Oxford University Press, 2006),
138.
5 **few followed this mandate either:** For discussion on the size of daggers and
bayonets, see BNF, *mss. français*, 16847, fols. 10–11; for ordinances
against carrying pistols, see fol. 14; A. P. Trout, *City on the Seine: Paris in
the Time of Richelieu and Louis XIV* (New York: St. Martin's Press,
1996), 173–174.
5 **kept a knife at her bedside precisely for that task:** On Madame Surqualin,
see Saint-Germain, *La Reynie*, 98.
5 **pick a fight:** A. Hussey, *Paris: The Secret History* (New York: Bloomsbury
Publishing, 2010), 163.
6 **worked as apprentices to a woodcarver:** J. D. Melish, "Order and the People: Men, Women, and the Courts in Control of Male Public Violence in a
Parisian Faubourg under Louis XIV" (Ph.D. Diss., University of Michigan, 2005), 4, 55–76.
6 **nearly three-quarters of a day's pay:** Ibid., 59.
6 **that a duchess paid for similar services:** Melish, 61.
7 **"Day and night they kill here":** G. Patin, *Lettres choisies du feu Mr. Guy
Patin.* (Paris: Chez Jean Petit, 1692).
7 **from the violent world outside:** For more on the Tardieu murders, see A.

Lebigue, *Les Dangers de Paris au XVIIe siècle: L'Assassinat de Jacques Tardieu, Lieutenant Criminel au Châtelet de sa femme, 24 août 1665* (Paris: Albin Michel, 1991), and P. F. Riley, *A Lust for Virtue: Louis XIV's Attack on Sin in Seventeenth-Century France* (Westport, CT: Greenwood Press, 2011), 16–17.

8 **crumpled to the floor:** Riley, *Lust for Virtue*, 16–17.

9 **filled the large dining room:** J. Saint-Germain, *Madame de Brinvilliers, La Marquise aux poisons* (Paris: Hachette, 1971), 14.

10 **until he could find a more profitable pursuit:** *A Narrative of the Process Against Madam Brinvilliers and Her Condemnation and Execution, for Having Poisoned Her Father and Two Brothers* (London: Jonathan Edwyn, 1676), 3.

10 **to live her life exactly as she wished:** The marquis would later flee the country in an attempt to hide from his creditors; E. Pirot, *Relation des vingt-quatre dernières heures de la vie de Marie-Madeleine d'Aubray, Marquise de Brinvilliers*, ed. G. Rouillier (Paris: Robert Laffont, 1883), 4.

11 **"yours with all my heart":** Saint-Germain, *Brinvilliers*, 36.

11 **never to be heard from again:** E. Dutray-Lecoin and A. Fargette, "Le désordre social et politique, la main du roi s'y oppose," *La Bastille, ou, l'enfer des vivants: À travers les archives de la Bastille* (Paris: Bibliothèque Nationale de France, 2010), 86.

11 **"made to disappear":** F. Funck-Brentano, *Les Lettres de Cachet* (Paris: Libraire Hachette, 1926), xxii, 15–18. Louis XIV made ample use of *lettres de cachet*. Between 1661 and 1715 (the years of his reign) Louis sent 2,309 people to the Bastille on his signature alone; this does not include other *lettres de cachet* ordering others into exile, convents, or hard labor in the colonies.

13 **"strange heat in his entrails":** *Mémoire du procès extraordinaire d'entre Dame Thérèse Mangot, veuve de feu Messire Antoine Daubray, vivant lieutenant civil, demanderesse, accusatrice et appellante, d'une sentence du present mois de mars. Contre le nommé La Chaussée, prisonnier ès prisons de la conciergerie. et la Dame De Brinvilliers, absente et fugitive* (Paris: n.p., 1672), 84.

13 **divided his assets among his daughter and her two brothers:** For reasons that are not clear, d'Aubray did not include his other daughter—about whom we know very little—in his will; F. Funck-Brentano, *Le Drame des poisons* (Paris: Hachette, 1902), 79.

13 **"in such extreme peril":** D'Aubray d'Offemont to Colbert, 10 September 1666, F. Ravaisson, *Archives de la Bastille* (4: 9).

13 **d'Aubray was dead:** G. Patin, "M. d'Aubray d'Offemont à Colbert," 10 September 1666 (4: 10).

13 **could not be capable of poisoning her own father:** "Mémoire de M. de la Reynie," n.d. (6: 396).

14 **an illness he had battled several years earlier:** *Factum en forme de requête pour Damoiselle Angélique Domaigné et le Sieur Baron de Divette son beau-père, accusés de l'empoisonnement, autres crimes* (Paris: Veuve Dupont, 1681), 58. Danjou, 79.

CHAPTER 2
City of Light

16 every aspect of French political, economic, and social life: See J. Soll, *The Information Master: Jean-Baptiste Colbert's Secret State Intelligence System*, (Ann Arbor: University of Michigan Press, 2009).

16 "too much trouble reading them": Ibid., 78.

16 rather than social, political, or economic advantage: Saint-Germain, *La Reynie*, 21.

18 "if this is agreeable to you": October 4, 1665, BNF, *Mélanges de Colbert*, 132, fol 188, cited in Saint-Germain, *La Reynie*, 24.

18 quiet seriousness: The marquis de Sourches described La Reynie as having "much intellect... he spoke little and had an air of seriousness"; see P. Clément, *La police de Paris sous Louis XIV* (Paris: Didier et Cie, 1866), 68.

18 "what was causing its disorders": Saint-Germain, *La Reynie*, 15.

18 Châtelet complex: While La Reynie's headquarters were at the Châtelet, he worked often in his sprawling estate on the rue du Bouloi, north of the Louvre, near Les Halles, Nabour, 60.

18 "the threats of your courtiers": P. J. Stead, *The Police of France* (New York: Macmillan, 1983), 15.

19 no "better man or a more hardworking magistrate" for the job: A. Somerset, *The Affair of the Poisons: Murder, Infanticide, and Satanism at the Court of Louis XIV* (New York: St. Martin's Press, 2004), 126.

19 "establish law and order in Paris": La Reynie to Séguier, June 24, 1667 in Clément, *Police*, 68–69.

21 "as it was in the countryside": A. Franklin, *Estat, noms et nombre de toutes les rues de Paris en 1636, d'après le manuscrit inédit de la bibliothèque nationale; précédés d'une étude sur la voirie et l'hygiène publique à Paris depuis le XIIe Siècle*, Vol. 10 (Paris: Éditions de Paris, 1988), 129.

21 in the well-populated halls of the Louvre: A. Williams, "Domestic Espionage and the Myth of Police Omniscience in Eighteenth-Century Paris," *Consortium on Revolutionary France 1750–1850: Proceedings* 7 (1979), 57.

21 "in order to rid their box of the unpleasant smell": Maland, 247.

21 "the streets are so clean now": Saint-Germain, *La Reynie*, 74.

22 "each person in the quarter shall contribute": Edict, 1 September 1667, in Delamare, Administration de la Police, fol 153. Edict, 1 Septembre 1667 in Delamare, *Collection formé par Nicolas Delamare sur l'administration de la police de Paris et de France*, BNF, mss. français 21740.

23 in their Sunday sermons: P. F. Riley, "Hard Times, Police and the Making of Public Policy in the Paris of Louis XIV," *Historical Reflections/Réflexions Historiques* 10, no. 2 (1983).

23 the majority of Paris's streets: W. Schivelbusch, "The Policing of Street Lighting," *Yale French Studies* 73 (1987): 61, see also E. Defrance, *Histoire de l'éclairage des rues de Paris* (Paris: Imprimerie Nationale, 1904), 37.

23 whips, canes, and swords: A-P. Herlaut, *L'éclairage des rues à Paris à la fin du XVIIe et au XVIIIe Siècles* (Paris: P. Renouard, 1916), 226.

23 "almost as light as daytime": J. Dejean, *How Paris Became Paris: The*

Invention of the Modern City (New York: Bloomsbury, 2014), 137. Cottelet was writing in 1671.

24 **"an opportunity to repent":** La Reynie to Colbert, 19 November, 1671 in Clement, *Police*, 428.

25 **hospitals, public charities, and orphanages:** Saint-Germain, *La Reynie* 92, 95. Riley, *Lust for Virtue*, 42–43.

25 **the streets are much less muddy:** The author of the letter was the musician Charles Coypeau d'Assoucy; cited in Defrance, 42.

25 **"eternalize his memory":** *Mercure Galant*, April 23, 1672, 280.

25 **"Security and Clarity of the City 1669":** Defrance, 38.

CHAPTER 3
The Street at the End of the World

27 **Court of Miracles:** H. Sauval and C. B. Rousseau, *Histoire et recherches des antiquités de la ville de Paris* (Paris: Charles Moette, 1733), 513–514.

27 **"without any miracles":** Ibid.

27 **"Stop thief!":** Ibid, 513.

28 **life and death:** R. Briggs, *Witches and Neighbors: The Social and Cultural Context of European Witchcraft* (New York: Penguin, 1988), 69.

28 **among household remedy manuals:** A good example of a standard *grimoire* is the one found among Voisin's belongings at the time of her arrest. "Secrets véritables et éprouvés en premier lieu pour le mariage," Archives de la Bastille, ms. 10355, fol. 365.

29 **"you, Madame, are a marquise":** S. Mechior-Bonnet and A. de Tocqueville, *Histoire de l'adultère* (Paris: Éditions de la Martinière, 2000), 13.

29 **known for removing red marks and sunspots:** Confrontation between Marguerite de Henard and Voisin, n.d. (Ravaisson, 5: 370); see also Mongrédien, *La Vie Quotidienne sous Louis XIV*, for preparations used in daily life that we would now consider odd or superstitious.

29 **aphrodisiac properties:** M, Wilson, *Poison's Dark Works in Renaissance England* (Lewisburg, PA: Bucknell University Press, 2013), 189-190. The remnants of the amniotic sac of newborn foals, called "hippomane," were similarly prized for their love-inspiring properties.

30 **a love powder:** "M. de la Reynie à M. de Louvois," 1680 (4: 14).

30 **"causes titillation and delight":** J. Marten, *A Treatise of the Venereal Diseases*, 1711: 91.

30 **after swallowing a mixture of ground cantharis and nettles:** Amboise Paré, *Oeuvres complètes* (Paris: J-B Baillère, 1841), vol. 3, 326–329.

30 **"corroded and burnt parts of humors":** Ibid.

31 **"who had gotten herself into trouble":** Frances Mossiker, *The Affair of the Poisons: Louis XIV, Madame de Montespan, and One of History's Great Unsolved Mysteries* (New York: Knopf, 1969), 177.

31 **more than 2,500 aborted children:** Vautier interrogation, 2 November 1679 (6: 37).

32 **"You'll see soon enough if you are with child":** Interrogation of Voisin's daughter, 28 March 1680 (6: 198).

32 **her next meal or glass of wine:** For an inventory of items found in Lepère's home, see Archives de la Bastille, ms. 10342, fols. 78–87.

32 a resounding yes: Interrogation of Voisin's daughter, 28 March 1680 (6: 198).
32 injected into the woman's uterus: Lepère interrogation, 27 May 1679 (5: 379–380).
32 "wonderful for the womb": J. Riddle, Contraception and Abortion from the Ancient World to the Renaissance (Cambridge, MA: Harvard University Press, 1992), 140.
32 the Church condemned: T. R. Forbes, The Midwife and the Witch (New Haven: Yale University Press, 1966), 118.
33 baptizing the aborted fetuses: Lepère interrogation, 27 May 1679 (5: 380). Voisin and Lepère confrontation, 15 June 1679 (5: 406); on midwifery and witchcraft, see Malleus Maleficarum; Forbes; and H. Tucker, Pregnant Fictions: Childbirth and the Fairy Tale in Early-Modern France (Detroit, MI: Wayne State University Press, 2003) 55–75.
34 performed abortions: Descriptions based on Lesage interrogation, 15 July 1680 (6: 249–250); Interrogation of Voisin's daughter, 13 August 1680 (6: 288–289); details of the preparation of the toad poison provided by Voisin, in reference to Bosse ("Procès-Verbal of the Voisin Question," 19 February 1680, 6: 150–151). There is every reason to believe that the two women used the same or similar methods. Voisin makes frequent reference to toad poison in interrogations.
34 rinsed between uses: Chéron interrogation, 27 March 1679 (5: 300).
34 ready for their next customer: Lesage interrogation, 5 July 1680; see also ibid., 15 July 1680. Ravaisson (6: 249); interrogation of Voisin's daughter, 13 August 1680 (6: 289).

CHAPTER 4
To Market

This chapter is based on those portions of Marie-Marguerite Voisin's testimony that are sufficiently confirmed in La Reynie's interrogations of other suspects; see 4: 198, 6: 120, 165–166, 194–198, 294, 298.

35 coin clutched tightly in her fist: Interrogation of the Daughter Voisin, 28 March 1680 (6: 194).
36 red wig and a gray cape: Vigoureux interrogation, 18 February 1679 (5: 215). Vigoureux testified that Lesage wore a gray bouracan; these were cloaks made of goat hair or, less commonly, of camel hair.
37 burned that one in the fire: Vigoureux interrogation, 18 February 1679 (5: 215).
38 preparing for Holy Communion: Lesage places this episode at the end of 1667 or the beginning of 1668; that is, after the king and Montespan became lovers, Lesage interrogation, 15 November 1680 (6: 356–366); BNF, mss. français 7608, fols. 269–271.
38 same blessing as the host and the wine: Lesage interrogation, 15 November 1680. (6: 357).
39 "Indubitably," he added: Ibid.
39 a few months later: Interrogation of Mariette at Châtelet, June 30, 1668

(4: 11); interrogation of Lesage and Mariette at Tournelle, September 26, 1668 (4: 11–13); La Reynie to Louvois, 1680 (4: 13–15); draft of letter, La Reynie to Louvois, n.d. (6: 372–374).

40 **"I don't believe it"**: Guy Patin, cited in Ravaisson, 4: 11.

CHAPTER 5
Agitation without Disorder

43 **more than thirty thousand horses**: Standen, 189; *Mémoires de Coligny*, 123-124, cited in C. Rousset, *Histoire De Louvois et de son administration politique et militaire* (Paris: Didier et cie, 1863), 105.

43 **"the pomp that accompanies the king on this trip"**: Bussy-Rabutin to the Comte de Coligny, *Mémoires de Coligny* 123–124, cited in C. Rousset, *Histoire de Louvois et de son administration politique et militaire* (Paris: Didier et cie, 1863), 105.

45 **"peace as a dowry"**: A. Fraser, *Love and Louis XIV: The Women in the Life of the Sun King* (New York: Anchor Books, 2007), 54.

45 **"round all over"**: Visconti, 161.

46 **"people who get along"**: Renee, *Les Nièces de Mazarin*, 177.

46 **pairing for a king**: *Mémoires de Madame de Motteville*, ed. M. Petitot, 34: 367; See Renée, 179.

47 **"easy to love"**: Fraser, 59.

47 **a royal child would soon be on its way**: Ibid., 62.

48 **awkward young girl**: N. N. Barker, *Brother to the Sun King: Philippe, Duke of Orléans* (Baltimore: Johns Hopkins University Press, 1988), 74.

48 **failed to "entertain" his new wife**: Ibid., 79.

48 **"find themselves with her [*chez elle*]"**: Marie-Madeleine Pioche de la Vergne La Fayette, *Histoire d'Henriette d'Angleterre* (Paris: Charavay Frères, 1882), 40.

48 **"something about her that made one love her"**: Fraser, 65.

48 **"the arbiter of all that is delightful"**: Ibid.

49 **filled the air**: La Fayette, 43.

CHAPTER 6
The Dew and the Torrent

50 **"Greek statue"**: C. Saint-André, *Henriette D'Angleterre et la Cour de Louis XIV* (Paris: Plon, 1933), 59.

50 **among court insiders**: Fraser, 113.

51 **sister-in-law's home**: He was joined by Marie-Thérèse, his wife; Philippe and Henrietta Anne's eldest daughter, Anne Marie Louise (Mademoiselle); and the countess of Soissons.

51 **graceful tomboy**: Fraser, 73.

51 **"as if you were saying yes"**: A. Houssay, *Mademoiselle de La Vallière et Madame de Montespan: Études historiques sur la cour de Louis XIV* (Paris: Henri Plon, 1860), 29.

51 **for her sins**: Madame de Sévigné described her appreciatively as a "little

violet hiding under the grass, who was embarrassed to be a mistress, to be a mother, to be a duchess; never will there be another like her," September 1, 1680. Sévigné (2: 1066).

53 "but I myself am not interested": Fraser, 109.

53 not to count on ever seeing one *denier*: J. Lemoine and A. Lichtenberger, *De La Vallière à Montespan* (Paris: Calmann-Lévy, 1902), 137–138.

54 most precious and expensive pair of earrings: Ibid., 147–148.

54 "present myself in front of the queen": J. Lair, *Louise de La Vallière et la jeunesse de Louis XIV d'après des documents inédits, avec de nouveaux portraits, plans, documents et notes* (Paris: Plon-Nourrit, 1902), 199.

54 "as much wit or beauty as she does": Madame de Chartier, cited in Phelps, 448.

54 carriage ride alone: Saint-Maurice, 31.

54 trumping the Dew: See Sévigné 1: 342, 1: 665–666, 2: 342–343, 3: 304.

CHAPTER 7
The Door Marked 1

55 silk-upholstered beds and chairs: Saint-Maurice, 71.

55 in the royal tents: Clément, *Montespan*, 44.

56 "will serve as her closet": Rousset 1: 311, n. 2.

56 "as much to complain about": Lair, 172.

56 "slept all day long": Petitfils, *Montespan*, 41.

56 his lover, Madame de Montespan: Montpensier, 4: 55, cited in Lair, 202–203.

57 "I am prudent": Ibid., 52, cited in ibid., 204.

57 in her quarters: Ibid., 62.

58 end of the Allée Royale: P. de Nolhac, *Histoire du château de Versailles: Versailles sous Louis XIV*, vol. 2 (Paris: Chez Émile-Paul, 1911), 64.

58 rustic wooden roller coaster: Ibid., 61.

58 "measured by Versailles": Cited in R. W. Berger, "The Chronology of the Envelope of Versailles," *Architectura* 10, no. 2 (1980): 117. Scholars debate whether the letter was written in 1663 or 1665; regardless of the date, it is a plea that Colbert made with each phase of Versailles construction.

59 king's relationship with Madame de Montespan: Details of the party are drawn from Félibien, the programs distributed to guests, and accounts by Scudéry and Sévigné, as well as Nolhac's *Histoire du Château de Versailles*.

60 in his city of light: See Le Blant "Notes," 441–465. The couple had two children, Gabriel-Jean Nicolas and Gabrielle Nicolas.

60 the king was in love: Bluche, 190.

CHAPTER 8
"He Will...Strangle Me"

61 "spoil" the king with it: Petitfils, *Montespan* 56, quoting Saint-Simon and Madame Dunoyer.

62 in a gesture of mourning: Petitfils, *Montespan*, 59; Clément, *Montespan*,

15. While some historians have doubted whether this actually occurred, given Montespan's eccentricities and passionate outbursts, it is not unlikely. In the summer of 1669, Monsieur de Montespan's indignation once again attracted the attention of the Crown. The company of guards for which Montespan served as captain assaulted a visiting dignitary in the small southern village of Roussillon. When word of the confrontation reached Louvois, he resolved that it was time for the Crown to be done with Montespan once and for all. Louvois wrote to the judge reviewing the case that he must "attempt, in one way or another, to implicate Montespan so that he can be charged without suspicion." Louvois concluded his letter: "You can guess the reason for it" (cited in Lair, 274). Charged with insubordination, Montespan fled to Spain immediately afterward.

62 "L'Innocente": Montespan had seven children in all with the king; each time she wore a *robe battante,* the court knew she was pregnant, Franklin, 15: 240.

64 "his court in shame": Cited in Barker, 106.

64 "share in his disgrace": Montpensier, 8: 250, translation in M. A. E. Green, *Lives of the Princesses of England: From the Norman Conquest,* vol. 6 (London: Longman, Brown, Green, Longman & Roberts, 1854), 531.

65 "while saying that he missed me": La Fayette, *Histoire d'Henriette d'Angleterre,* 119.

CHAPTER 9
The Golden Viper

69 their pharmacological uses: Recounted by Charas in *Nouvelles expériences sur la vipère,* 63–75.

70 snake flesh: A trace amount of dried snake flesh was key to the preparation of theriac. Believing in the idea that like-cures-like (*simila similibus curantur*), doctors and apothecaries also recommended small amounts of theriac—and the toxins it contained—as a preventive measure to reduce the effects of an eventual poisoning (Nockels Fabbri, 252).

70 "so quickly and efficiently": Ibid., 70.

72 highest quality possible: Ibid., 8.

72 "best pharmaceutical rules": "Certificat de Messieurs les Docteurs de la Faculté de Medecine de Paris" 10–12.

CHAPTER 10
"Madame Is Dying, Madame Is Dead!"

This chapter draws from Madame de La Fayette's *Histoire de Madame Henriette d'Angleterre,* contemporary correspondence (4: 23–47), memoirs (*Mémoires de Madame de Montpensier, Journal d'Olivier Ormesson*), references by Bossuet and Primi Visconti, and a number of biographies (Baillon, *Henriette-*

Anne d'Angleterre, Duchesse d'Orléans, sa vie et sa correspondence; Nancy Barker, *Brother to the Sun King: Philippe, Duke d'Orléans;* Jacqueline Duchêne, *Henriette d'Angleterre, duchesse d'Orléans;* Mary-Anne Everett Green, *Lives of the Princesses of England,* vol. 6.; Claude Saint-André, *Henriette d'Angleterre et la cour de Louis XIV).* I have discounted Saint-Simon's much-later account of Henrietta Anne's death, which makes detailed claims about the chevalier of Lorraine's involvement. It is not certain that Henrietta Anne died of poison, but if she did, either Philippe, the chevalier, or both could have been responsible.

73 **"on whom someone had put on some rouge":** Montpensier, *Mémoires,* 4: 137.
73 **gave her away:** Ibid.
73 **"I cannot bear it":** La Fayette, 128.
74 **contained poison:** Chicory was often administered for digestive problems as well as liver concerns, including jaundice, see L. Bourgeois, *Receuil des Secrets* 1, 5: 57–58.
74 **"this is unjust":** La Fayette, 129.
74 **"nor embarrassed by Madame's opinion":** La Fayette, 130.
74 **"I shall not be alive tomorrow":** La Fayette, 136.
74 **"I have been poisoned":** Ibid., 130.
75 **through to the stomach:** M. Boscher, "Mémoire d'un chirurgien du roy d'Angleterre qui a esté present à l'ouverture du corps de Madame royale de France," *Lives of the Princesses of England,* vol. 6 (London: Henry Colburn, 1855), 586.
75 **like "breadcrumbs":** Ibid.
75 **"an extraordinary quantity of bile":** Ibid.
75 **"or lesions of any part":** Ibid.
75 **"very boiling bile":** Ormesson, 594.
75 **"pierced and rotten":** Ibid.
76 **"Madame is dead!":** Voltaire, *Le Siècle de Louis XIV,* trans. in L. Hilton, *Athénaïs: The Life of Louis XIV's Mistress, the Real Queen of France* (Boston: Little, Brown and Company, 2002), 81.

CHAPTER 11
Poison in the Pie

These accounts are drawn from *Mémoire du process extraordinaire contre Madame de Brinvilliers & de la Chausée Valet de Monsieur Sainte-Croix* (1676); *Mémoire du procèz extraordinaire contre la Dame de Brinvilliers* (1676); *Arrest de Parlement...contre Dame Marie Marguerite d'Aubray espouse du Sieur Marquis de Brinvilliers* (16 July 1676); *Factum pour Dame Marie Madeleine d'Aubray, Marquise de Brinvilliers accusée* (1676); *Factum du procèz extraordinairement fait à La Chaussée Valet de Sainte-Croix, pour raison des empoisonnemens des Sieurs d'Aubray Lieutenants Civils;* A Narrative Of the Process Against Madam Brinvilliers; and Of Her Condemnation and Execution for Having Poisoned Her Father and Two Brothers (1676). Secondary sources include Erika Carroll, "Potions, Poisons, and 'Inheritance Powders': How Chemical Discourses Entangled 17th Century France in the Brinvilliers

Trial and Poison Affair"; Jacques Saint-Germain, *Madame de Brinvilliers;*
Clara de Milt, "Christopher Glaser"; Paul Friedland, *Seeing Justice Done: The
Age of Spectacular Capital Punishment in France;* Edward Peters, *Torture;* Lisa
Silverman, *Tortured Subjects: Pain, Truth, and the Body in Early-Modern
France.* Details of Brinvilliers's imprisonment at the Conciergerie and her execu-
tion are drawn from the priest Pirot's account, *La Marquise de Brinvilliers,
récits de ses derniers moments.*

77 **both highly respected lawyers:** The eldest son, Antoine, had inherited the
position of civil lieutenant following his father's death. Tensions between
the criminal and civil domains of Châtelet had diminished following the
edict of 1667 that named La Reynie as police lieutenant. La Reynie clearly
had the upper hand in all matters but maintained cordial relations with the
civil lieutenant. François d'Aubray lived just a few doors down from La
Reynie on the rue du Bouloi, near the Louvre.

78 **"your men would poison me!":** *A Narrative of the Process Against Madam
Brinvilliers, and Her Condemnation and Execution For Having Poisoned
Her Father And Two Brothers: Translated out of French* (London: Jona-
than Edwyn, 1676), 7.

79 **possibility of poisoning:** Ibid.

CHAPTER 12
An Alchemist's Last Words

80 **witnesses to the process:** French law required that, immediately after a
person's death, surviving family members to arrange for a postmortem
inventory of the deceased's belongings.

81 **most precious possessions:** My account of the key is from Picard's testimony of July 21, 1677 (4: 299–301). This conflicts with the evidence presented in the court case against Madame de Brinvilliers (*Mémoire du
procez extraordinaire contre la Dame de Brinvilliers*), in which the pros-
ecuting attorney explains that the key was found simply on a bookshelf in
Sainte-Croix's home.

81 **in May 1670:** Narrative, 9.

82 **"without opening the packet":** Ibid., 10.

CHAPTER 13
The Faithful Servant

84 **to avoid detection:** *Factum du procez extraordinairement fait à La
Chaussée,* 3.

85 **box's contents:** Lebel confirmed that La Reynie was part of the process and
that it was La Reynie who provided him with the items found on La
Chaussée during his arrest. Archives de la Bastille, ms. 10336, fol. 8.

85 **"nothing that one could have used as poison":** Archives de la Bastille, ms.
10338, fol. 5.

85 **no further tests were necessary:** Ibid., fol. 8.

86 **damage to its organs:** Ibid., fol. 4.

86 **"curdled blood":** Ibid., 10338 fol. 8.

86 "as if it had been burned": Ibid., 10338, fol. 8.
87 "contained in the case described above": See ibid., 10338 fols. 8 and 9, for
the underlined portions of Lebel's report.
87 pain to be inflicted: During the Affair of the Poisons, few if any orders for
the Preliminary Question (*Question préparatoire*) were imposed pretrial.
Moreover, criminals sentenced to death also received the more intense
Extraordinary Question (*Question extraordinaire*) rather than the Ordinary Question (*Question ordinaire*). To minimize potential confusion
between these different forms of "questions," I refer to postsentencing torture as the Question.
87 "rendered useless for life": T. Smollett, *Travels through France and Italy
(1766)*, cited by L. Silverman, *Tortured Subjects: Pain, Truth, and the
Body in Early Modern France* (Chicago: University of Chicago Press,
2001), 96.
88 "affrighted to see it": Evelyn, *Diary*, 3: 28–29, cited by Silverman, 97.
88 increased the water's pressure on the stomach: Gibson, 219. The Question
of Madame Chanfrain, a minor player in the Affair of the Poisons, con-
firms this. The two questioners explicitly warn the accused that water torture would most certainly "run the risk of suffocating her, given the weight
of her body and the effect of her chest [on her stomach]" (5: 481).
88 to dull the pain: Silverman, 94, 145.
88 "last minutes of a wretched life": *Narrative*, 11. See also "Extrait du
procès-verbal de la question de La Chaussée," 24 March 1676 (4: 67–69).
89 "great mind to poison" her as well: *Narrative*, 13.

CHAPTER 14
"Brinvilliers Is in the Air"

90 much less romantic: *Narrative*; Sévigné, May 1, 1678, 2: 281; L. W. Mollenauer, *Strange Revelations: Magic, Passion, and Sacrilege in Louis
XIV's France* (University Park: Pennsylvania State Press, 2007), 12;
"Mémoire de M. de la Reynie," n.d. (6: 396).
91 "that person should be arrested": Louvois de M. Descarrières, 16 March
1676.
92 wrapped with cords and hairpins: Jacques, 141–142.
92 bitter rivals: For rivalries between Colbert and Louvois, see Farrère,
71–93, and Mongrédien, *Madame de Montespan et l'affaire des poisons*
(Paris: Fayard, 1953), 161–168.
93 needed to push water through them: Visconti, 68.
93 "who wants to save it": "Mémoire au roi," 22 July 1666. Clément, *Lettres,
instructions et mémoires de Colbert*, Vol. 7, ccxxii.
93 "not because of favoritism": Louis XIV, *Mémoires*, cited in P. Sonnino,
Louis XIV and the Origins of the Dutch War (Cambridge, England: Cambridge University Press, 1988), 17.
94 "satisfy the king and the public": Colbert to Harlay, 9 April 1679 (4: 174).
While other scholars have not insisted on the jurisdictional debates between
Louvois and Colbert in the Brinvilliers case, the extant correspondence is
telling. Louvois dominates the correspondence from mid-March until the
second week of April 1676, at which point Colbert takes over.

94 "such an extraordinary matter": Cited in P. Friedland, *Seeing Justice Done: The Age of Spectacular Capital Punishment* (Oxford, England: Oxford University Press, 2012), 147. Primi Visconti also fueled rumors that Brinvilliers had tested her poison by tainting sweets and giving them to hospital patients and the homeless (279).

94 "you have been able to find out": Clément, *Affaire des Poisons* 114–115.

95 "heart was pricked": *Narrative*, 18.

95 The references to Glaser: Glaser's name also remains eponymous for potassium salt, called "Glaser's salt," as well as for the mineral Glaserite, a naturally occurring crystalline potassium sulfate. C. de Milt, "Christopher Glaser," *Journal of Chemical Education* 19, no. 2 (1942): 53.

95 He wrote the first textbook: Glaser's *Treatise* included a preparation for "Infernal stone or perpetual caustic" (fused nitrate sticks). "'Tis called Infernalis, partly from its black color, and partly from its caustic burning quality" as well as other substances that could prove deadly to humans. To the magistrates' frustration, however, Glaser had returned to his native Switzerland and could not be extradited. Glaser, *Traité de la chimie*, cited in de Milt, 54.

95 the marquise's lawyer asserted: *Mémoire du procès extraordinaire contre Madame de Brinvilliers & de La Chaussée Valet de Monsr. Sainte-Croix. Pour raison des empoisonmens des diverses personnes...et l'Arrest de la Cour donné contre la dite Dame, 16 juillet 1676* (Amsterdam: Henry & Theodore Boom, 1676), 63.

95 "is not one to be trusted": Plumitif de la Tournelle, 26 June 1676 (4: 227).

95 "She disgusts us": Pirot, 45.

96 "the salvation of her soul": Ibid., 30.

96 "her poisons will outlive her": Pirot, 46.

96 "who your accomplices are": Ibid., 59.

97 "what I will do, Messieurs": P. Pirot, *La Marquise de Brinvilliers: Récit de ses derniers moments*, edited by G. Rouiller (Paris: Alphonse Lemerre, 1883), 2: 160.

97 "my husband five times": Plumitif de la Tournelle, n.d. (4: 243).

98 "made me shiver": Cited in Friedland, 147.

99 "or a pearl necklace": Mongrédien, 32–33.

99 could have hoped for her: Pirot, 2: 172.

99 "'turn us all into poisoners'": Sévigné, 2: 342–343.

99 "I'd ruin them all": Mongrédien, 34; Somerset, 44; Mollenauer, 16–17.

100 found by the authorities: "Mémoire de M. de la Reynie sur le fait touchant les abominations, le sacrifice de l'enfant pour La des Oeillets et pour l'étranger prétendu Milord Anglais," n.d. (6: 396).

CHAPTER 15
House of Porcelain

104 by potential suitors: Clément, *Montespan* 79–80, 82. Petitfils, *Montespan*, 151.

104 again in 1672 and 1673: Montespan had seven children in all with the king, four boys and three girls, born in 1669, 1670, 1672, 1673, 1677, 1678. With the exception of Françoise Marie, all were named Louis or Louise.

104 **"her powder lights very quickly"**: Saint-Maurice, cited in Fraser, 119.
104 **legitimized their three children**: December 1673. This was not first time he had bestowed such status on the children he fathered outside of marriage. To soften the blow of his rejection of La Vallière, he legitimized the couple's first daughter in 1667.
104 **"augment considerably his sentiments"**: Cited in Clément, *Montespan*, 44.
104 **caught his eye**: As Mademoiselle des Oeillets was one of Madame de Montespan's personal attendants, it is entirely possible that the ever-practical Athénaïs put her maid in the king's way in order to assert some control over his dalliances.
105 **found her fortune at court**: J. Lemoine, *Madame de Montespan et la légende des poisons* (Paris: Leclerc, 1908), 39.
105 **true to its name**: Description of the Trianon de Porcelain is from Cowen, Jones, and Félibien.
106 **at Françoise's feigned ignorance**: Petifils, *Montespan*, 157.
107 **stones of all colors**: Clément, *Montespan*, 47–48.
107 **"fit for a chorus girl"**: *Mémoires de Luynes*, 9: 255–256; see also Bonnassieux, *Clagny*, 50.
107 **"nothing is impossible"**: Clément, *Montespan*, 51.
107 **"one can ever imagine"**: 4: 21.
107 **"to better her reign"**: Petitfils, *Montespan*, 163.
108 **"why God would make me suffer"**: Maintenon, *Correspondence générale* 1: 221, cited in Clément, *Montespan*.
108 **"good friends"**: Sévigné, 2: 878, 982.
108 **the king's future**: Clément, *Montespan* 82–83.
108 **"the ministers of Jesus Christ"**: Riley, *Lust*, 88.
109 **being refused communion**: Clément, *Montespan*, 57.
109 **"like a man who had been crying"**: See C. Adams, "'Belle comme le jour': Beauty, Power, and the King's Mistress," *French History* 29 (2015): 170.
109 **"love will have the upper hand"**: Madame de Scudéry to Bussy-Rabutin, *Correspondance de Bussy-Rabutin*, 3: 34.
109 **"pensive and sighing"**: Lemoine, 33.
109 **eclipsed the queen's eleven on the second**: Clément, *Montespan*, 46. In a later confirmation of her decline in status, Montespan moved to smaller quarters in 1680.
110 **"grown to formidable proportions"**: Maintenon, *Lettres*, 2: 389.
110 **appear slimmer than she actually was**: Gibson, "Attitudes Toward Obesity in 17th-Century France" 224; see also Clément, *Montespan*, 429.

CHAPTER 16
Offering

111 **the man frightened her**: Confrontation of Lesage and Voisin, 19 May 1670 (5: 369).
111 **spun around and ran**: Interrogation of Voisin's daughter, 5 July 1680 (6: 237).
111 **also in her house**: To her later recollection, his first visit was sometime in 1672 or 1673 (6: 294–298).

112 dramatic flair about her: Madame des Oeillets, Voisin arrest, 12 March 1679 (6: 244); La Reynie, "Observations à mettre sur la liasse des actes envoyés suivant l'ordre du roi." (6: 420–421).

113 than to make the journey again: Declaration de la fille de la Voisin, 12 July 1680, BNF, mss. français 7608, fol. 170 (6: 24–246).

113 at Lepère's home: Both the elder Voisin and her daughter testified that Marie-Marguerite refused to take coaches after a certain point after having had "bad experiences" in the coach. Voisin was obliged to send a male courier in her daughter's place; see La Reynie's summary of interrogations, 12 July 1680 (6: 241). On the birth of Marie-Marguerite's child and her choice of midwife, see Vautier interrogation, 2 November 1679 (6: 37); Romani interrogation, 25 July 1680 (6: 263–268).

113 toward her mother was now gone: Voisin's daughter's childbirth and Lepère's role as midwife in birth confirmed by Margo, Voisin's servant, and Lepère, "Confrontation de la Lepère à Margo," 3 July 1679 (6: 424–425). "Procès-Verbal de la Présentation de La Lepère à la Question," 12 August 1679 (5: 452–453).

CHAPTER 17
"The Sneakiest and Meanest Woman in the World"

115 the most luxurious of carriages: Vigoureux interrogation, 4 January 1679 (5: 162), Archives de la Bastille, ms. 10341, fol. 12.

115 like the most devoted of lovers: Bosse interrogation, 5 January 1679 (5: 169).

115 who claimed to be Faurye: Leroy interrogation, 4 July 1678 (5: 70) Archives de la Bastille, ms. 10341, fol. 25.

115 died just a few days later: Somerset, 124–126; La Reynie to Ponchartrain, 7 March 1692 (7: 151).

116 "keep your children off my property": Sarmant and Soll, 94.

117 "to enlighten him on it": Louvois to La Reynie, February 1677 (4: 283). La Reynie details both his actions and his thoughts on the La Grange case as well as his interrogations of Bosse, Vigoureux, and Poulaillon in a letter addressed to Chancellor Pontchartrain on March 7, 1692 (7: 150–164); for his interrogation of Poncet, see 20 February 1677 (4: 277–283).

118 "you also wrote them in code": Poncet interrogation, 20 February 1677 (4: 279).

118 "did you receive from them": Ibid.

118 "prisoner at Châtelet": Ibid. (4: 281).

118 "tell her secrets directly to His Majesty": Ibid. (4: 282).

119 "the sneakiest and meanest woman in the world": La Reynie to Pontchartrain, 7 March 1677.

119 La Reynie asked to see the letters: La Grange (7: 151). 23 February 1677 (4: 283–284).

119 La Grange insisted: La Grange interrogation, 26 April 1677 (4: 287).

120 "expense of my enemies": Quoted in Treasure, Louis XIV 174.

120 "transferred to the Bastille": Le Tellier to La Reynie, 8 June 1677 (4: 291).

CHAPTER 18
"Burn after Reading"

122 passed daily through the compound: Saint-Germain, *La Reynie* 12–13.
122 "you will lose me forever": 5: 180–181, n. 2.
123 "it is enough to know only of the intent": Ibid.
123 "Burn after reading": Ibid.
124 uncovering its author: Colbert to La Reynie, 12 October 1677 (4: 308).
124 his approval of the request: Seignelay to the First President (of the *parlement*) Novi, 19 November 1678 (5: 152–153).
125 "begin the procedure you are proposing": Colbert to La Reynie, 28 November 1678 (5: 155–156).

CHAPTER 19
Dinner Guests

126 to perform on Poulaillon's husband: Vigoureux interrogation, 4 January 1679 (5: 159); Archives de la Bastille, ms. 10341, fols. 10–11.
127 bracelet, encrusted with precious jewels: Vigoureux interrogation, 4 January 1679 (5: 159); Archives de la Bastille, ms. 10341, fols. 10–11.
127 left with a vial of poison: Colbert to La Reynie, 28 November 1679 (5: 157, n. 1).
129 obscenity-laden missives directed against the wardens: From personal tour of upper levels of the dungeons, March 2014.
129 apothecaries for testing: Red wax was typically used by La Reynie's officiers for seals; see Archives de la Bastille, ms. 10347, fol. 1 and elsewhere.
130 down for questioning first: all dialogue from "Interrogation of Vigoureux," 4 January, 1679, Archives de la Bastille, ms. 10341, fols. 9–18 (5: 157–164). Though the historical record does not tell us precisely where in the tower the police chief's initial interrogations took place, in all likelihood they happened in Charles V's formal counsel room on the second floor with its large fireplace.
132 to question Bosse: Interrogation of Marie Mariettte, Widow Bosse, 5 January 1679 (5: 167–175); Archives de la Bastille, ms. 10341, fols. 24–45. La Reynie questioned Bosse a day earlier, on January 4, but only briefly. "Interrogation of Bosse, dit Belamour," 4 January 1679 (5: 164–167), Archives de la Bastille, ms. 10341, fols. 7–8.
132 powders and liquids found in her home: For the search-and-seizure record as well as the various documents found in her home, see Archives de la Bastille, ms. 10342, fols. 78–87.
132 "put the idea in my head": Interrogation of Marie Mariette, Widow Bosse, 5 January 1679 (5: 173–175); Archives de la Bastille, ms. 10341, fols. 32–34. Ravaisson's transcription of the interrogation is incomplete. Moreover the transcriptions do not include La Reynie's interrogation of Bosse on 18 January 1679, 21 January 1679 (Archives de la Bastille, ms. 10341, fols. 100–107, 144–147), or interrogations of Vigoureux on 19 January 1679, 21 January 1679, 23 January 1679, 29 January (Archives de la Bastille, ms. 10341, fols. 128–131, 134–136, 148–150, 168–171).

CHAPTER 20
The Question

134 **betting that Louvois would win:** for rivalries between Colbert and Louvois, Claude Farrère, *Jean-Baptiste Colbert*, 71–93; Mongrédien, *L'Affaire des poisons*, 161–168.
134 **to enhance the glory of the king:** A. Corvisier, *Louvois* (Paris: Fayard, 1983), 389.
135 **"freezes out those who come to him":** Visconti, 3.
135 **"war, glory, dominion, and self-worship":** *The Age of Louis XIV*, 17.
135 **time of relative peace:** "Barely had the *Te Deum* been celebrated to honor the victorious peace of Nimègue and the Affairs [regarding poison] bubbled back up again," Rousset, 270.
136 **to the *parlement*:** Louvois to Chancellor Le Tellier, 5 February 1679 (5: 178–179).
136 **three years earlier:** All dialogue for La Grange interrogation from Procès-verbal of the Question for La Grange and Nail [Launay], 6 February 1679 (5: 180–193). Archives de la Bastille, ms. 10341, fols. 571–600.
139 **as documented by the interrogation record:** All dialogue for the Launay interrogation from Procès-verbal of the Question for La Grange and Nail [Launay], 6 February 1679 (5: 180–193). Archives de la Bastille, ms. 10341, fols. 571–600.
139 **"dying from the force of the torments":** Procès-verbal of the Question for La Grange and Nail [Launay], 6 February 1679 (5: 192).
140 **had let La Grange and Launay off too gently:** Ibid., n. 1. See La Reynie's sustained reflections on the La Grange interrogation and other related events in his letter to Louvois, 28 January 1681 (6: 417–419) and "Mémoire de La Reynie sur le fait touchant les abominations . . ." (6: 393–403, 417–419).
141 **"powders, poisons, or similar things":** Procès-verbal of the Execution, 8 February 1679 (5: 194–200).

CHAPTER 21
Monsters

142 **former servant, a woman named Monstreux:** Perrine Monstreux interrogation, February 13 1679 (5: 202–212). The description of Poulaillon's sentence in the Chambre Ardente (5 June 1679, 5: 386–387 and 7: 176–177) is taken from La Reynie's observations many years later on the occasion of Madame de Poulaillon's request for clemency (18 May 1697, 7: 176–177). La Reynie's letter to Pontchartrain in 1697 gives the date for the Chambre as 7 June 1679, not 5 June as indicated by Ravaisson.
143 **"strong and ugly fat woman":** Monstreux interrogation, 13 February 1679 (5: 206).
143 **"It will put him to sleep":** Ibid. (5: 209).
144 **instructed Monstreux once again:** Ibid.
144 **"find yourself in trouble":** Ibid.
144 **"put it in his wine":** Ibid.

145 to evade arrest: La Chéron interrogation, 25 February 1679 (5: 223, n. 1).
145 few would think to look for her: See Archives de la Bastille, ms. 10342, fol. 128.
145 "every one one of them will die": La Chéron interrogation, 27 March 1679 (5: 300). See also La Chéron testimony, 25 February 1670 (5: 226).
146 two apothecaries to Bosse's home: Archives de la Bastille, ms. 1324, fols. 42–44; Nass, *Les empoisonnements sous Louis XIV d'après les documents inédits de l'affaire des poisons: 1679–1682* (Paris: Carré et Naud, 1898), 145–149.
147 La Reynie interrogated Bosse again at Vincennes: Interrogation of Bosse, 12 March 1679 (5: 244–248); Archives de la Bastille, ms. 10342, fols. 60–68.
147 apothecaries the day before: Ravaisson reproduces a large portion of this interrogation. However, sections are missing in the transcription; for this see Archives de la Bastille, ms. 10342, especially fols. 60–62 and 65–68.
148 "a clear liquid for Madame Poulaillon": Ibid., fol. 65.

CHAPTER 22
Quanto

151 Seven separate royal ordinances: 1643, 1655, 1661, 1663, 1664, 1665, 1666. Delamare, *Traité de la Police* 1: 459–466.
152 stolen winnings: nouvelles à la main, 1671 (4: 50–51).
152 devastating losses was stunning: Clément, *Montespan*, 107; *Lettres inédites de Feuquières*, 4: 277.
153 Carmelite convent: Clément, *Montespan*, 86.
153 wrote to her priest: Ibid., 89.
153 disappointed and bitter: Lemoine, 49.
153 "very good heart": Choisy, *Mémoires*, 174; Orléans, *Correspondence complète*, 390.
154 could access through a shared staircase: Visconti, *Mémoires*, 208–209.
154 gift from the king: Bush, *Memoirs of the Queens of France*, 2: 178.
154 trademark curls: The hairstyle remained popular at court for more than ten years, long after Fontanges's favor diminished at court, until Louis tired of it and instructed women at court to wear their hair straight and unadorned. "I can't describe to you the stir this caused at Versailles," Madame de Sévigné wrote. See Bussy-Rabutin, *Correspondence*, 6: 485–486, and Sévigné, 15 May 1691, 10: 24.
154 "edge of a high precipice": Lettre de Madame de Scudéry à Bussy, 18 January 1679, cited in Clément, *Montespan*, 110.
155 formal separation of the couple's assets: L. Delavaud, *La cour de Louis XIV en 1671: Madame De Montespan, Colbert & Louvois.* (Paris: Levé, 1912), 4.
156 with profanity: Bussy-Rabutin, 18 May 1680.
156 "without Monsieur Colbert": Madame de Montmorency to Bussy-Rabutin, 18 June 1679; see also Bussy, 18 May 1680; Sévigné, 25 May 1680.
156 "marry a prince!": Visconti, 289.
157 "very knowledgeable in it": Rousset, 2: 561.
157 "striking them in secret": François-Timoléon de Choisy, *Mémoires de l'abbé de Choisy*, 66–67.

CHAPTER 23
Search and Seizure

158 **the Châtelet commissioner on duty:** Jacques Camuset should not be confused with the commissioner responsible for inventorying Sainte-Croix's home, whose full name was Sébastien Camuset Picard but is referred to most often in the record as Picard.

158 **that she would be arrested:** La Reynie suspected that Voisin had burned the most incriminating papers before her arrest, including those relating to Madame Leféron and Madame Dreux, Procès-verbal of Voisin's Question, 19 February 1680 (6: 156).

159 **desired effect:** Camuset's report on the seizure and inventory of Voisin's home can be found in Archives de la Bastille, ms. 10342, fols. 48–50. It is reproduced only in part in Ravaisson; original documents found at Voisin's home constitute the bulk of Archives de la Bastille, ms. 10357.

159 **from her cell for questioning:** Dialogue from Voisin interrogation, 17 March, 1679 (5: 257–267), Archives de la Bastille, ms. 10342, fols. 69–79.

160 **a flood swept the bridge:** See Voisin interrogation, 17 March 1679 (5: 267). Ravaisson notes that, in a 1664 complaint against his wife, Marie-Marguerite's father is named as a "bonnetier" who had established a shop on the Pont Marie. The original Pont-Marie was swept away in a flood in 1658, which was around the time that Marie-Marguerite was born. While a temporary bridge restored the link across the river in 1660, work did not begin in earnest until 1667. The bridge was not finished until 1670—at which time Marie-Marguerite would have been twelve. Interrogation records suggest that the husband was still unemployed at this time.

160 **"chiromancy" skills:** Voisin claimed that she learned her skills at the age of nine, Bosse interrogation, 27 March 1679 (5: 297).

161 **at Montmartre:** Ibid. (5: 259).

161 **paid a handsome price:** Ibid. (5: 269).

161 **"we found at your house?":** This portion of the interrogation is not included in Ravaisson's transcription; see Archives de la Bastille, ms. 10342, fols. 76–77.

162 **to the interrogation room together:** Confrontation of Bosse and Voisin, 28 March 1679 (5: 303–310).

163 **Leféron did not listen, she said:** Leroux admitted during the Question that she gave Voisin a vial of poison for Madame Leféron, Procès-verbal of Question of La Leroux," 5 April 1680 (6: 199–203).

163 **it was evidence enough:** Included on the list, which La Reynie sent to the king the same day: Mesdames Lepère, Saint Martin, Bergerot, Monaco, Duval, Rollet, Catau, Simon, and Philbert, among others, Archives de la Bastille, ms. 10342, fol. 77; see also interrogations of 15 and 28 March 1679.

163 **to ensure the security of the prison:** In May 1679 Desgrez received a second bonus—as did the notary Sagot, Louvois to La Reynie, 20 May 1679 (5: 374).

CHAPTER 24
A Noble Pair

164 **poisoned her husband:** March 21, see Louvois's letter to La Reynie, 22 March 1679 (5: 284–285).

165 **"over the fear [the arrests] are causing":** Saville to Coventry, April 1679 (5: 335).

165 **"one of their siblings gives them":** Petitfils, *Affaire*, 124.

165 **guards accompanying the police chief:** Louvois to Desgrez, 22 March 1679 (6: 283).

165 **while frisking the suspect:** Archives de la Bastille, ms. 10342, fol. 92.

165 **was gone now:** All dialogue from Lesage interrogation, 22 March 1679 (5: 285–289). A large portion of this interrogation is not reproduced in Ravaisson; see Archives de la Bastille, ms. 10342, fols. 100–111.

166 **a *very* nasty woman:** Lesage interrogation, 22 March, 1679 (5: 287); A large portion of this interrogation is not reproduced in Ravaisson.

166 **with bravado:** Archives de la Bastille, ms. 10342, fols. 114–117.

167 **following her there two days later:** See Louvois to La Reynie, 11 April 1679 (5:333); "Procès-verbal of Madame de Dreux's capture," 11 April 1679 (5: 334), Archives de la Bastille, ms. 10343, fols. 69–70. Degrez was accompanied by twelve guards when he arrested Dreux.

167 **one or two questions:** Leféron interrogation, 13 April 1679 (5: 336); Dreux interrogation, 16 April 1679; Partial transcription of Archives de la Bastille, ms. 10343, fols. 107–109 in 5: 336–337.

168 **gone to her all the same:** Dreux interrogation, 16 April 1670 (5: 337). On April 20 Dreux's husband petitioned the tribunal to allow her legal counsel. His petition was ignored. Archives de la Bastille, ms. 10343, fols. 128–129.

168 **dispensing poisons:** On March 8, 1679, Louis informed La Reynie via Louvois that he intended to appoint a special committee to try suspects who were imprisoned at Vincennes. The king named the eleven men who would sit on the committee (Boucherat, Breteuil, Bezons, Voisin [a state counselor, no relation to Madame Voisin], Fieubet, Pelletier, Pommereuil, d'Argouges, Fortin, Turot, Ormesson, and La Reynie). The king requested that La Reynie begin preparing for the eventual trials. One month later, on April 7, Louis formally announced by *lettre patente* his wish to create the private tribunal, see Louvois to La Reynie, 8 March 1679. (5: 237).

168 **the king did not yield:** *Mercure Galant,* March 1679: 341–342. See also Mongrédien, 41.

168 **primary arms depot for France:** Sauval, 330–332.

169 **detective, prosecutor, and judge:** Somerset, 150.

169 **they had collected:** In the pages that follow I refer infrequently to Claude Bazin de Bezons. Bezons assisted La Reynie in the interrogations at Vincennes through August 1679, which corresponds to the moment when the tribunal began its lengthy review of evidence against suspected poisoners (Archives de la Bastille, ms. 10345, fols. 243–249, 332–354, 357–364). From 30 August 1679, La Reynie's name alone figures in interrogation records. It is likely, then, that Bezons was reassigned to the Arsenal in order to facilitate the tribunal's review of interrogation records and other evidence collected by La Reynie. While Bezons was present at many of the interroga-

tions and sat as a judge at the tribunal (as did La Reynie), I concur with Mongrédien that his role was "only secondary" to that of La Reynie (168).

CHAPTER 25
The Burning Chamber

170 **the Question:** BNF, *mss. francais*, 7608, fols. 20–21.

171 **what was said:** All we have left are a few sentences indicating that Vigoureux confirmed that Lesage and his priestly companion Mariette performed sacrilegious masses for Madame Philbert and that the marquis of Luxembourg, Louvois's nemesis, had also used their services. "Résumé du Procès-verbal de Question de La Voisin," 9 May 1679. BNF, *mss. français* 7608, fols. 20–21 (5: 260).

171 **"from a head wound":** Ibid.

171 **screaming along with it:** "Procès-verbal de la Chambre," 4–6 May 1679 (5: 363); "Résumé du Procès-verbal de Question de la Bosse" (5: 360–361); "Procès-verbal de pronunciation et d'exécution de l'arrêt" 10 May 1679 (5: 362–364).

172 **take care of any sick prisoners:** Louvois to La Reynie, 14 May 1679 (5: 367).

172 **no new insights:** Confrontation between Voisin and Lesage, 18–19 May 1679 (5: 367–369).

172 **to question Madame de Poulaillon:** "Procès-verbal de la Chambre," 5 June 1679 (5:386–387); La Reynie to Pontchartrain, 18 May 1697 (7: 175–177).

172 **to do the job for her:** La Reynie to Pontchartrain, 18 May 1697 (7: 175).

172 **"presence of mind":** "Procès-verbal de la Chambre," 5 June 1679 (5: 387, n. 2).

172 **then beheaded:** "Procès-verbal de la Chambre" (5: 386–387).

173 **"She was very polite":** La Reynie to Pontchartrain, 18 May 1697 (7: 175).

173 **Château of Saint-Germain:** Procès-verbal de question de La Chéron, 19 June 1679 (5: 417).

173 **to be burned alive:** Ravaisson suggests that she was strangled first (5: 413).

174 **"I will not lie":** Ibid. (5: 417).

174 **place de Grève:** Ibid. (5: 418).

174 **the following day:** "Procès-verbal de la question de Lepère," 11 August 1679 (5: 451–452); "Procès-verbal de presentation de la Lepère à la question" (5: 452–453).

175 **"Saint-Germain":** Procès-Verbal de la question de Belot, 10 June 1679 (5: 392–399).

175 **"servants of Paris are at risk":** Madame de Scudéry, cited in Mongrédien, 44. Bourdelot, cited in Petitfils, *Affaire*, 125. Further intensifying things, Parisians also began sending *placets* to Louvois and La Reynie containing "information" about neighbors, colleagues, and family members who bought or used poison; for example, see BNF, *mss. français*, 7608, fol. 28.

175 **business selling charms:** Archives de la Bastille, ms. 10343, fols. 347–350; she was first questioned at Vincennes on May 20.

176 **buried immediately:** See Archives de la Bastille, ms. 10345, fols. 607–608, for the detailed physician's report, which is not included in Ravaisson's transcriptions. Louvois also references the death in his letter to the king (16 September 1679); (5:477).

CHAPTER 26
"Beginning to Talk"

177 **"and my family"**: Interrogation of Voisin, 12 September 1679 (5: 468).

178 **"thank God."**: Ibid. (5: 470).

178 **bone-wasting disease:** In an earlier interview, Leféron claimed it was smallpox. "Résume de l'interrogatoire de Madame Leféron," 16 April 1679 (6: 336).

179 **"she is guilty":** "Confrontation de La Voisin à Mesdames Dreux et Leféron," 16 September, 1679 (5: 479).

179 **"I warned her husband:** "Note autographe de M. de La Reynie sur une declaration de Lesage, du 17 Septembre 1679" (5: 473).

179 **"order them to be used":** "King to La Reynie," 21 September 1679 (5: 483). BNF, *mss. français*, 7608, fols. 98–99.

179 **denied knowing her:** "Interrogatoire de la Voisin," 22 September 1679 (5: 483). However, Voisin's apparent success motivated other women to seek her help in securing similar positions at court. Voisin admitted on 24 October 1679 that a woman named Vertemart offered her 400 *livres* for a place in Montespan's entourage, which she claimed to have refused (6: 29–30, 59–60).

180 **firm in her assertion:** "Interrogatoire de la Vertemart," 30 September, 1679 (5: 491).

180 **the duke of Luxembourg:** Lesage interrogation, 27 March 1679 (5: 293).

180 **alleged transgressions to the king:** Louvois to the king 8 October 1679 (5: 501–502).

180 **"nothing compared to…interrogation":** Ibid.

181 **the dungeon:** Mongrédien downplays the significance of this "abnormal and surprising" visit, explaining that La Reynie was the one who requested it. While this was what Louvois explained to the king in his letter the following day, it is far from certain that the minister was simply complying with La Reynie's request. It would have been unusual for La Reynie to give direction to Louvois, whom he regarded as a messenger for the king. The tenor and content of the investigations took a sharp turn following Louvois's visit to Lesage, which leads me to believe that the minister saw this as an opportunity to influence the course of the investigations.

181 **"change his behavior":** Louvois to La Reynie, 11 October 1679 (6: 18).

181 **her servant:** The paper had been signed by Vivonne, the duchess of Angoulême, the duchess of Vitry, and the princess of Tingry.

181 **"dreadful":** "Déclaration de Lesage," 14 October 1679 (6: 19).

181 **"many strange things":** "Déclaration de Lesage," 26 September and 14 October 1679 (5: 490, 6: 19). Lesage also claimed that the card cheat the marquis de Cessac had once been a client. Voisin similarly continued to confess the names of her many clients.

182 **"against those named":** Louvois to M. de La Reynie, 16 October 1679 (5: 25).

182 **"persons of quality":** "Déclaration de La Voisin," 9 October 1679 (6: 3–6); "Déclaration de La Voisin," 10 Octobre 1679 (6: 7). The tribunal called Roure in for questioning on 23 January 1680; See Archives de la Bastille, ms. 10347, fol. 108.

182 **might return:** Voisin made the assertion a third time on 16 January 1680 (6: 103–104).
182 **"even farther up":** "Déclaration de La Voisin," 9 October 1679 (6: 3–6).
182 **to his wife:** She was assisted by fellow malcontent the marquis de Vardes, who served in the king's personal guard and similarly fumed that the king had stolen the heart of Henrietta Anne whom he had tried to bed. For more on the scandal of the Spanish letter, see La Fayette, *Histoire d'Henriette d'Angleterre*; Motteville, *Mémoires;* Ormesson, *Mémoires;* Tellier, "Mémoire à M. Bezons."
182 **exiled her to the provinces:** Motteville, *Mémoires.*
182 **company of his wife:** Motteville 3: 294, cited in Somerset, 82.
183 **"inconceivable aversion":** Renée, *Les Nièces de Mazarin,* 179, citing *Entretiens de Colbert et de Bloin,* 1701. Louis, on the other hand, felt "neither pain nor sadness," Motteville, *Mémoires* 4: 83; for the count's death, see Petitfils, *Affaire,* 13–14.
183 **get rid of her husband:** Abbot of Estrades to Pomponne, 28 April, 1679, (5: 352–353).
183 **the duke of Vendôme:** Just as Louis's mother had arranged for the young king to lose his virginity to a chambermaid, rumor had it he was considering the duchess of Bouillon to serve as the object of his son's first affections, Somerset, 272.
183 **and hand it to Lesage:** On 28 October 1679 Lesage confirmed that Bouillon had been a former client (6: 33).
184 **a few coins for his trouble:** Lesage interrogation, 28 October 1679 (6: 31–36).
184 **after supper:** BNF, *mss. français,* 7608, fol. 96.
184 **La Reynie wrote:** Ibid.

CHAPTER 27
Fortune-Teller

185 **sold-out performance of** *The Fortune-Teller***:** Clarke, "La Devineresse"; Clarke, *The Guénégaud Theater in Paris (1673–1680),* vols. 1–2; The play drew a large crowd every night, forcing ticket takers to turn away more than four hundred people at the door with each performance, so great was the demand both for its subject matter and for its special effects.
186 **Jobin's brother in disguise:** Donneau de Visé and Thomas Corneille, *La Devineresse ou les faux enchantemens,* edited by Julia Prest, *MHRA Critical Texts* (12), 2007.
186 **the Opéra:** Saint-Germain, *La Reynie* 100.
186 *Phèdre et Hippolyte***:** Clarke, "La Devineresse," 233.
187 **murderers in his city:** Saint-Germain, 145. This said, the play would not have been allowed to be performed if he did not approve of it. The police had the right to censure any play that went against good morals or that disrespected the king. La Reynie issued annual ordinances beginning in 1670 that announced "extraordinary treatment against those who, inside and outside or nearby theaters or the Opera, excite tumult or disturb presentations" (BNF *Mélanges Colbert,* 166, cited in Saint-Germain, 149). For

debates on La Reynie's involvement in the composition of *The Fortune-Teller*, see Clarke, "La Devineresse," 222.

187 **the duchess of Bouillon:** 16 January 1680. BNF, *mss. français*, 10347, fol. 91.

187 **"respect and obedience to the king":** Dialogue from Bouillon interrogation, 29 January 1680 (6: 123); *Mémoire de la Marquis de la Fare* 65: 249; Visconti, 288.

189 **"disguised as a judge":** *Mémoire du Marquis de La Fare,* 65: 249; see also Visconti, 288. It is possible that the last exchange about the devil is apocryphal. The accounts contained in Visconti's and the marquis de La Fare's memoirs were proudly circulated by the Bouillons and may have been exaggerated. Madame de Sévigné's description is not an eye witness account, but likely approaches closer to the truth. In any case there is consensus that the duchess of Bouillon proved to be a hostile witness.

189 **"ask such dumb questions":** Saint-Germain, 21; Sévigné, 31 January 1680; Voltaire, *Oeuvres complètes*, 13 ("Lettre de Ferney du 13 décembre 1767").

190 **"put me in prison":** Choisy, *Mémoires* 63: 224.

190 **chased her from their city:** Primi Visconti, 292. Visconti claimed, likely apocryphally, that La Reynie wanted the tribunal to investigate his as well but was rebuffed.

190 **"to my people":** Renée, 216.

191 **dismissed him:** BNF, *mss. français*, 7608, fol. 97; some reports suggest that La Reynie spent two hours with the king that morning, "Brayer to Mazauges," 7 February 1680.

191 **as they always had:** BNF, *mss français* 7608, fol. 97.

191 **for blasphemy and witchcraft:** For an especially thorough account of Luxembourg's imprisonment and the animosities between Louvois and the duke, see B. Fonck, *Le Maréchal de Luxembourg*, 2014, Kindle edition.

191 **encouraging him to flee, thus signaling his guilt:** J. P. Cénat, *Louvois: Le Double de Louis XIV*, 2015, Kindle edition.

192 **"my full confidence":** From Sévigné, 26 January 1680. Robert also signed a request to question Feuquières around the same time. See Archives de la Bastille, ms. 10347, fol. 106.

192 **"continue the proceedings against him":** Louvois to Boucherat, 24 January 1680 (6: 107).

192 **bowels of the prison:** Luxembourg, *Lettre secrète de Mr. de Luxembourg sur son emprisonnement à la Bastille*, 49–50.

192 **"for such little things":** Sévigné, February 1680, 2: 598.

192 **a hoax:** BNF, *mss français* 7608, fols. 336, 341.

193 **follow established procedures:** Fonck, *Le Maréchal de Luxembourg*, Kindle edition.

193 **physical evidence against him:** Description based on Luxembourg, *Lettre secrète*; Interrogation of Landard, 28 January 1680 (6: 113–114); Interrogation of Lesage, 9 February 1680 (6: 130–144).

194 **exiled Luxembourg from Paris:** Louis rescinded the punishment the following year, in 1680.

194 **"all will be taken care of":** Petitfils, *Affaire*, 124.

CHAPTER 28
"From One Fire to Another"

195 **at the Bastille:** Account of Voisin's trial, torture, and execution from Procès-verbal de l'interrogation de La Voisin, 19 February 1680 (6: 150–156); Suite du Procès-verbal de Question de La Voisin, 20 February 1680 (6: 156–181); Procès-verbal d'exécution de La Voisin, écrit par Sagot, 22 February 1680 6: 181–182); see also BNF, *mss. Français* 7608, fols. 226–227.

196 **Morel entered the room:** For reasons unknown, Morel replaced Terode as surgeon present during the tortures, Terode attended the earlier torture of Chéron.

196 **"Madame Alluye":** Suite du Procès-verbal de Question de La Voisin, 20 February 1680 (6: 174, 175).

197 **The questioning was over:** Ibid., 180.

197 **middle of the stone floor:** Procès-verbal de Question de La Voisin, 22 February 1680 (6: 180).

197 **"at the heart of it all":** Ibid.

198 **ball of heat and smoke:** Description from Antoine Coypel, cited in Mongrédien.

198 **"pass from one fire to another":** Sévigné, 2: 852.

198 **"will surprise us all":** Mongrédien, 71.

CHAPTER 29
The Poisoner's Daughter

201 **"unburden herself" of her memories:** See Interrogation of Voisin's daughter, 28 March 1680 (6: 194–198). Voisin's daughter was interrogated on 28 March 1680 (6: 194–198), 5 July 1680 (6: 234–238), 12 July 1680 (6: 241–246), 13 August 1680 (6: 288–292), 20 August 1680 (6: 294–298), 22 August 1680 (6: 299-305) 1680. Ravaisson's transcription is mostly reliable. However, it is worth noting that some information is missing for 12 July 1680 (BNF, *mss. français* 7608, fol. 61); 13 August 1680 (BNF, *mss. français* 7608, fol. 182); and 20 August 1680 (BNF, *mss. français*, fols. 239–249).

202 **Madame Pelletier snapped:** Interrogation of Voisin's daughter, 28 March 1680. (6: 196).

202 **got what she deserved:** Ibid. Marie-Marguerite's father was also poisoned at the same time, as well as on a number of other occasions. Likely the only thing standing between him and a sure death was his apparent friendship with the public executioner for the city of Paris. If Monsieur Voisin happened to die, the executioner threatened, he would make sure a full autopsy was performed—and would also tell every detail he knew about Madame Voisin's "business" (6: 31); Somerset, 153.

203 **the noblewoman Leféron:** See Confrontation of Bosse against Voisin, 28 March 1679 (5: 303–309); Confrontation of Voisin against Bosse, 28 March 1679 (5: 309–310); Lesage interrogation, 16 September 1680 (5: 309–311).

203 **submit their entreaties:** Somerset, 255.

204 "'a piece of paper'": Interrogation of Voisin's daughter, 5 July 1680 (6: 234–238).

204 dismissed entirely: While Philbert was not a member of the nobility, she had strong connections at court through her second husband, a court musician.

204 Marie-Marguerite explained: Compte rendu au Roy par M. de La Reynie sur le placet que La Voisin devoit presenter à Sa Majesté, le lendemain ou sur lendement de sa detention. BNF, *mss. français*, 7608, fol. 70.

205 "disgusting things": Interrogation of Voisin's daughter, 13 August 1680 (6: 289). BNF, *mss. français*, 7608, fol. 70.

205 "whom I name": Interrogation of Voisin's daughter, summary by La Reynie, 12 July 1680, BNF, *mss. français*, 7608, fols. 69–73 (6: 241–246). See also BNF, mss. français, 7608, fols. 179. Interrogation of the Wife Vautier. 8 August 1680. BNF, *mss français* 7608, fol 186, 190.

206 "just on hearsay": Interrogation of Voisin's daughter, 12 July 1680 (6: 245).

206 earnest and convincing: Projet de lettre de M. de la Reynie à Louvois, 2 September 1680; See also BNF, *mss. français*, 7608, fol. 275v.

206 "unbelievable things": Compte rendu au roi par M. de la Reynie du placet que la Voisin devait presenter à S.M. le lendemain ou surlendemain de la détention, n.d. (6: 320). BNF, *mss. français*, 7608, fol. 144. Marie-Marguerite's story also rang true when La Reynie interrogated another of Voisin's colleagues, Madame Vautier. Voisin had bragged to Vautier over dinner that she needed to go to Saint-Germain to meet the king and hoped a "beautiful fortune" would come of it. Interrogation of the wife Vautier, 8 August 1680, BNF, *mss. français* 7608, fols. 186, 190.

206 "than to declare the truth": Interrogation of Voisin's Daughter, 12 July 1680 (6: 246).

207 "follows his example": Bussy-Rabutin to the Marquis of Trichâteau, 30 April 1680.

207 "charmed by her": Sévigné, 17 July 1680; 18 September, 1680.

207 "my eyes have seen the king cry": Houssaye, 297.

208 "poisoned her milk": Princesse Palatine, *Correspondance complète*, 1: 199; Clément, *Montespan*, 115. Did La Reynie believe that Fontanges was poisoned? Clément believes so, ibid., 116.

208 died of natural causes: "Fragment du Procès-verbal de Madame de Fontanges," n.d. (6: 486).

CHAPTER 30
Sacrifices

209 "as she is with poison": Interrogation of Voisin, 10 October 1679.

209 prayers backwards: Interrogation of Filastre, 26 May 1680 (6: 211–214); 5 June 1680; 12 June 1680 (6: 216–218); 15 June 1680 (6: 223).

210 its evil mother: Interrogation of Filastre, 22 December 1679 (6: 64–66); 26 May 1680 (6: 211–214); interrogation of Simon, 28 May 1680, BNF, *mss. français*, 7608, fol. 288. See also Interrogation of Le Royer, 13 June 1680 (6: 218–219). One of Guibourg's colleagues, Father Leroyer, had a very different story to tell. He said Simon had told him that Filastre signed a

contract with the devil in the presence of Simon. Following the birth, the two women sold the child for sacrifice, never to see it again.

210 **Leroyer could not say:** Interrogation of Leroyer, 13 June 1680 (6: 218–219); interrogation of Guibourg, 26 June 1680 (6: 230–232).

210 **"take advantage of my weaknesses":** Interrogation of Guibourg, 26 June 1680 (6: 232).

211 **"my servants":** Excerpt from the interrogation of Guibourg, 10 October, 1680, BNF, *mss. français*, 7608, fol. 23 (6: 335). Stories of killing children for magical or demonic purposes circulated in Europe from the beginning of the fifteenth century and helped contribute to the flurry of witch-hunts during the Inquisition. In sermons priests described in great detail the supposed practices of witches. Among the most famous books in Europe was the bestselling *Malleus Maleficarum* (The Hammer of Evil), which quoted a sorceress's recipe for creating flying brooms: "We steal [deceased children] secretly from the tomb and boil them in a cauldron until all the flesh is made almost drinkable, the bones having been pulled out. From the more solid matter, we make a paste suitable for our desires and arts and movements by flight." Once the paste was smeared on a chair or a piece of wood, the witch could then levitate into the air.

211 **love potion:** Interrogation and declaration of Guibourg, 10 October, 1680, BNF, *mss. français*, 7608, fols. 160, 235–236.

211 **both former and present:** Louvois to La Reynie, 25 June 1680 (6: 229).

212 **better wine to inmates:** Louvois to La Reynie, 18 July 1680 (6: 260); 21 July 1680 (6: 262). Louvois to Ferronnay, 22 July 1680 (6: 263).

212 **"just one mass":** The description of Filastre's Question and torture is taken from Procès-verbal de la question de La Filastre, 30 September 1680 and 1 October 1680, BNF, *mss. français*, 7608, fols. 277–280 and 280–286, respectively. It is noteworthy that Ravaisson's transcription in the Archives de la Bastille does not contain La Reynie's summary of the 30 September session, BNF, *mss. français*, 7608, fols. 277–280. For 1 Octobre 1680, see (6: 324–326).

213 **while she was in labor:** Procès-verbal de la question de La Filastre, 1 October 1680, BNF, *mss. français*, 7608, fol. 281. Ravaisson's transcription is incomplete.

213 **through the pain:** Ibid., fol. 283.

213 **justify her actions:** Ibid.

214 **she admitted:** Declaration of Filastre before the execution, BNF, *mss. français*, 7608, fol. 286.

214 **interrogated her:** Interrogation of Jean Chanfrain, 9 August 1680 (6: 281–283). Chanfrain's name is also spelled Chanfrin in the interrogation records.

214 **"It is none of your business":** Ibid., 282. The scene repeated itself with the birth of her next two children, who were twins, after she handed them to Guibourg immediately after their birth.

215 **"of Madame de Montespan":** Interrogatoire de la fille Voisin, 9 October 1680 (6: 332–334). See also Declaration of Filastre, n.d., BNF, *mss. français*, 7608, fol. 80; Confrontation between Guibourg and Voisin's daughter, 23 October 1680, BNF, *mss. français*, 7608, fols. 237–238; Interrogation of Voisin's daughter, 30 August 1680, BNF, *mss. fran-*

çais, 7608, fols. 239 and 245–246. Ravaisson's transcription is incomplete.

215 change his mind: Mémoire de M. de la Reynie sur le fait touchant les abominations, le sacrifice de l'enfant pour La des Oeillets et pour l'étranger prétendu milord anglais, n.d. (6: 398).

216 "justice's failures": Second mémoire envoyé par M. de la Reynie, 11 Octobre 1680 (6: 339).

216 "darkness that surrounds me": Ibid.

216 whatever he felt necessary: Ibid., and "Mémoire de Sagot" ca. end of 1681. (6: 346–348).

CHAPTER 31
"A Strange Agitation"

217 Guibourg also blessed: Confrontation between Guibourg and Voisin's daughter, 23 October 1680, BNF, *mss. français*, 7608, fol. 237. This joint interrogation is not included in Ravaisson.

218 on the road to Versailles: Projet d'un rapport de M. de la Reynie au Roi (6: 364–375), n.d.

218 with anyone at court: La Reynie to Louvois, 22 October 1680 (6: 351).

219 saying her name aloud: Colbert, *Mémoire contre les faits calomnieux*, 419–420.

219 did not believe Oeillets one bit: Louvois to La Reynie, 24 November 1680; Louvois to La Reynie, BNF, *mss. français*, 7608, fol 193; note autographe de la Reynie, 15 February 1681.

220 totaled 442 people: BNF, *mss. français*, 7608, fol. 17.

220 "most general of terms": La Reynie to Louvois, 23 January 1681, BNF, *mss. français*, 7608, fol. 61. I cite here only the original, given its graphic complexies; for Ravaisson's transcription, see 6: 417–419.

220 "these sad affairs": Ibid., fol. 62.

220 "the public good": Ibid., fol. 63.

221 "strange agitation": Compte rendu au Roy par M. de la Reynie, BNF, *mss. français*, 7608, fols. 64–227, esp. 95, 102, 106, 109. La Reynie's "conjectures" initiated the review of evidence by Louvois, Colbert, and the king that resulted in reopening the tribunal in May 1681. Although La Reynie's letter is not dated, he would have had to compose his treatise before that date but after Louvois's meetings with Oeillets in November 1680, to which he makes reference in his treatise.

221 "for justice": Ibid., fols. 114, 141.

221 a secret court: Ibid., fol. 94.

221 two hundred pages: BNF, *mss. français*, 7608, fols. 6–14.

222 Claude Duplessis: Colbert, *Lettres instructions et mémoires* (6: 67–68, 407–430).

222 "such abominations": Clément, *Montespan* 99. See also Colbert, *Lettres instructions et memoires* (6: 417).

222 unable to identify Oeillets: Colbert, 420.

223 God-given wisdom in this matter: Ibid.

223 "desires of the king": Ibid., 422.

223 "the Affair would not end": Ibid., 423.
224 "no memory of it remains": Ibid., 424.
225 emptying Vincennes: BNF, *mss. français*, 7608, fol. 380.
225 remains unknown: Petitfils, *Affaire*, 235–237.
225 uncomfortably on the floor: Louvois to M. Chauvelin, 26 August 1682 (7: 112–113).
225 "smallest noise": Petitfils, *Affaire*, 237.

CHAPTER 32
Lock and Key

226 seals be removed: See BNF, *mss. français*, 7608, fols. 32–33 and 34–49, which contain an inventory of the documents in Sagot's home.
227 declared Madame de Sévigné: Sévigné, 3: 354.
228 "pull out their roots": *Edit du Roy pour la punition de différens crimes*, 3–4.
228 track all such sales: Ibid., 6–7.
228 "she has ever given me": Fraser, 197.
228 "He needs you": Maintenon, *Correspondence* générale, vol. 2, edited by Théophile Lavillée (Paris: Charpentier, 1865), p. 301.
229 "bubbly spirit": L'Abbé de Choisy, cited in Saint-Amand, 72.
229 more than passion: Saint-Amand, 68.
229 the Montorgeuil neighborhood: Lemoine convincingly refutes claims that Oeillets died in 1686 during sequestration, attributing Louvois's reference to her death as a misreporting. See Louvois to La Reynie (7: 134) and Lemoine, 41–42.
229 the couple once shared: Somerset, 142.
229 walked out the door: Ibid., 144.
230 the early hours of the morning: Ibid.
230 he made sure in his will: La Reynie's will and will addenda are reproduced in Nabour.

Epilogue

231 or the galleys: BNF, *mss. français*, 7608, fols. 1–2, which list each day the tribunal met, marking pauses between 28 August and 23 November 1679, 16 May and 3 August 1680, and 31 September 1680 and 16 May 1681, and include a supplementary accounting by La Reynie, BNF, *mss. français*, 7608, fol. 380.
232 well-protected courtyard: For a detailed presentation of the archive's history, see Funck-Brentano, *Archives de la Bastille: La Formation du Dépôt*.
233 slated for demolition: Funck-Brentano, *Archives*, 10. In 1684 the dungeon of Vincennes was decommissioned as a prison; the remaining records were transferred to the Bastille and were among many of those destroyed in 1789.
233 rediscovered them: Funck-Brentano, *Archives*, 12–13.
234 massive Bastille collection: Ravaisson's son, Louis, continued his father's work, publishing a seventeenth volume.

237 **"that I commit them all"**: Fraser, 181.
238 **"out of Vincennes"**: Ferronaye took offense to Louvois's letter, claiming to
     have difficulties with Desgrez. Unsurprisingly, Louvois shot back another
     letter, threatening once again to go to the king. Louvois to Ferronnaye, 8
     May, 1680 (6: 209–210). In a menacing letter to the jailer, Louvois wrote:
     "I will let you give some thought to what His Majesty would do if such
     rumors made it to [his] ears. I believe it is not necessary to tell you that, by
     whatever means necessary, it is important that this disorder cease now" (6:
     208). See also Louvois from Desgrez, 15 March 1680 (6: 191); Louvois to
     Ferronnaye, 2 May 1680 (6: 208).
238 **Louvois ordered Ferronnaye:** Louvois to Ferronnaye, 16 July 1680 (6:
     254).

Bibliography

MANUSCRIPTS

Archives Nationales
Série Y, Archives and reports of the Châtelet commissioners: 8958, 11019, 12495, 14355, 14371, 14505, 14506–14510, 15536, 15552, 15561, 15563–15567, 9498, 9532, 9537, 10018.
Bibliothèque de l'Arsenal
Archives de la Bastille, mss. 10338–10354.
Bibliothèque Nationale
Deliberations of Colbert's committee on the cleanliness and security of Paris (1666): *Manuscrits français*, 16847, 8118.
Police Reports (1669–1715): *Manuscrits français*, 8119–8125.
Papers of Nicolas de la Reynie: *Nouvelles acquisitions françaises*, 5247–5249; *mss. francais* 7608;
Procès criminal du chevalier de Rohan: *BNF mss. fonds français*, 7629.
University of Pennsylvania
Correspondence, Nicolas de la Reynie and Jean-Baptiste Colbert

Abbiatecci, André, François Billacois, Yves Castan, and Porphyre Petrovich. *Cahier des annales*, 33. Paris: Éditions EHESS, 1971.
Adams, Christine. "'Belle comme le jour': Beauty, Power, and the King's Mistress." *French History* 29 (2015): 161–181.
Albanese, Ralph, Jr. "Historical and Literary Perceptions on 17th-Century Criminality." *Stanford French Review* 4 (1980): 417–453.
Almond, Philip C. *The Devil: A New Biography*. Ithaca, NY: Cornell University Press, 2014.

Alphand, Adolphe, ed. *Atlas des anciens plans de Paris*. 3 vols. Paris: Imprimerie nationale, 1880.

Andrews, Richard Mowery. *Law, Magistracy, and Crime in Old Regime Paris, 1735–1789: Volume 1, the System of Criminal Justice*. Cambridge, England: Cambridge University Press, 1994.

Antoine, Michel. "Qui entrait au conseil du Roi ?" *La Revue administrative 52*, no. 3 (1999): 71–76.

Aubry, Gérard. *La Jurisprudence criminelle du Châtelet de Paris sous le règne de Louis XIV*. Vol. 10. Paris: Librairie générale de droit et de jurisprudence. Bibliothèque de sciences criminelles, 1971.

Audiger. *La maison réglée, ou l'art de diriger la maison d'un grand seigneur*. Paris: n.p., 1692.

de Baillon, Charles, comte. *Henriette-Anne d'Angleterre, Duchesse d'Orléans, sa vie et sa correspondance avec son frère Charles II*. Paris: Perrin et cie, 1886.

Baldwin, Martha. "The Snakestone Experiments: An Early Modern Medical Debate." *Isis 86*, no. 3 (September 1995): 394–418.

Barbiche, Bernard. "Le conseil du roi dans tous ses états: Questions de vocabulaire." *La Revue administrative 52*, no. 3 (1999): 20–26.

Barker, Nancy Nichols. *Brother to the Sun King: Philippe, Duke of Orléans*. Baltimore: Johns Hopkins University Press, 1988.

Barker, Sheila. "Poussin, Plague, and Early Modern Medicine." *Art Bulletin 86*, no. 4 (2004): 659–689.

Baron, Jeremy Hugh. "Paintress, Princess and Physician's Paramour: Poison or Perforation." *Journal of the Royal Society of Medicine 91* (1998): 213–216.

Barras, Vincent, and Michael Porret, eds. "Homo criminalis: Pratiques et doctrines médico-légales (XVI–XXe Siècles)." Special issue, *Equinoxe, revue de sciences humaines 22* (1999).

Bastien, Paul. "La parole du confesseur aupres des supplicés (Paris, XVIIe–XVIIIe Siècle)." *Revue historique 634*, no. 2 (2005): 283–308.

Beam, Sara. "Les canards criminels et les limites de la violence dans la France de la première modernité." *Histoire, économie et société 30*, no. 2 (June 2011): 15–28.

Beasley, Faith. *Revising Memory: Women's Fiction and Memoirs in Seventeenth-Century France*. New Brunswick, NJ: Rutgers University Press, 1990.

———. *Salons, History, and the Creation of Seventeenth-Century France: Mastering Memory*. Aldershot, England: Ashgate, 2006.

Beik, William. *Urban Protest in Seventeenth-Century France: The Culture of Retribution*. Cambridge, England: Cambridge University Press, 1997.

Benedict, Philip. *Cities and Social Change in Early Modern France*. Oxford: Routledge, 1992.

Bercé, Yves-Marie. "Aspects de la criminalité au XVIIe siècle." *Revue historique 239*, no. 1 (January 1968): 33–42.

Berger, Robert W. "The Chronology of the Envelope of Versailles." *Architectura 10*, no. 2 (1980): 105–133.

Bernard, Leon. *The Emerging City: Paris in the Age of Louis XIV*. Durham, NC: Duke University Press, 1970.

Berty, Adolphe. "Études historiques et topographiques sur le vieux Paris. Trois ilots de la cité compris entre les rues de la Licorne, aux fèves, de la lanterne, du haut Moulin et de Glatigny." *Revue Archéologique* 1 (1860): 197–215.

Bever, Edward. "Witchcraft, Female Aggression, and Power in the Early Modern Community." *Journal of Social History* 35, no. 4: 955–988.

Bée, Michel. "Le spectacle de l'exécution dans la France d'Ancien Régime." *Annales. histoires, sciences sociales* 38, no. 4 (1983): 843–862.

Bély, Lucien. "Secret et espionnage militaire au temps de Louis XIV." *Revue historique des armées* 263 (2011): 28–39.

Billacois, François. "Pour une enquête sur la criminalité dans la France d'Ancien Régime." *Annales. Histoire, Science Sociale* 22, no. 2 (1967): 340–349.

Blégny, Nicolas. *La doctrine des rapports de chirurgie.* N.p.: n.p., 1684.

de Boislisle, A. "Le secret de la Poste: Sous le règne de Louis XIV." *Annuaire-Bulletin de la Société de l'histoire de France* 27, no. 2 (1890): 229–245.

Bluche, François. *Louis XIV.* Paris: Fayard, 1986.

Bondois, Paul-M. "Les difficultés du ravitaillement parisien: Les projets de nouvelles Halles de 1663 à 1718." *Revue d'histoire moderne* 11, no. 24 (1936).

———. "Le commissaire Nicolas Delamare et le traité de la police." *Revue d'Histoire Moderne* 10, no. 19 (1935): 313–351.

Boorsch, Suzanne. "Fireworks!: Four Centuries of Pyrotechnics in Prints & Drawings." *Metropolitan Museum of Art Bulletin* 58, no. 1 (2000): 3–52.

Boscher, M. "Mémoire d'un chirurgien du roy d'Angleterre qui a esté present à l'ouverture du corps de Madame royale de France." *Lives of the Princesses of England.* Vol. 6. London: Henry Colburn, 1855.

Boudon–Millot, Véronique. "La thériaque selon Galien: Poison salutaire ou remède empoisonné?" *Le corps à l'épreuve. Poisons, remèdes et chirurgie: aspects des pratiques médicales dans l'Antiquité et au Moyen Âge* (2002): 45–56.

Boudon-Millot, Véronique, and Franck Collard, eds. *Le Corps à l'épreuve: poisons, remèdes et chirurgie: Aspects des pratiques médicales dans l'antiquité et au Moyen Age.* Collection Hommes et textes en Champagne. Reims: D. Guéniot: 2002.

Boulanger, Marc. "Justice et absolutisme: La grande ordonnance criminelle d'août 1670." *Revue d'histoire moderne et contemporaine (1954–)* 47, no. 1 (2000): 7–36.

Bournon, Fernand. *La Bastille: Histoire et description des bâtiments, administration, régime de la prison, événements historiques.* Paris: Imprimerie nationale, 1893.

Brittain, Robert P. "Cruentation in Legal Medicine and Literature." *Medical History* 9 (1965): 82–88.

Brock, I. W. "Vitalizing the Seventeenth Century." *Modern Language Journal* 19, no. 4 (January 1935): 241.

Bruzelius, Caroline. "The Construction of Notre-Dame in Paris." *Art Bulletin* 69, no. 4 (1987): 540–569.

Burger, Pierre-François. "Deux documents sur Amelot de La Houssay." *Dix-Septième Siècle* 33, no. 2 (1981): 199–202.

Burke, Peter. *The Fabrication of Louis XIV.* New Haven: Yale University Press, 1994.

————. *Popular Culture in Early Modern Europe.* London: Temple Smith, 1978.

Camden, Carroll, Jr. "Astrology in Shakespeare's Day." *Isis* 19, no. 1 (1933): 26–73.

Campbell, W. A. "The History of the Chemical Detection of Poisons." *Medical History* 25, no. 2 (1981): 202–203.

Carbasse, Jean-Marie. *Histoire du droit pénal et de la justice criminelle.* Paris: Presses universitaires de France, 2014.

Carrier, Hubert. *La presse de la Fronde (1648–1653): Les Mazarinades.* Geneva: Droz, 1989.

Carroll, Erika. "Potions, Poisons and 'Inheritance Powders': How Chemical Discourses Entangled 17th Century France in the Brinvilliers Trial and the Poison Affair." *Voces Novae: Chapman University Historical Review* 4, no. 1 (2012).

Carroll, Patrick E. "Medical Police and the History of Public Health." *Medical History* 46 (2002): 461–494.

Carroll, Stuart. *Blood and Violence in Early Modern France.* Oxford, England: Oxford University Press, 2006.

Catellani, Patrizia, and Renzo Console. "Moyse Charas (1619–1698): Farmacista e Scienziato Europeo del Seicento." *Atti e memorie* 21, no. 2 (August 2003).

————. "Moyse Charas, Francesco Redi, the Viper and the Royal Society of London." *Pharmaceutical Historian* 34, no. 1 (March 2004): 2–10.

————. "Moyse Charas nell'Eloge di Condorcet." *Atti e memorie* 9, no. 1 (2006): 17–26.

Cénat, Jean-Philippe. *Louvois: Le Double de Louis XIV.* Paris: Tallandier, 2015.

Chagniot, Jean. "Le guet et la garde de Paris à la fin de l'Ancien Régime." *Revue d'histoire moderne et contemporaine (1954–)* 20, no. 1 (1973): 58–71.

Chapman, Sara E. *Private Ambition and Political Alliances: The Phélypeaux de Pontchartrain Family and Louis XIV's Government, 1650–1715.* Rochester, NY: University of Rochester Press, 2004.

Charas, Moyse. "Certificat de Messieurs les Docteurs de la faculté de médecine de Paris, & de Messieurs les Gardes de la pharmacie." In *Thériaque d'Andromacus,* 10–12. Paris: Laurent d'Houry, 1682.

Charmasson, Thérèse. *L'astronomie, la cosmologie, l'astrologie, et les sciences divinatoires.* Heidelberg: Carl Winder University, 1988.

Chassaigne, Marc. *La lieutenance générale de police de Paris.* Geneva: Slatkine-Megariotis Reprints, 1975.

Chast, François. "Les origines de la législation sur les stupéfiants en France." *Histoire des sciences médicales* 43, no. 3 (2009): 293–305.

Chaunu, Pierre. "Sur la fin des sorcières au XVIIe siècle." *Annales. Histoire, Sciences Sociales* 24, no. 4 (1969): 895–911.

Chéreul, A. *Mémoires de Mlle de Montpensier.* Paris: Charpentier, 1858.

Choisy, François-Timoléon. *Mémoires pour server à l'histoire de Louis XIV par feu M. l'Abbé de Choisy.* Edited Georges Mongrédien. Paris: Mercure de France, 1979.

Chubak, Barbara. "Impotence and Suing for Sex in Eighteenth-Century England." *Urology* 71, no. 3 (March 2008): 480–484.

Cladel, Judith. *Mademoiselle de La Vallière*. Paris: Éditions d'art et de littérature, 1912.

Clark, Michael, and Catherine Crawford. *Legal Medicine in History*. Cambridge, England: Cambridge University Press, 1994.

Clark, Stuart. *Thinking with Demons: The Idea of Witchcraft in Early Modern England*. Oxford, England: Oxford University Press, 1997.

Clarke, Jan. "L'éclairage." In *La Réprésentation théâtrale en France au XVIIe siècle*, 119–140, edited by Pierre Pasquier and Anne Surgers. Paris: Armand Colin, 2011.

———. "'In the Eye of the Beholder'?: The Actress as Beauty in Seventeenth-Century France." *Seventeenth-Century French Studies* 25 (2003): 111–127.

———. "*La Devineresse* and the *Affaire des Poisons*." *Seventeenth-Century French Studies* 28 (2006): 221–234.

———. "Machine Plays at the Guénégaud: The Twilight of the Gods." *The Seventeenth Century* 12, no. 1 (1997): 85–110.

———. "Music at the Guénégaud Theatre 1673–1680." *Seventeenth-Century French Studies* 12 (1990): 89–110.

Clément, Pierre. *La police de Paris sous Louis XIV*. Paris: Didier et Cie, 1866.

———. *Trois drames historiques: Enguerrand de Marigny, Semblançay, le Chevalier de Rohan*. Paris: Didier et Cie, 1857.

———. *Madame de Montespan et Louis XIV: Étude historique*. Paris: Didier et Cie, 1868.

Coeyman, Barbara. "Social Dance in the 1668 Feste de Versailles: Architecture and Performance Context." *Early Music* 26, no. 2 (1998): 264–269, 271–278, 281–282, 284–285.

———. "Theatres for Opera and Ballet During the Reigns of Louis XIV and Louis XV." *Early Music* 18, no. 1 (1990): 22–37.

Colbert, Jean-Baptiste. *Lettres, instructions et mémoires de Colbert*. Edited by Pierre Clément. Vols. 5–7. Paris: Imprimerie Impériale, 1869.

Collard, Franck. *Le crime de poison au Moyen Âge 2003*. Paris: Presses Universitaires de France, 2003.

———. "Recherches sur le crime de poison au Moyen Âge." *Journal des savants* 1, no. 1 (1992): 99–114.

Colyar, H. A. de. "Jean-Baptiste Colbert and the Codifying Ordinances of Louis XIV." *Journal of the Society of Comparative Legislation* 13, no. 1 (1912): 56–86.

Contant, J. P. *L'enseignement de la chimie au jardin royal des plantes de Paris*. Cahors, France: I. Couselant, 1952.

Cooper, George. *Poison Widows: A True Story of Witchcraft, Arsenic, and Murder*. New York: St. Martin's, 1999.

Coquery, Natacha. "Les hôtels parisiens du XVIIIe siècle: Une approche des modes d'habiter." *Revue d'histoire moderne et contemporaine* 38 (1991): 205–230.

Corbin, Alain. *The Foul and the Fragrant: Odor and the French Social Imagination*. Cambridge, MA: Harvard University Press, 1988.

Cornu, Marcel. *Le procès de la Marquise de Brinvilliers, 1672–1676. Discours prononcé à l'ouverture de la conférence du stage des avocats au conseil d'état et à la cour de cassation*. Paris: n.p., 1894.

Corvisier, A. "Les gardes du corps de Louis XIV." *XVIIe siècle* 45 (1959): 265–291.

Corvisier, André. *Louvois*. Paris: Fayard, 1983.

Crawford, Catherine. "Legalizing Medicine: Early Modern Legal Systems and the Growth of Medico-Legal Knowledge." *Legal Medicine in History*. Cambridge, England: Cambridge University Press, 1994.

Cummings, Mark. "Elopement, Family, and the Courts: The Crime of 'Rapt' in Early Modern France." *Proceedings of the Western Society for French History* 4 (1976): 118–125.

Cumston, Charles Greene. "Remarks on the History of Forensic Medicine From the Renaissance to the Nineteenth Century." *Green Bag* 22 (1910): 685–691.

Danis, Robert. *La Première Maison Royale de Trianon, 1670–1687*. Paris: Morancé, 1926.

Davis, Ben. "A History of Forensic Medicine." *Medico-Legal Journal* 53, no. 1 (1985): 9–23.

Davis, Natalie Zemon. *Fiction in the Archives: Pardon Tales and Their Tellers in Sixteenth-Century France*. Stanford, CA: Stanford University Press, 1987.

———. *Fiction in the Archives: Pardon Tales and Their Tellers in Sixteenth-Century France*. Stanford, CA: Stanford University Press, 1987.

Defrance, Eugène. *Histoire de l'éclairage des rues de Paris*. Paris: Imprimerie Nationale, 1904.

DeJean, Joan. *The Essence of Style: How the French Invented High Fashion, Fine Food, Chic Cafés, Style, Sophistication, and Glamour*. New York: Simon & Schuster, 2006.

———. *How Paris Became Paris: The Invention of the Modern City*. New York: Bloomsbury, 2014.

———. "The Work of Forgetting: Commerce, Sexuality, Censorship and Molière's *Le Festin De Pierre*." *Critical Inquiry* 29, no. 1 (2002): 53–80.

Delamare, Nicolas. *Traité de la police*. Paris: J. et P. Cot, 1705.

Delavaud, Louis. *La cour de Louis XIV en 1671: Madame de Montespan, Colbert & Louvois*. Paris: Levé, 1912.

Depauw, Jacques. "Pauvres, pauvres mendiants, mendiants valides ou vagabonds?: Les hésitations de la législation royale." *Revue d'Histoire Moderne & Contemporaine* 21, no. 3 (1974): 401–418.

Depping, G. B., ed. *Correspondance administrative sous le règne de Louis XIV*. Vol. 2. Paris, Imprimerie Nationale, 1851: 561–680.

Derblay, Claude. *Un Drame sous Louis XIV: L'Affaire du Chevalier de Rohan*. Paris: Nouvelle Edition, 1945.

Desprat. Jean-Paul. *Madame de Maintenon (1635–1719), ou le prix de la réputation*. [2003]. Paris: Perrin, 2015.

Detourbet, Robert. *L'espionnage et la trahison*. Paris: L. Larose, 1898.

———. *La procédure criminelle au XVIIe siécle*. Edited Detourbet. Paris: A. Rousseau, 1881.

Devaux, Jean. *L'Art de faire les rapports en chirurgie*. Paris: Laurent d'Houry, 1703.

d'Ormesson, Olivier Lefèvre. *Journal d'Olivier Lefèvre d'Ormesson, et extraits des mémoires d'André Lefèvre d'Ormesson*. Edited André Chéreul. Paris: Imprimerie Royale, 1861.

Duchêne, Jacqueline. *Henriette d'Angleterre, Duchesse d'Orléans.* Paris: Fayard, 1995.

Dulong, Claude. "L'assassinat de la Du Parc." *La revue des deux mondes* (1965): 334–344.

———. *La vie quotidienne des femmes au grand siècle.* Paris: Hachette Littérature, 1984.

Duramy, Benedetta Faedi. "Women and Poisons in 17th Century France." *Chicago-Kent Law Review* 87 (2012): 347–370.

Dutray-Lecoin, Élise, and Arlette Fargette. "Le désordre social et politique, la main du roi s'y oppose." *La Bastille, ou l'enfer des vivants: À travers les archives de la Bastille.* Paris: Bibliothèque Nationale de France, 2010. 86–90.

Dwyer, Deirdre M. "Expert Evidence in the English Civil Courts, 1550–1800." *Journal of Legal History* 28, no. 1 (2007): 93–118.

Dyer, Walter A. "The French Decorative Styles: I. Louis XIV (1643–1715)." *Art World* 3, no. 3 (1917): 240–242.

Eamon, W. *Science and the Secrets of Nature: Books of Secrets in Medieval and Early Modern Culture.* Princeton: Princeton University Press, 1996.

Edit du roy portant règlement contre ceux qui se disent devins, & contre les empoisonneurs. Vennes, France: n.p., 1682.

Ekberg, Carl J. "From Dutch to European War: Louis XIV and Louvois Are Tested." *French Historical Studies* 8, no. 3 (1974): 393–408.

Emmanuelli, Francois-Xavier. "Ordres du roi et lettres de cachet en provence à la fin de l'ancien régime: Contribution à l'histoire du climat social et politique." *Revue historique* (1974): 357–392.

Esmein, Adhémar. *Histoire de la procédure criminelle en France.* Paris: L. Laure et Forcel, 1882.

Esmonin, Ed. "Les mémoires de Louis XIV." *Revue d'histoire moderne* 2, no. 12 (1927): 449–454.

Etablissement de porte-flambeaux et porte-lanterne à louage dans la ville et faubourgs de Paris et toutes autres villes du royaume par lettres patentes du roi vérifiées en parlement, et règlement fait par ladite cour des salaires desdits porte-flambeaux et porte-lanternes. Paris: Veuve Dugast, 1662.

Fabbri, Christiane Nockels. "Treating Medieval Plague: The Wonderful Virtues of Theriac." *Early science and medicine* 12, no. 3 (2007): 247–283.

Fabre, Jean. *Essai médico-historique sur la vie, et principalement sur la mort de Madame Henriette-Anne Stuart, duchesse d'Orléans.* Paris: Champion, 1912.

Factum en forme de requête pour Damoiselle Angélique Domaigné et le Sieur Baron de Divette son beau-père, accusés de l'empoisonnement, autres crimes. Paris: Veuve Dupont, 1681.

Farr, James R. *A Tale of Two Murders: Passion and Power in Seventeenth-Century France.* Durham, NC: Duke University Press, 2005.

Felix, Fred W. "Moyse Charas, maître apothicaire et docteur en médecine." *Revue d'histoire de la pharmacie* 90, no. 333 (2002): 63–80.

Félibien, André. *Description sommaire du chasteau de Versailles.* Paris: G. Desprez, 1674.

Félibien, Michel. *Histoire de la ville de Paris.* Vol. 1. Paris: G. Desprez, 1725.

Félibien des Avaux, Jean-François. *Description sommaire de Versailles, ancienne et nouvelle. avec des figures.* Paris: Antoine Chrétien, 1703.

Ferrier, David. "Historical Notes on Poisoning." *British Medical Journal* 1, no. 597 (June 15, 1872): 601.

Flint-Hamilton, Kimberly. "Legumes in Ancient Greece and Rome: Food, Medicine, or Poison?" *Journal of the American School of Classical Studies at Athens* 68, no. 3 (1999): 371–385.

Fonck, Bertrand. *Le Maréchal de Luxembourg et le commandement des armées sous Louis XIV.* Seyssel, France: Editions Champ Vallon, 2014.

Forbes, Thomas Rogers. *The Midwife and the Witch.* New Haven: Yale University Press, 1966.

Fraile, Pedro. "The Construction of the Idea of the City in Early Modern Europe: Perez de Herrera and Nicolas Delamare." *Journal of Urban History* 36, no. 5 (September 1, 2010): 685–708.

Franklin, Alfred. *Estat, noms et nombres de toutes les rues de Paris en 1636, d'après le manuscrit inédit de la bibliothèque nationale; Précédés d'une étude sur la voirie et l'hygiène publique à Paris depuis le XIIe Siècle.* Paris: Editions de Paris, 1988.

Fraser, Antonia. *Love and Louis XIV: The Women in the Life of the Sun King.* New York: Anchor Books, 2007.

French, Roger. "Foretelling the Future: Arabic Astrology and English Medicine in the Late Twelfth Century." *Isis* 87, no. 3 (1996): 453–480.

Frenkel, F. E. "Sex-Crime and Its Socio-Historical Background." *Journal of the History of Ideas* 25, no. 3 (July 1964): 333–352.

Friedland, Paul. *Seeing Justice Done: The Age of Spectacular Capital Punishment in France.* Oxford, England: Oxford University Press, 2012.

Frostin, Charles. *Les Pontchartrain, ministres de Louis XIV: Alliances et réseau d'influence sous l'Ancien Régime.* Rennes, France: Presses Universitaires de Rennes, 2006.

Funck-Brentano, Frantz. *Les Archives de la Bastille: La Formation du Dépôt.* Dole, France: Ch. Blind, 1890.

———. *Catalogue des manuscrits de la Bibliothèque de l'Arsenal.* Paris: Plon, 1892.

———. *Le Drame des poisons.* Paris: Hachette, 1902.

———. *Les Lettres de cachet.* Paris: Libraire Hachette, 1926.

Gaskill, Malcolm. "The Displacement of Providence: Policing and Prosecution in Seventeenth- and Eighteenth-Century England." *Continuity and Change* 11, no. 3 (1996): 341–372.

———. "Reporting Murder: Fiction in the Archives in Early Modern England." *Social History* 23, no. 1 (1998): 1–30.

Gattrell, Victor A. C., Bruce Lenman, and Geoffrey Parker. *Crime and the Law: The Social History of Crime in Western Europe Since 1500.* London: Europa Publications, 1980.

Gauvard, Claude. "Paris, le parlement et la sorcellerie au milieu du XVe Siècle." In *Finances, pouvoirs, et mémoire: Mélanges offerts à Jean Favier*, edited by Jean Kerhervé and Albert Rigaudière, 85–111. Paris: Fayard, 1999.

Gavret, J. *Le vray style pour proceder au chastelet de Paris, tant en matières civiles que criminelles.* Paris: n.p., 1658.

Gélis, Jacques. "Sages-femmes et accoucheurs: L'obstétrique populaire au XVIIe et XVIIIe siècles." *Annales. Histoire, Sciences Sociales* 32, no. 5 (1977): 927–957.

Geremek, Bronislaw. "Criminalité, vagabondage, paupérisme: La marginalité à l'aube des temps modernes." *Revue d'histoire moderne et contemporaine* 21, no. 3 (1974): 337–375.

Gilbert, Emile. *Philtres, charmes, poisons: Antiquité, moyen age, renaissance, temps modernes.* Paris: Imprimerie de Veuve Renou, Maulde et Cock, 1880.

Glaister, John. "The Medical Profession and the Police." *Police Journal* (1930): 201.

Goldsmith, Elizabeth C. *The Kings' Mistresses: The Liberated Lives of Marie Mancini, Princess Colonna, and Her Sister Hortense, Duchess Mazarin.* New York: Public Affairs, 2012.

Gowing, Laura. "Secret Births and Infanticide in Seventeenth-Century England." *Past & Present* 156 (1997): 87–115.

Grancsay, Stephen V. "The Charles Noé Daly Bequest of Firearms." *Metropolitan Museum of Art Bulletin* 30, no. 10 (1935): 189–192.

Green, Mary Anne Everett. *Lives of the Princesses of England: From the Norman Conquest.* Vol. 5. London: Longman, Brown, Green, Longman & Roberts, 1854.

Gruyer, Paul. *Saint-Germain, Poissy, Maisons, Marly-le-Roi.* Paris: Henri Laurens, 1922.

Guéry, Alain. "Les finances de la monarchie française sous l'Ancien Régime." *Annales. Histoire, Sciences Sociales* 33, no. 2 (1978): 216–239.

Hamscher, Albert N. "The Conseil Privé and the Parlements in the Age of Louis XIV: A Study in French Absolutism." *Transactions of the American Philosophical Society* 77.2 (1987): i–vii, 1–162.

———. *The Royal Financial Administration and the Prosecution of Crime in France, 1670–1789.* Newark: University of Delaware Press, copublished with Lanham, MD. Rowman and Littlefield, 2012.

Harding, Vanessa. "Whose Body? A Study of Attitudes Towards the Dead Body in Early Modern Paris." In *The Place of the Dead: Death and Remembrance in Late Medieval and Early Modern Europe.* Edited by Bruce Gordon and Peter Marshall. Cambridge, England: Cambridge University Press, 2000. 170–187.

Harris-Warrick, Rebecca. "Ballroom Dancing at the Court of Louis XIV." *Early Music* 14, no. 1 (1986): 40–49.

Herlaut, Auguste-Philippe. *L'éclairage des rues à Paris à la fin du XVIIe et au XVIIIe Siècles.* Paris: P. Renouard, 1916.

Heuzé, Paul. *La cour intime de Louis XIV: D'après les manuscrits du temps et les documents de la bibliothèque de Versailles.* Paris: A. Charles, 1902.

Hillairet, Jacques, and Pascal Payen-Appenzeller. *Dictionnaire historique des rues de Paris.* Vol. 2. Paris: Éditions de minuit, 1963.

Hilton, Lisa. *Athénaïs: The Life of Louis XIV's Mistress, the Real Queen of France.* Boston: Little, Brown and Company, 2002.

Hopkins, Tighe. *Dungeons of Old Paris.* New York; London: G. P. Putnam & Sons, 1897.

Houssay, Arsène. *Mademoiselle de La Vallière et Madame de Montespan: Etudes historiques sur la cour de Louis XIV.* Paris: Henri Plon, 1860.

Hurt, John J. *Louis XIV and the Parlements: The Assertion of Royal Authority.* Manchester, England: Manchester University Press, 2004.

Hussey, Andrew. *Paris: The Secret History.* New York: Bloomsbury Publishing USA, 2010.

Hutton, R. "The Making of the Secret Treaty of Dover, 1668–1670." *Historical Journal* 29, no. 2 (1986): 297–318.

Hyde, Elizabeth. "The Stuff of Kingship: Louis XIV, the Trianon de Porcelaine, and the Material Culture of Power." *Proceedings of the Annual Meeting of the Western Society for French History* 30 (2002): 191–201.

Imbert, J., and P. Guénois. *La pratique judiciaire, tant civile que criminelle.* Lyon: François Arnoullet, 1619.

Isambert, F.-A., ed., *Receuil général des anciennes lois françaises.* Paris: Berlin-Le-Prieur, 1821.

Jackson, Mark. "Suspicious Infant Deaths: The Statute of 1624 and Medical Evidence at Coroners' Inquests." In *Legal Medicine in History*, edited by Michael Clark and Catherine Crawford, 64–86. Cambridge, England: Cambridge University Press, 1994.

Jones, Carol A. G. *Expert Witnesses: Science, Medicine, and the Practice of Law.* Oxford, England: Clarendon Press, 1994.

Jones, Colin. *Paris: The Biography of a City.* New York: Penguin, 2006.

———. "Plague and Its Metaphors in Early Modern France." *Representations* 53 (1996): 97–127.

Jousse, Daniel. *Traité de la justice criminelle en France.* Paris: Debure père, 1771.

Kahn, Axel, and Yvan Brohard. *Une Histoire de la pharmacie: Remèdes, onguents, poisons.* Paris: Martinière, 2012.

Kalifa, Dominique. "Crime Scenes: Criminal Topography and Social Imaginary in Nineteenth-Century Paris." *French Historical Studies* 27, no. 1 (2004): 175–194.

Kargon, Robert. "Expert Testimony in Historical Perspective." *Law and Human Behavior* 10, nos. 1/2 (1986): 15–27.

Kavanagh, Thomas M. "Gambling, Chance and the Discourse of Power in Ancien Régime France." *Renaissance and Modern Studies* 37, no. 1 (January 1994): 31–46.

Kettering, Sharon. "The Household Service of Early Modern French Noblewomen." *French Historical Studies* 20, no. 1 (1997): 55.

———. "Patronage and Politics During the Fronde." *French Historical Studies* 14, no. 3 (1986): 409–441.

Kimball, Fiske. "The Development of the 'Cheminée à la royale'." *Metropolitan Museum Studies* 5, no. 2 (1936): 259–280.

———. "Mansart and Le Brun in the Genesis of the Grande Galérie de Versailles." *Art Bulletin* 22, no. 1 (March 1940): 1.

Kimball, Marie. "Some Genial Old Drinking Customs." *William and Mary Quarterly* 2, no. 4 (1945): 349–358.

Kingsley, Rose, and Camille Gronkowski. "Types of Old Paris Houses. Article 1.—Hôtel de Lauzun, Louis XIV Period." *Burlington Magazine for Connoisseurs* 1, no. 1 (March 1903): 84–85, 87–89, 91–93, 95–97, 99–100.

Koslofsky, Craig. "Court Culture and Street Lighting in Seventeenth-Century Europe." *Journal of Urban History* 28, no. 6 (2002): 743–768.
———. *Evening's Empire: A History of the Night in Early Modern Europe.* Cambridge, England: Cambridge University Press, 2011.
———. "Princes of Darkness: The Night at Court, 1650–1750." *Journal of Modern History* 79, no. 2 (June 2007): 235–273.
"La Devineresse." *Mercure Galant* (January 1689): 344–349.
Ladurie, Emmanuel Le Roy. "Auprès du roi, la cour." *Annales. Histoire, Sciences Sociales* 38, no. 1 (1983): 21–41.
La Fayette, Marie-Madeleine Pioche de la Vergne. *Histoire d'Henriette d'Angleterre* (Paris: Charavay Frères, 1882).
Lafont, Olivier. "La pratique de l'art de l'apothicaire au XVIIe siècle : Information fournie par deux inventaires après décès." *Revue d'histoire de la pharmacie* 80, no. 295 (1992): 453–466.
Laingui, André. *Histoire du droit pénal.* Paris: Presses universitaires de France, 1985.
Lair, Jules. *Louise de La Vallière et la jeunesse de Louis XIV D'après des documents inédits, avec de nouveaux portraits, plans, documents et notes.* Paris: Plon-Nourrit, 1902.
Laistner, M. L. W. "The Western Church and Astrology During the Early Middle Ages." *Harvard Theological Review* 34, no. 4 (October 1941): 251–275.
Lamont-Brown, Raymond. *Royal Poxes and Potions: The Lives of Court Physicians, Surgeons, and Apothecaries.* Stroud, England: Sutton Publishing, 2001.
Laqueur, Thomas. "Bodies, Death, and Pauper Funerals." *Representations* 1 (February 1983): 109–131.
Lebigre, Arlette. *L'Affaire des poisons.* Paris: Editions Complexe, 1989.
———. *La justice du roi: la vie judiciaire dans l'ancienne France.* Paris: Albin Michel, 1988.
———. "La Naissance de la police en France." *L'Histoire* (Jan. 1979): 5–12.
———. *Les Dangers de Paris Au XVIIe siècle: L'assassinat de Jacques Tardieu, Lieutenant Criminel au Châtelet et de sa femme, 24 Août 1665.* Paris: Albin Michel, 1991.
———. "Madame de Sévigné et les grands procès de son temps." *Histoire de la justice* 10, no. 1 (2010): 25–33.
———. *Nicolas de La Reynie, premier préfet de police, La France de la monarchie absolue, 1610–1715,* edited by Joel Cornette. Paris: Seuil, 1997.
Le Blant, Robert. "Notes sur Jean de Garibal." *Revue de l'histoire de l'Amérique française.* 15, no. 1 (1961): 104–122.
Lebrun, François. "Le 'traité des superstitions' de Jean-Baptiste Thiers. Contribution à l'ethnographie de la France du XVIIe siècle." *Annales de Bretagne et des pays de l'Ouest* 83, no. 3 (1976): 443–465.
———. *Se soigner autrefois: Médecins, saints et sorciers aux XVIIe et XVIIIe siècles.* Paris: Seuil, 1995.
Leclant, Jean. "Le café et les cafés à Paris (1644–1693)." *Annales. Histoire, Sciences Sociales* 6, no. 1 (1951): 1–14.
Legué, Gabriel. *Médecins et empoisonneurs au XVIIe siècle.* Paris: Charpentier, 1895.

Lemoine, Jean. *Les des Oeillets: Une grande comédienne, une maîtresse de Louis XIV: Étude et Documents*. Paris: Perrin, 1938.
———. "Madame de La Fayette et Louvois." *Revue de Paris* 14, no. 5 (1907): 65–86.
———. *Madame de Montespan et la légende des poisons*. Paris: Leclerc, 1908.
Lemoine, Jean, and André Lichtenberger. *De La Vallière à Montespan*. Paris: Calmann-Lévy, 1902.
Le Nabour, Eric. *La Reynie: Le policier de Louis XIV*. Paris: Perrin, 1990.
Leong, Elaine. "Making Medicines in the Early Modern Household." *Bulletin of the History of Medicine* 82, no. 1 (2008): 145–68.
Léoni, Sylviane. *Le poison et le remède: Théâtre, morale, et rhétorique en France, en Italie, 1694–1758*. Oxford, England: Voltaire Foundation, 1998. Studies on Voltaire and the Eighteenth Century, 360.
Levantal, Christophe. *Louis XIV: Chronographie d'un Règne*. Vol. 1. Paris: Infolio, 2009.
Levy, Joel. *Poison: A Social History*. Stroud, England: History Press, 2011.
Lister, Martin. *Voyage de Lister à Paris en 1698*. Paris: Société des bibliophiles, 1873.
Loar, C. "Medical Knowledge and the Early Modern English Coroner's Inquest." *Social History of Medicine* 23, no. 3 (Dec. 1, 2010): 475–491.
Lough, John. *France Observed in the Seventeenth Century by British Travellers*. Stocksfield, England: Oriel Press, 1985.
Louvois, François Michel Le Tellier, marquis de. *Letters of Louvois*. Edited by Jacques Hardre. Chapel Hill: University of North Carolina Press, 1949.
Luxembourg, François-Henri de Montmorency, duke of. "Lettre secrette de M. de Luxembourg sur son emprisonnement à la Bastille." In *Mémoires pour servir à l'histoire du Maréchal Duc de Luxembourg*. La Haye: Benjamin Gibert, 1758: 36–88.
Lynn, John A. "Recalculating French Army Growth During the Grand Siecle, 1610–1715." *French Historical Studies* 18, no. 4 (1994): 881–906.
———. *The Wars of Louis XIV 1667–1714*. New York: Routledge, 2013.
Maes, L. "Empoisonnement, Procédure Inquisitoriale, Torture, et Peine de Mort au Début du XVIII Siècle." *Revue historique de droit français et étranger* 55 (1977): 59–72.
Maintenon, Madame de. *Correspondence générale*. Vol. 2. Edited by Théophile Lavallée. Paris: Charpentier, 1865.
Malandain, Gilles. "Les mouches de la police et le vol des mots. Les gazetins de la police secrète et la surveillance de l'expression publique à Paris au deuxième quart du XVIIIe siècle." *Revue d'histoire moderne et contemporaine (1954–)* 42, no. 3 (1995): 376–404. http://www.jstor.org/stable/20530082. Accessed June 28 2014.
Manal, Roland. "Comment travaillait un roi Louis XIV administrateur et grand commis de l'état." *La Revue administrative* 22, no. 127 (1969): 17–30. http://www.jstor.org/stable/40778887.
Mann, James G. "The Influence of Art on Instruments on War." *Journal of the Royal Society of Arts* 89, no. 4599 (1941): 740–784.
Matthews, Leslie G. "Nicolas Cabry: Master Apothecary of Paris." *Pharmaceutical History* 17, no. 1 (March 1987): 4–6.

Maza, Sarah. *Private Lives and Public Affairs: The Causes Célèbres of Prerevolutionary France.* Berkeley: University of California Press, 1993.

McClive, Cathy. "Blood and Expertise: The Trials of the Female Medical Expert in the Ancien-Régime Courtroom." *Bulletin of the History of Medicine* 82, no. 1 (2008): 86–108.

McMahon, Vanessa. "Reading the Body: Dissection and the 'Murder' of Sarah Stout, Hertfordshire, 1699." *Social History of Medicine* 19, no. 1 (Feb. 20, 2006): 19–35.

Mechior-Bonnet, Sabine, and Aude de Tocqueville. *Histoire de l'adultère.* Paris: Editions de la Martinière, 2000.

Mémoire du procès extraordinaire d'entre Dame Thérèse Mangot, veuve de feu Messire Antoine Daburay, vivant lieutenant civil, démanderesse, accusatrice et appellante, d'une sentence du présent mois de mars. Contre le nommé La Chaussée, prisonnier ès prisons de la conciergerie. et la Dame De Brinvilliers, absente et fugitive. Paris: n.p., 1672.

Merlin, Hélène. *Public et littérature en France au XVIIe siècle.* Paris: Belles Lettres, 1994.

Merrick, Jeffrey. "The Cardinal and the Queen: Sexual and Political Disorders in the Mazarinades." *French Historical Studies* 18, no. 3 (1994): 667–699.

———. "Chaussons in the Streets: Sodomy in Seventeenth-Century Paris." *Journal of the History of Sexuality* 15, no. 2 (May, 2006): 167–203.

Michelet, Jules. "Décadence morale du XVIIe Siècle, La Brinvilliers." *Revue des Deux Mondes* 26 (1860): 538–561.

Miller, John. "Henriette-Anne." In *Oxford Dictionary of National Biography.* Edited by H. C. G. Matthew and Brian Harrison. Oxford: Oxford University Press, 2004.

Miller, Minnie A. "The French Periodical Press During the Reign of Louis XIV." *French Review* 5, no. 4: 301–308.

Milliot, Vincent. "Saisir l'espace urbaine: Mobilité des commissaires et controle des quartiers de police à Paris au XVIII siècle." *Revue d'histoire moderne et contemporaine* 50, no. 1 (2003).

Milt, Clara de. "Christopher Glaser." *Journal of Chemical Education* 19, no. 2 (1942): 53–60.

———. "Early Chemistry at the Jardin du Roi." *Journal of Chemical Education* 18, no. 11 (1941): 502–509.

Minois, Georges. *Le couteau et le poison: L'assassinat politique en Europe (1400–1800).* Paris: Fayard, 1997.

Molinier, Emile. "French Furniture of the Seventeenth and Eighteenth Centuries. Article 1—The Louis XIV Style—Introduction." *Burlington Magazine for Connoisseurs* 1, no. 1 (1903): 24–27, 30–33, 36–37.

Mollenauer, Lynn Wood. *Strange Revelations: Magic, Passion, and Sacrilege in Louis XIV's France.* University Park: Penn State University Press, 2007.

Mongrédien, Georges. *Madame de Montespan et l'affaire des poisons.* Paris: Fayard, 1953.

———. "Racine et la mort de la Du Parc." *Cahiers Raciniens* 8 (1960): 489–494.

Monter, William. "Toads and Eucharists: The Male Witches of Normandy, 1564–1660." *French Historical Studies* 20, no. 4 (1997): 563–595.

Moogk, Peter N. "The Liturgy of Humiliation, Pain, and Death: The Execution of Criminals in New France." *Canadian HIstorical Review* 88, no. 1 (2007): 89–112.

Mossiker, Frances. *The Affair of the Poisons: Louis XIV, Madame de Montespan, and One of History's Great Unsolved Mysteries.* New York: Alfred A. Knopf, 1969.

Mousnier, Roland. *Paris au XVIIe siècle.* Paris: Centre de documentation universitaire, 1969.

Muchembled, Robert. *Le roi et la sorcière: L'europe des bûchers, XVe–XVIII Siècle.* Paris: Desclée-Mame, 1993.

Muir, Edward, and Guido Ruggiero. "Introduction: The Crime of History." *History from Crime.* Baltimore: Johns Hopkins University Press, 1994. vii–xviii.

Murray, Stephen O. "Homosexual Acts and Selves in Early Modern Europe." *Journal of Homosexuality* 16, nos. 1–2 (1988): 457–477.

A Narrative of the Process Against Madam Brinvilliers and Her Condemnation and Execution, for Having Poisoned Her Father and Two Brothers. London: Jonathan Edwyn, 1676.

Nass, Lucien. *Les empoisonnements sous Louis XIV d'après les documents inédits de l'affaire des poisons: 1679–1682.* Paris: Carré et Naud, 1898.

Neville, Roy G. "Christopher Glaser and the 'Traité de la Chymie,' 1663." *Chymia* 10 (January, 1965): 25–52.

Nickel, Helmut. "Arms & Armors: From the Permanent Collection." *Metropolitan Museum of Art Bulletin* 49, no. 1 (1991): 1–64.

Nivelle, Maître. *Factum pour Dame Marie Magdelaine D'Aubray, Marquise de Brinvilliers, accusée contre Dame Marie Therese Mangot, veuve du Sieur D'Aubray, lieutenant civil accusatrice; et monsieur le procureur general.* Paris: De l'imprimerie de Thomas Le Gentil, 1676.

Nolhac, Pierre de. *Histoire du château de Versailles: Versailles sous Louis XIV.* Vol. 2. Paris: Chez Émile-Paul, 1911.

Nutton, Vivian. "The Seeds of Disease: An Explanation of Contagion and Infection from the Greeks to the Renaissance." *Medical History* 27 (1983): 1–34.

O'Hara, Stephanie Elizabeth. "Tracing Poison: Theater and Society in Seventeenth-Century France." *Dissertation Abstracts International,* 2004.

Oliver, Reggie. "The Poisons Affair." *History Today* 51, no. 3 (March 2001): 28.

Oresko, Robert. "Homosexuality and the Court Elites of Early Modern France: Some Problems, Some Suggestions, and an Example." *Journal of Homosexuality* 16, no. 1–2 (1989): 105–128.

Orléans, Charlotte-Elisabeth, duchess d' (née Princesse Palatine). *Correspondance complète.* Edited by M. G. Brunet. Vol. 1. Paris: Charpentier, 1863.

Oster, Emily. "Witchcraft, Weather and Economic Growth in Renaissance Europe." *Journal of Economic Perspectives* 18, no. 1 (2004): 215–228.

Paige, Nicholas. "L'affaire des poisons et l'imaginaire de l'enquête: De Molière à Thomas Corneille." *Littératures Classiques* 40 (2000): 195–208.

Parascandola, John. *King of Poisons: A History of Arsenic.* Washington, DC: Potomac Books, 2012.

Paré, Amboise. *Oeuvres Completes*. Paris: J-B Baillère, 1841.

Parker, James, Alice M. Zrebiec, Jessie McNab, Clare Le Corbeiller, and Clare Vincent. "French Decorative Arts During the Reign of Louis XIV, 1654–1715." *Metropolitan Museum of Art Bulletin* 46, no. 4 (1989): i, 10–64.

Pastore, Alessandro. "Médecine légale et investigation judiciaire: Expérimenter le poison sur les animaux en Italie a l'époque moderne." *Revue d'Histoire des Sciences Humaines* 22 (2010): 17–35.

Patin, Guy. *Lettres choisies de feu Mr. Guy Patin*. Vol. 2. Paris: Jean Petit, 1692.

Perez, Stanis. *La santé du Louis XIV. Une biohistoire du roi-soleil*. Paris: Editions Champ Vallon, 2007.

Perkins, Wendy. "Perceptions of Women Criminals: The Case of Mme de Brinvilliers." *Seventeenth-Century French Studies* 17 (1995): 99–110.

Petry, Yvonne. "'Many Things Surpass Our Knowledge': An Early Modern Surgeon on Magic, Witchcraft and Demonic Possession." *Social History of Medicine* 25, no. 1 (Feb. 1, 2012): 47–64.

Phan, Marie-Claude. "Les déclarations de grossesse en France (XVIe–XVIIIe Siècles): Essai institutionnel." *Revue d'histoire moderne et contemporainne* 22, no. 1 (1975): 61–86.

Pharamond, Annette. "A Hermeneutic of Poison." Rochester, NY: University of Rochester, 1995.

Piasenza, Paolo. "Juges, lieutenants de police et bourgeois à Paris aux XVII et XVIII siècles." *Annales. Histoire, Sciences Sociales* 45, no. 5 (1990): 1189–1215.

Pirot, Edmé. *Relation des vingt-quatre dernières heures de la vie de Marie-Madeleine d'Aubray, Marquise de Brinvilliers*. Edited by G Rouillier. Paris: Robert Laffont, 1883.

Placet, François. *La superstition du temps, reconnue aux talismans, figures astrales et status fatales*. Paris: Veuve Gervais Alliot, 1668.

Planche, James Robinson. *A Cyclopedia of Costume, or a Dictionary of Dress Including Notices of Contemporaneous Fashions on the Continent; A General Chronological History of the Costumes of the Principal Countries of Europe, From the Commencement of the Christian Era to the Accession of George the Third*. 2 vols. London: Chatto & Windus, 1876.

Pomata, Gianna. "Praxis Historialis: The Uses of Historia in Early Modern Medicine." In *Historia: Empiricism and Erudition in Early Modern Europe*, edited by Gianna Pomata and Nancy Sirais, 105–146. Cambridge, MA: MIT Press, 2005.

Pomet, Pierre. *Le marchand sincère, ou traité général des drogues simples et composées, renfermant dans les 3 classes des végétaux, des animaux et des minéraux tout ce qui est l'objet de la physique, de la chimie, de la pharmacie et des arts les plus utiles à la société des hommes... avec un discours qui explique leurs différents noms, les pays d'où elles viennent, la manière de connoître les véritables d'avec les falsifiées et leurs propriétez, où l'on découvre l'erreur des anciens et des modernes... il est à remarquer que toutes les drogues dont il est parlé dans ce nouveau traité ont été démontrez publiquement l'année dernière au jardin royal à Paris....* Paris: Pomet, 1695.

Porter, Roy. "The Rise of the Physical Examination." In *Medicine and the Five Senses*, edited by William Bynum, 179–197. Cambridge, England: Cambridge University Press, 1993.

Porter, Roy, and Mikulás Teich, eds. *Drugs and Narcotics in History*. Cambridge, England: Cambridge University Press, 1995.

Prest, Julia. "Silencing the Supernatural: *La Devineresse* and the Affair of the Poisons." *Forum for Modern Language Studies* 43, no. 4 (October 1, 2007): 397–409.

Prevost, Claude-Joseph. *Principes de jurisprudence sur les visites et rapports judiciaires des médecins, chirurgiens, apothicaires et sages-femmes*. Paris: Guillaume Desprez, 1753.

Pyne, Stephen J. *Voice and Vision: A Guide to Writing History and Other Serious Nonfiction*. Cambridge, MA: Harvard University Press, 2009.

Rabier, Christelle. "Écrire l'expertise, traduire l'expérience: Les rapports des chirurgiens parisiens au XVIIIe siècle." *Rives Méditerranéennes* 44 (2013): 39–51.

Ranum, Orest. "Lèse-Majeste Divine: Transgressing Boundaries by Thought and Action in Mid-Seventeenth Century France." *Proceedings of the Western Society for French History* 68–80.

———. *Paris in the Age of Absolutism: An Essay*. University Park: Pennsylvania State University Press, 2004.

Ravaisson-Mollien, François. *Archives de la Bastille*. Vols. 4–7. Paris: A. Durand et Pedone-Lauriel, 1870.

Ravel, Jeffrey S. "Husband-Killer, Christian Heroine, Victim: The Execution of Madame Tiquet, 1699." *Seventeenth-Century French Studies* 32, no. 2 (December, 2010): 120–136.

Ravel, Jeffrey Scott. "The Police and the Parterre: Cultural Politics in the Paris Public Theater, 1680–1789." *Dissertation Abstracts International*, 1992.

Reinhardt, Steven G. "Crime and Royal Justice in Ancien Régime France: Modes of Analysis." *Journal of Interdisciplinary History* 13, no. 3 (1983): 437.

Reinharez, Claudine, and Josselyne Chamarat. "Boutiques Parisiennes à Décor." *Ethnologie française* 6.2 (1976): 163–180.

Rénée, Amédée. *Les Nièces de Mazarin: Etudes de moeurs et de caractères au XVII siècle*. 3rd Ed. Paris: Firmin Didot Frères, 1857.

De Renzi, Silvia. "Witnesses of the Body: Medico-Legal Cases in Seventeenth-Century Rome." *Studies in History and Philosophy of Science* 33 (2002): 219–242.

———. "Medical Expertise, Bodies, and the Law in Early Modern Courts." *Isis* 98, no. 2 (2007): 315–322.

Revel, Jacques. "Autour d'une épidémie ancienne: La peste de 1666–1670." *Revue d'histoire moderne et contemporaine (1954–)* 17, no. 4 (1970): 953–983.

Rey, Michel. "Police et sodomie à Paris au XVIIIe siècle: Du Péché au Désordre." *Revue d'histoire moderne et contemporaine* 29, no. 1 (1982): 113–124.

Richardson, Joanna. "Madame de Montespan and the Affair of the Poisons." *History Today* 13, no. 11 (November 1963): 588–592.

Riley, Philip F. "Hard Times, Police and the Making of Public Policy in the Paris of Louis XIV." *Historical Reflections/Réflexions Historiques* 10, no. 2 (1983): 313–334.

———. "Louis XIV: Watchdog of Parisian Morality." *The Historian* 36, no. 1 (1973): 19–33.

———. *Michel Foucault*, "Lust, Women, and Sin in Louis XIV's Paris." *Church History* 59, no. 1 (1990): 33–50.

———. "The Policing of Sin in Louis XIV's Paris." *South Atlantic Quarterly* 75, no. 4 (September 1976): 510–524.

———. "Witchcraft and Forensic Medicine in Seventeenth-Century Germany." In *Languages of Witchcraft: Narrative, Ideology, and Meaning in Early Modern Culture*, edited by Stuart Clark, 197–215. New York: Palgrave Macmillan, 2001.

———. "Women and Police in Louis XIV's Paris." *Eighteenth-Century Life* 4, no. 2 (1977): 37–42.

Robisheaux, Thomas Willard. *The Last Witch of Langenburg: Murder in a German Village*. New York: W. W. Norton, 2009.

Roos, Anna Marie. "'Magic Coins' and 'Magic Squares': The Discovery of Astrological Sigils in the Oldenburg Letters." *Notes and Records of the Royal Society of London* 62, no. 3 (September 20, 2008): 271–288.

Roosen, William J. "The Functioning of Ambassadors Under Louis XIV." *French Historical Studies* 6, no. 3 (1970): 311–332.

Rosasco, Betsy. "Masquerade and Enigma at the Court of Louis XIV." *Art Journal* 48.2 (1989): 144.

Rosenthal, Lloyd L. "The Development of the Use of Expert Testimony." *Law and Contemporary Problems* 2, no. 4 (1935): 403–418.

Rosset, François. *Mémoire du procès extraordinaire contre la Dame de Brinvilliers prisonnière en la Conciergerie du palais, accusée*. Les Histoires tragiques de nostre temps. Lyon: Benoist Vignieu, 1701.

Rousset, Camille. *Histoire de Louvois et de son administration politique et militaire*. Paris: Didier et cie, 1863.

Royer, J. P. *Histoire de la justice en France: De la monarchie absolue à la république*. Paris: Presses Universitaires de France, 1995.

Rudolph, Julia. "Gender and the Development of Forensic Science: A Case Study." *English Historical Review* 123, no. 503 (August 2008): 924–946.

Rule, John C. "Jean-Frédéric Phélypeaux, Comte de Pontchartrain et Maurepas: Reflections on His Life and His Papers." *Louisiana History* 6, no. 4 (1965): 365–377.

Saint-Amand, Imbert de. *Les Femmes de Versailles: La Cour de Louis XIV et la cour de Louis XIV*. Paris: Dentu, 1886.

Saint-André, Claude. *Henriette d'Angleterre et la cour de Louis XIV*. Paris: Plon, 1933.

Saint-Germain, Jacques. *La Reynie et la police au grand siècle d'après de nombreux documents inédits*. Paris: Hachette, 1962.

———. *Madame de Brinvilliers, La Marquise aux poisons*. Paris: Hachette, 1971.

Sargent, Rose-Mary. "Scientific Experiment and Legal Expertise: The Way of Experience in Seventeenth-Century England." *Studies in History and Philosophy of Science Part A* 20, no. 1 (March 1989): 19–45.

Sarmant, Thierry, and Mathieu Stoll. "Le style de Louvois: Formulaire administratif et expression personnelle dans la correspondance du secrétaire d'état de la guerre de Louis XIV." *Annuaire-Bulletin de la Société de l'histoire de France* (1997): 57–77.

Sauval, Henri, and Claude-Bernard Rousseau. *Histoire et recherches des antiquités de la ville de Paris*. Paris: Charles Moette, 1733.

Sawyer, Jeffrey K. *Printed Poison: Pamphlet Propaganda, Faction Politics and the Public Sphere in Early Seventeenth-Century France*. Berkeley: University of California Press, 1990.

Schivelbusch, Wolfgang. "The Policing of Street Lighting." *Yale French Studies* 73 (1987): 61.

Selimonte, Michel. *Le Pont Neuf et ses charlatans*. Paris: Plasma, 1980.

Shapiro, Barbara J. "Testimony in Seventeenth-Century English Natural Philosophy: Legal Origins and Early Development." *Studies in History and Philosophy of Science, Part A* 33, no. 2 (2002): 243–263.

Sheehan, Jonathan. "The Alters of Idols: Religion, Sacrifice, and the Early Modern Polity." *Journal of the History of Ideas* 67, no. 4 (2006): 649–674.

Silverman, Lisa. *Tortured Subjects: Pain, Truth, and the Body in Early Modern France*. Chicago: University of Chicago Press, 2001.

Smith, Angie. "Weighed in the Balance?: The Corporation of Apothecaries in Bordeaux, 1690–1790." *Journal of the Social History of Medicine* 16, no. 1 (2003): 17–37.

Smith, S. Halikowski. "The Physician's Hand: Trends in the Evolution of the Apothecary and His Art Across Europe (1500–1700)." *Nuncius* 24, no. 1 (2009): 97–125.

Smith, Sydney. "The Development of Forensic Medicine and Law-Science Relations." *Journal of Public Law* 3 (1954): 304–319.

———. "The History and Development of Forensic Medicine." *British Medical Journal* (March 24, 1951): 599–607.

Smoller, Laura Ackerman. "The Crime of Poison in the Middle Ages." *American Historical Review* 115, no. 4 (October 2010): 1209–1210.

Smyth, Frank. *Cause of Death: The Story of Forensic Science*. New York: Van Nostrand Reinhold, 1980.

Soll, Jacob. *The Information Master: Jean-Baptiste Colbert's Secret State Intelligence System*. Ann Arbor: University of Michigan Press, 2009.

Soman, Alfred. "La décriminalisation de la sorcellerie en France." *Histoire, économie, société* 4, no. 2 (1985): 181.

———. "La justice criminelle, vitrine de la monarchie française." *Bibliothèque de l'ecole des chartes* 153.2 (1995): 291–304.

———. "Les procès de sorcellerie au parlement de Paris (1565–1640)." *Annales: Economies, Societes, Civilisations* 32, no. 4 (1977): 790–814.

———. "The Parlement of Paris and the Great Witch Hunt (1565–1640)." *Sixteenth Century Journal* 9, no. 2 (July 1978): 30.

———. "Sorcellerie, justice criminelle et société dans la France moderne (l'ego-histoire d'un Américain à Paris)." *Histoire, Économie et Société* 12, no. 2 (June 1993): 177–217.

————. *Sorcellerie et justice criminelle: Le parlement de Paris,(16e–18e siècles)*. Aldershot, England: Variorum, 1992.

Somerset, Anne. *The Affair of the Poisons: Murder, Infanticide, and Satanism at the Court of Louis XIV*. New York: St. Martin's Press, 2004.

Sondheim, Moriz. "Shakespeare and the Astrology of His Time." *Journal of the Warburg Institute* 2, no. 3 (1939): 243–259.

Sonnino, Paul. *Louis XIV and the Origins of the Dutch War*. Cambridge, England: Cambridge University Press, 1988.

Soula, Mathieu. "La roue, le roué et le roi: Fonctions et pratiques d'un supplice sous l'Ancien Régime." *Revue historique de droit français et étranger* 3 (2010): 343–364.

Spawforth, Tony. *Versailles: A Biography of a Palace*. New York: Macmillan, 2010.

Stark, Marnie P. "Mounted Bezoar Stones, Seychelles Nuts, and Rhinoceros Horns: Decorative Objects as Antidotes in Early Modern Europe." *Studies in the Decorative Arts* 11, no. 1 (2004): 69–94.

Stead, Philip John. *The Police of France*. New York: Macmillan, 1983.

Stephens, Walter. *Demon Lovers: Witchcraft, Sex, and the Crisis of Belief*. Chicago: University of Chicago Press, 2002.

Stephenson, Marcia. "From Marvelous Antidote to the Poison of Idolatry: The Transatlantic Role of Andean Bezoar Stones During the Late Sixteenth and Early Seventeenth Centuries." *Hispanic American Historical Review* 90, no. 1 (February 1, 2010): 3–39.

Stokes, Hugh. *Madame de Brinvilliers and Her Times, 1630–1676*. London: John Lane, 1912.

Tedeschi, John. "The Question of Magic and Witchcraft in Two Unpublished Inquisitorial Manuals of the Seventeenth Century." *Proceedings of the American Philosophical Society* 131, no. 1 (1987): 92–111.

Thiers, Jean-Baptiste. *Traité des superstitions: Qui regardent les sacremens selon l'écriture Sainte, les décrets des conciles, et les sentimens des Saints Pères, et des théologiens*. Vol. 4. Paris: Antoine Dezalier, 1704.

Thiery, Daniel E. "Exploring Medieval Crime and Punishment." *History: Reviews of New Books* 38, no. 4 (2010): 116–118.

Thorburn, Malcolm. "Reinventing the Night-Watchman State?" *University of Toronto Law Journal* 60, no. 2 (2010): 425–443.

Thorndike, Lynn. "The True Place of Astrology in the History of Science." *Isis* 46, no. 3 (1955): 273–278. http://www.jstor.org/stable/226346. Accessed Jan. 10, 2014.

Thuillier, Guy. "Les pauvres en 1661: Une audience de Louis XIV." *La Revue administrative* 48, no. 285 (1995): 242–244. http://www.jstor.org/stable/40770237. Accessed Jan. 6, 2014.

Tillay, Alain. "La liberté du travail au faubourg Saint-Antoine à l'épreuve des saisies des jurandes parisiennes (1642–1778)." *Revue d'histoire moderne et contemporaine* 44, no. 4 (1997): 634–649.

Totelin, Laurence M. V. "Mithradates' Antidote: A Pharmacological Ghost." *Early Science and Medicine* 9, no. 1 (2004): 1–19.

Treasure, Geoffrey. *Louis XIV*. Edinburgh: Pearson Education, 2001.

Trout, Andrew P. *City on the Seine: Paris in the Time of Richelieu and Louis XIV*. New York: St. Martin's Press, 1996.

Tucker, Holly. *Blood Work: A Tale of Medicine and Murder in the Scientific Revolution*. New York: W. W. Norton, 2011.

————. *Pregnant Fictions: Childbirth and the Fairy Tale in Early-Modern France*. Detroit: Wayne State University Press, 2003.

Ultée, J. Maarten. "The Suppression of 'Fêtes' in France, 1666." *Catholic Historical Review* 62, no. 2 (1976): 181–199.

Urry, Alfred. "La crue de Janvier 1677 à Paris." *Annales de Géographie* 19, no. 106 (1910): 343–349.

van Klooster, H. S. "Three Centuries of Rochelle Salt." *Journal of Chemical Education* 36, no. 7: 314–318.

Villeneuve, Roland. *Le poison et les empoisonneurs célèbres*. Paris: La Palatine, 1960.

Vincent, Clare. "Magnificent Timekeepers: An Exhibition of Northern European Clocks in New York Collections." *Metropolitan Museum of Art Bulletin* 30, no. 4 (February 1972): 154–165.

Visconti, Primi. *Mémoires sur la cour de Louis XIV, 1673–1681*. Edited by Jean-François Solnon. Paris: Perrin, 1988.

Visé, Donneau de, and Thomas Corneille. *La Devineresse ou les faux enchantemens*. Edited by Julia Prest. *MHRA Critical Texts* 12 (2007), 1–164.

Watson, Katherine. *Forensic Medicine in Western Society: A History*. New York: Routledge, 2010.

Welch, Ellen R. "State Truths, Private Letters, and Images of Public Opinion in the Ancien Régime: Sévigné on Trials." *French Studies* 67, no. 2 (2013): 170–183.

Wilhelm, Jacques. *La vie quotidienne des parisiens au temps du roi-soleil, 1660–1715*. Paris: Hachette, 1977.

Williams, Alan. "Domestic Espionage and the Myth of Police Omniscience in Eighteenth-Century Paris." *Consortium on Revolutionary Europe 1750–1850: Proceedings* 8 (1979): 253–260.

Wilson, Miranda. *Poison's Dark Works in Renaissance England*. Lewisburg, PA: Bucknell University Press, 2013.

Wolf, John B. "The Formation of a King." *French Historical Studies* 1, no. 1 (1958): 40–72.

Wright, Peter. "Astrology and Science in Seventeenth-Century England." *Social Studies of Science* 5, no. 4 (1975): 399–422.

Index

Page numbers beginning with 247 refer to endnotes.